# The Films
## of Donald Pleasence

# The Films
## of Donald Pleasence

### by
### Christopher Gullo

BearManor Media

2012

The Films of Donald Pleasence

© 2012 Christopher Gullo

For information, address:

BearManor Media
P. O. Box 71426
Albany, GA  31708

bearmanormedia.com

Typesetting and layout by John Teehan

Published in the USA by BearManor Media

ISBN—1-59393-212-X

# TABLE OF CONTENTS

## DEDICATION

To my son Anthony Gullo

Who continues to make me proud at every moment of his life.

And to Donald Pleasence, O.B.E., for providing so many
enjoyable performances.

# ACKNOWLEDGEMENTS

I would like to thank the following individuals and institutions for their invaluable assistance in the research and writing of *The Films of Donald Pleasence*: Michael G. McGlasson, for so generously editing my book in bits and pieces; Ben Ohmart and BearManor Media, for publishing my project; Linda Pleasence, Angela Pleasence, Joy Jameson, John Carpenter, Kevin Connor, John Dark, John Mayall, Sylvester McCoy, Michael Pattinson, Robert Weinback, Gerrard Potterton, Don Calfa, Martyn Burke, Ulli Lommel, Gonzalo Suarez, Jeff Bridges, Lawrence Douglas, Don Pedro Colley, Oliver Tobias, David Worth, Jeremy Bulloch, George Wilbur, Reverend Mother Dolores Hart, Dick Warlock, Donald MacDonald, Renee Glynne, Tony Britton, David Birney, Frank Stallone, Shirley Eaton, Ira von Furstenberg, Annie Korzen, Howard Grey, Tony Battock (for kindly tracking down some of the more difficult to find films), Tony Earnshaw, Brian Peters, Edward T. Peters, Nancy Vaskas, David Vaskas, John Gibbon, Salvador Fortuny Miro, John Gullide, Sean Sobczak, Pat Halliday; Lynda Naylor, Nottingham Central Library; Philip Robinson, Nottingham City Council, Sheffield Forum; Kevin Bradford, Randy Vest; and, of course, my wife, Beth Anne Gullo.

# A LETTER OF APPRECIATION

Dear Christopher:

I wish to thank you for your interest in my husband Donald Pleasence and I am sure he would be very flattered. Donald was a great actor and a very good and gentle man; he was also a great father who loved his daughters and was very proud of them. He has lovely grandchildren who loved him so much. He was a true gentleman and a loyal friend. When he worked on stage on the revival of *The Caretaker* with Colin Firth, Donald told me that Colin would become a great actor. I wish Donald were alive today to see how great Colin Firth has become. Donald also loved and admired the one and only Harold Pinter and stayed friends with Peter Vaughn, one of England's most talented actors, until the day he died; they both had a wicked sense of humour.

Donald always stayed true to his working class roots and was always happy to see his close friends like David Warner and Ian McShane doing well in their careers. He also loved working in the United States and was a true admirer of John Carpenter. My good friend Don Calfa was one of Donald's best friends and in my opinion is one of America's great actors. Donald was also very proud of his children's book *Scouse the Mouse* and was bitterly disappointed when due to circumstances beyond his control, the book never took off. His great friend Gerald Potterton was the illustrator of both the book and the album cover and of course is a great illustrator and film director. His good friend and marvelous agent Joy Jameson was very special to Donald because she and her then-partner Tessa Sutherland were always there for him.

I miss Donald and there's never an hour in any day that I don't think of him. I will love him until the day I die; he meant the world to me and still does. I would like to thank you and your publisher for this tribute to my husband, a very talented actor, a funny man and a true English gent with a big generous heart. My dear, I wish you were here to read it.

– Linda Pleasence

# INTRODUCTION

**W**elcome to my tribute to Donald Pleasence. I noticed that when I mentioned to friends and family that I was writing this book, they would often say two things—first, that they remember Pleasence from films like *Halloween* and *The Great Escape*, and TV shows like *Columbo*; and second, what made me choose to write a book on Pleasence? My answer is that he deserves one. I was surprised to learn that my book is the very first one devoted to Pleasence, a man whose film career stretched from the 1950s to the 1990s; a man who starred in Hollywood hits and productions around the world; a man who proudly served his country in World War II as he was horrified to hear of what was going on in the Nazi concentration camps; a man who brought to life the wondrous character of Bernard Jenkins in Harold Pinter's *The Caretaker* and repeated this feat in both London and New York; a man beloved by his fans for his iconic character of Dr. Loomis in the *Halloween* film series started by John Carpenter.

To share a little of my own initial interest in Donald Pleasence, I actually saw my first Pleasence film while in school when a science teacher showed us *Fantastic Voyage*. Besides the science angle of seeing all the body parts, I was intrigued by Pleasence's character, who turns out to be a saboteur and eventually meets a rather nasty end. I later saw Pleasence in the first two *Halloween* films and was hooked, and started looking for his appearances in various films in my weekly *TV Guide* and circling them to remind myself of what to watch.

So here it is—my tribute to the great Donald Pleasence for all of his wonderful performances that kept me entertained while growing up. Thank you.

– Christopher Gullo

# DONALD PLEASENCE:
# A BIOGRAPHY

**A**s a young boy growing up in the small town of Worksop, England, Donald Pleasence always dreamed of becoming an actor. Interestingly enough, Worksop is located next to Nottinghamshire, home of the fabled Sherwood Forest and the alleged home of the legendary Robin Hood and of which Pleasence would eventually star as Prince John in the 1950s British television series *The Adventures of Robin Hood*. Economically, Worksop was a working-class area and was greatly aided by the discovery of coal deposits which led to the creation of the local coal mining industry. In turn, in 1849, this new industry led to the construction of the Manchester, Sheffield, and Lincolnshire Railway that would later play a major role in the careers of the Pleasence clan.

Donald's paternal grandfather James Pleasence was born in 1856 in Banningham, Norfolk, and although he started out as a marble polisher working in Leeds, he soon made a career change to a signalman at Notton Station near Barnsley. In order to be close to where he worked as a signalman, James and his wife Agnes took up residence in Notton Station, where Thomas Stanley Pleasence, Donald's father, was born on October 2, 1887, one of seven children. By 1901, due to his position with the railway, James had moved his family to East Retford, and several years later, following in his father's footsteps, Thomas also found employment with the railway as a lowly railway clerk. By the age of fifteen, Thomas was working for the London and North Eastern Rail Company out of Conisborough Station, and in 1911, another transfer with the railway forced the Pleasence family to move back to Worksop.[1]

Around this time, Thomas began courting a young woman named

Alice Armitage, born on February 23, 1888, and raised in America, where her mother passed away when Alice was quite young; she then came to England to live with her grandparents in Thornton, York. Thomas fell in love with Alice and on June 10, 1913, they became man and wife at the Wesleyan Chapel in Nottinghamshire. One year later, Thomas and Alice's first child was born, a son named Ralph, and after working for a number of years as a railway clerk, Thomas was eventually promoted to Station Master which proved very helpful because Alice was expecting another child. Donald Pleasence, Thomas and Alice's second and last child, was born on October 5, 1919 at 62 Potter Street, Worksop, where Thomas and Alice raised their two sons and where they attended Ecclesfield Grammar School. The acting bug bit Donald early in life; his first role at age seven was in the Scunthorpe Players production of *Passers By*.[2] His mother even entered him and his brother Ralph in local musical festivals, where young Donald would recite poems, such as "The Highwayman" by Alfred Noyes. In a 1964 interview with the *New York Times*, Donald Pleasence noted that "There were always verse-speaking classes. You had to announce the full title and the author clearly with the best diction. I won a great many prizes. My mother still has a drawer full of them."[3] Donald's father raised his two sons as followers of the Socialist Party and as Methodists; thus, Donald remained a life-long Labour supporter and was always actively involved in following the political scene. However, he chose not to follow the religious teachings of Methodism and became a self-proclaimed atheist.

Continuing the family trade, Ralph Pleasence eventually went on to work with his father in an entry-level position with the railroad which became a Pleasence family profession that demanded hard work but provided low pay. After toiling away for many years as a lowly railroad worker, Ralph was promoted to the position of station master. As for Donald, his parents were very concerned about his choice to become an actor and insisted that he continue his studies at school. Donald obeyed his parents' wishes and excelled in school by maintaining very high marks and reaching matriculation at the scholarship level. While in A levels at school, seventeen year-old Donald made his way to London and won a scholarship to the Royal Academy of Dramatic Art, but because the scholarship did not include housing and his parents could not afford to pay for it, he returned home. Donald then found a position collecting tickets for the railroad, another entry-level position that he maintained while searching out acting jobs.

After a year and a half of searching, Donald managed to get his foot in the door and in May of 1939 was hired as an assistant stage manager at the Playhouse in Jersey, but unlike assistant stage managers of today, Donald's position was the lowest rung on the theatre ladder and required him to do errands like making tea for very little money. In fact, Donald's dedication to acting would require him to live hand to mouth until he was in his 40s.

It was at this venue, run by Lawrence Naismith, that Donald made his first professional appearance in the role of Hareton Earnshaw in *Wuthering Heights*, due in part to the director liking his strong Northern accent. Unfortunately, on the night after his debut, Prime Minister Neville Chamberlain declared that England was going back to war with Germany, and while this might have hampered many beginning hopefuls, there was no looking back for Donald. Within three years following his debut at the Playhouse, he reached London and appeared as Curio in Shakespeare's *Twelfth Night* at the Arts Theatre Club where he began to earn acclaim for his performances. One of the plays at the Club was a popular role that Donald would help to create and repeat in the film version—Harold Pinter's *The Caretaker*. At the Stratford Theatre, Donald appeared in another Shakespearean play opposite a young actor whom he would become very good friends with, none other than Robert Shaw. [4] During this time and while learning his craft, Donald met a young actress named Miriam Raymond. The two fell in love and married in 1941 and soon after were blessed with their first child Angela who would one day become an actress in her own right. Donald and Miriam eventually had another daughter whom they named Jean, and for the time being, everything seemed to be going right on track.

However, the Second World War would not allow Donald Pleasence to escape unscathed, even though he considered himself as a pacifist and a conscientious objector, a moral position that would force him to defend his beliefs in court and to be found innocent or face going to prison. In the meantime and during the very early days of the war, Donald worked as a lumberjack in the Lake District, but what eventually made him decide to join the war effort was reading about the horrors of the concentration camps in the newspapers. Always a brave man and wishing to help those in need, Donald enlisted in the

Royal Air Force in early 1944 as a wireless radio operator, and by the summer was flying missions for the RAF in the 166ᵗʰ Squadron Bomber Command.

During one specific flight on August 7 to Fontenay le Marmion, France, Pleasence filled in as radio operator for an officer Buckland who fell ill. This flight was part of Operation Crossbow, a bombing mission in support of the Canadian army. Taking off at 21.27 hours, Pleasence and the rest of the crew under the command of Edward T. Peters joined 1,019 other aircraft, including 614 Lancasters, 392 Halifaxes, and 13 Mosquitoes, and attacked five aiming points in front of Allied ground troops. This mission was quite successful, hitting German strong points and the roads around them that were well-cratered after the attack.[5]

In August and following Operation Crossbow, Pleasence resumed his duties with his regular bomber crew; however, little did he know that he would soon experience a living nightmare. After flying in sixty missions, Pleasence went up again on August 31 for a raid over Agenville, France, but during this flight, Pleasence's plane was shot down by the Germans. Director and friend Gerald Potterton later revealed what Pleasence told him concerning this harrowing incident:

> "Donald told me once of his experience as a radio operator in the RAF bomber command. His plane had just crossed the English Channel when the navigator radioed the crew 'French coast below!' Donald said all of a sudden there was a big white flash and he found himself under his parachute and falling into a field of German soldiers."[6]

Luckily, Pleasence survived the crash but was captured by the Germans and marched back into Germany to be held at prisoner of war camp Stalag Luft I, where he spent the remainder of 1944 and into 1945 until the camp was liberated by advancing Russian troops on April 30, 1945. Actor Don Calfa, who was also good friends with Pleasence, recounts a story Pleasence told him of his time in the concentration camp—

> "His plane was shot down and the Germans surrounded him with guns drawn. Donald figured he was going to get killed so

when the Germans said pack up your chute, he told them to go fuck themselves, you pack it up. So the Germans packed up the chute and they marched Donald off to meet the Commandant. In the Commandant's quarters, they started undressing him and pulling out all of these rubbers that he used for antistatic as a radioman. And the Commandant looked at all the rubbers and said, 'Well, you won't need those here.' The Commandant also told Donald, 'I'm from Dresden. I'm an aristocrat and I lost everything; my family and my house. Why would you English bomb Dresden? It wasn't even a military town.' At this point, Donald knew he was going to have trouble in the camp. The first week he was there, the guards woke him up every morning to be shot. They would take the prisoners out, line them up and then say, 'Nah, not today.' This must have affected Donald for the rest of his life because when we were working on *The Rainbow Boys*, one night I heard Donald screaming. The next morning I saw his then-wife Meira and asked why Donald was screaming and she told me that he was having a nightmare that he was back in the camp and that it was not uncommon."[7]

Although tortured by the experience, Pleasence did not allow the Nazis to strip him of his humanity; in fact, he actually started a theatre group in the camp in order to entertain his fellow prisoners. Later in his life, Pleasence gave an interview in which he made an amusing point at the expense of his former captors—"The camp was called Stalag Luft 1, and *The Great Escape* took place in Stalag Luft 3. I don't know what happened to Stalag Luft 2. Nobody ever heard of it. It's very un-Germanic that they missed it out."[8]

During the war, Donald became acquainted with a fellow soldier named Peter Vaughan who was also interested in acting and would become Donald's best friend. After the war, Donald and Peter shared an apartment in Bayswater, London while trying to find the odd acting job here and there. Over the years, they worked together professionally a number of times with the first major pairing being in the 1966 play of the week *The Move after Checkmate*. Later in their careers, they teamed up in films like *The Pied Piper* and *Malachi's Cove*.

After Pleasence was liberated from the camp and discharged as a flight lieutenant, he returned home to England and threw himself back into his acting career full force, perhaps as a way of dealing with his painful experiences during the war. Initially doing some theatre in London's West End, Pleasence had by 1948 joined the Birmingham Repertory Theatre and starred in a number of productions, such as *The Comedy of Errors*. On Christmas Day of 1948, Pleasence starred in the musical *Bears of Bay-Rum* along with Eric Porter, another actor in the troupe making his start in the theatre. During this run, Pleasence moved his family to Archway, London, residing at 68 Hargrave Park Lane, N. 19. Pleasence continued at Birmingham for another two years before moving on in 1950 to an even bigger theatre group—the Old Vic Company run by Laurence Olivier.

For Donald Pleasence, working for Olivier must have seemed like a dream come true, due to his admiration for the great actor and the fact that he actually performed with Olivier, which led to them becoming good friends. The Old Vic had such great success with their productions of *Antony and Cleopatra* and *Caesar and Cleopatra* that Olivier decided to take his troupe to New York City to perform on Broadway with Pleasence being among the actors chosen to embark on the ship *Franconia* out of Liverpool, arriving in the city on December 11, 1951. At this time, Donald was thirty-two years old and took four bags with him on the trip. His destination was 9 Rockefeller Plaza. After touring with the Old Vic on Broadway for a few months, Donald eventually boarded the same ship and headed back to Liverpool, where he arrived on April 22, 1952 and immediately headed home to his new residence at 220 Kew Road, in Richmond, Surrey.[9]

At the London theatres, Pleasence continued to get accolades for his performances, such as the North Country shoemaker Willie Mossop in *Hobson's Choice*. Perhaps wishing to test his talents, Pleasence adapted and produced the Robert Louis Stevenson story *Ebb Tide* which he had performed at the Edinburgh Festival and Royal Court Theatre in London during the 1952 season. During this same year, Pleasence branched out into another medium—television, and appeared in a bit part as Second Batlon in *The Dybbuk*, a Jewish story about a malicious possessing spirit, an interesting start considering that later in his career Pleasence would come face-to-face with another malicious spirit named Michael Myers.

Pleasence's success on the stage continued and in 1953 he acted opposite Michael Redgrave in *The Tragedy of King Lear* at the Stratford Memorial Theatre; one year later, Pleasence made his theatrical film debut as Tromp in *The Beachcomber*. This was followed by several supporting roles in television and film as Pleasence's career continued to gain momentum. However, by the mid 1950s, Pleasence, like many of his young contemporary British actors, decided to try his luck in Hollywood. Having previously toured with Olivier on Broadway, Pleasence must have thought it would be easier the second time around. This time, Pleasence took a flight to New York City and arrived on December 11, 1955, yet his stay would be short-lived, as the American Actors Union was busy protesting against English actors taking their jobs. Pleasence was one among four other actors that the Department of Immigration, backed up by the Actors Equity Association, decided to refuse entry into the United States. The Actors Equity spokesman referred to Pleasence and the other actors as "bit players and undistinguished." [10] With no other choice, Pleasence returned home to England.

Once back in England and still determined to further his career, Pleasence continued his streak of bit parts in film and television. His first big TV break turned out to have a connection to his childhood via the role of Prince John in *The Adventures of Robin Hood*, set in Sherwood Forest, which was not far from his childhood home in Worksop. This long-running series with British actor Richard Greene as Robin Hood was enormously popular in England, and most importantly for Pleasence, it was picked up in the States by CBS for rebroadcasting on Monday nights. In 1958, Pleasence ended his run as Prince John and obtained a supporting role in the classic theatre drama *Look Back in Anger* with mega-star Richard Burton.

Meanwhile, Pleasence's relationship with his wife Miriam Ramond had become strained after many years of hardship and eventually decided to end their marriage. Donald then met Josephine Crombie, a one-time actress who had switched to a career as a professional nurse, and soon they were married. Out of this union, two daughters came into the life of Donald Pleasence—Polly Jo and Lucy.

Pleasence started out the 1960s by producing and hosting his own television series *Armchair Mystery Theatre* which would make him a household name. As Donald explained it in 1975, "I was tired of people half-recognizing me in the street. Instead of being "that actor" on TV, I became Donald Pleasence. I became instantly known, and I found it very nice." [11] Certainly, Pleasence had successfully made the leap from theatre to television, but success in film continued to elude him. This however did not prevent his fellow actors from noticing Pleasence's budding talent. Tony Britton, who played a scientist in the 1960 espionage thriller *Suspect*, recalls working with Pleasence in the role of a black market dealer—"We worked together previously at Stratford doing theatre. He was very funny and made me laugh both on stage and off. Donald was an entirely distinctive and original performer."[12] In late 1960, Pleasence made the momentous decision to return to his theatrical roots which would prove to be quite beneficial for his career as an actor.

If Pleasence was happy to finally become a "known" actor, he must have been ecstatic upon his triumphant return to the theatre in a role that brought him into the international spotlight, that of Mac Davies/ Bernard Jenkins the tramp in playwright Harold Pinter's smash hit *The Caretaker*. Interestingly, production director Donald McWhinnie recommended Pleasence for the role of the tramp as a result of hearing him on the radio and felt that his voice would work well with the character's mood swings.[13] *The Caretaker* opened with great success on April 27, 1960 at the Arts Theatre Club in London and tells the story of Aston, who takes in a homeless tramp following a bar fight and offers him a job as the caretaker of the house. The tramp stays the night and after meeting Aston's brother Mick decides to fix up the house, which quickly pits one brother against the other. *The Caretaker* concludes with Mick and Aston making up with the tramp left out, alone with his unsuccessful schemes and pleas. Also in the production was Alan Bates as Mick and Pleasence's good friend Robert Shaw, replacing Peter Woodthorpe who did the London run as Aston.

In a 1961 interview, Pleasence provided some background on how this production came about—"This play was put on originally in London for five hundred pounds or about $15,000 American dollars and we all worked for ten pounds a week. The money that can be invested in a London play can be very small, so it's not so desperately essential that a play be a great success." [14] However, *The Caretaker* did become a great success and after its run in London headed for Broadway with one hundred and sixty-five performances. For his role as the tramp, Pleasence won the 1960 British Critics Award for Best Performance of the Year and was also nominated for a Tony Award for Best Actor during the Broadway run. In an interview conducted during the Broadway production of *The Caretaker*, Pleasence was asked how he approached his role as the tramp:

> "I do not use any set methods, not even 'The Method.' All the real work is done in the rehearsal period. The play is on top of me all the time and I am constantly thinking about it. Even when I leave the theatre, I'll mumble the lines to myself or think about the way the character walks or holds himself. The process of creation goes on all the time."[15]

After the successful run of *The Caretaker*, Pleasence returned to theatrical films and television, appearing in *Spare the Rod*, *No Place Like Homicide!* and *Lisa*. Shirley Eaton, the beautiful nurse Linda Dickson in *No Place Like Homicide!*, said of her costar, "Donald was a very 'pleasant' actor to work with even though I had little time with him on-screen. I found him to be quiet and focused during the filming." [16]

Jeremy Bulloch, one of the mischievous students in *Spare the Rod*, relates, "I have great memories of working with Donald Pleasence on *Spare the Rod*. He played a rather strict head teacher and being only fifteen years old, I was rather in awe. It was a great film to work on and Geoffrey Keen was another great actor to have met. It was a long time ago but I always remember Donald Pleasence giving us tips on how to play certain scenes and I took his advice. I consider myself very lucky to have been in a film with such a professional man." [17]

Dolores Hart (now Reverend Mother), one of Donald's co-stars in *Lisa*, relates that "Mr. Pleasence was the epitome of excellence as a craftsman. I was so impressed by his presence on the set and his sureness with lines and everything our director said to him. He had my total respect and admiration though I never spoke to him about this. It would seem out of character." [18]

Pleasence then appeared in Rod Serling's ever-popular series *The Twilight Zone* in the 1962 classic episode *The Changing of the Guard* in which he portrays Ellis Fowler, an aging professor being forced to retire. Thinking that he has wasted his life as a teacher, Fowler becomes depressed and considers suicide, but is surprised to see some of his past (and passed on) students back in his classroom to visit their old professor and tell him how much his lessons and teachings changed their lives.

*The Changing of the Guard* is quite emotional and Pleasence provides a spot-on performance as the old professor who suddenly realizes his true value as a human being and teacher. Interestingly, Pleasence's role as the professor was written expressly for him after the producers of the play saw him as the elderly tramp in *The Caretaker*. In an interview conducted in 1962, Pleasence described his reasoning behind choosing certain parts:

> "One reason why I do all kinds of parts is quite apart from having to earn money. I hate doing nothing. I am very neurotic about it. I like to work all the time until I discover I need a break, then I like to go on holiday. I have always found television a fascinating medium, imperfect though it is in many ways, because it combines film and theatre. There are many things you can actually do better on television than in other media. There are big effects that you can create in the theatre which you would find difficult to do in television or on film. There are small effects on television, subtleties, which you could not possibly do in the theatre. Big close-ups can be fascinating to an actor who has spent most of his life in the theatre." [19]

In 1963, the acting career of Donald Pleasence took off in a new direction through his involvement in an "A-list" Hollywood film called *The Great Escape*. Playing opposite major stars like Steve McQueen, James Garner, Richard Attenborough, and Charles Bronson, Pleasence struck a chord with viewers as the sympathetic Flight Lieutenant Colin Blythe, a.k.a. "The Forger." Because Pleasence was the only member of the cast to have actually been a prisoner of war during World War II, he offered some suggestions to director John Sturges concerning inaccuracies in the period costumes. At first, Sturges dismissed Pleasence's suggestions, but when a member of the cast explained to him that Pleasence had been a POW during the war, he invited him to look over all of the details of the film's production.

Joy Jameson, Pleasence's long-time agent, relates that *The Great Escape* was her client's favorite film from among his movies—"*The Great Escape* was definitely Donald's choice and it was a fantastic role which and led to him appearing in more Hollywood films. I remember

Donald telling me he was critical of the length of the S.S. officers' great coats in the film because he had actually been a prisoner of war." [20]

Also in 1963, Pleasence appeared in the long-awaited film version of *The Caretaker* with screenplay credit going to Pinter and re-titled *The Guest* for the U.S. market. Returning along with Pleasence were his co-stars Robert Shaw and Alan Bates, and thanks to director Clive Donner, Pinter's story was showcased before a much wider audience, creating a legions of new fans. Among them were blues legends Eric Clapton and John Mayall:

> "As for Eric and I, and our devotion to *The Caretaker*, we became totally obsessive about the film and Harold Pinter's totally off the wall writings. We saw the movie over and over again when it was playing on Oxford Street. I forget the name of the cinema but we also bought the book of the play and spent long journeys on the road quoting excerpts from the film. One of Donald Pleasence's finest roles ever and that's saying something. Later that year, Eric and I did a couple of recordings for Mike Vernon's Purdah record label and for the B side instrumental, we name it 'Bernard Jenkins,' chuckling to ourselves at how people would be mystified at who this person was." [21]

The year also heralded Pleasence's return to the theatre in fine form for director Shirley Butler's production of *Poor Bitos* by playwright Jean Anouilh. First presented at the Duke of York Theatre in London on November 13, 1963, *Poor Bitos* is a political analogy that compares the movers of the French Revolution to the resistance leaders of post-World War II. The guests at a fancy dress party appear as French Revolutionary figures in order to humiliate a local prosecutor who comes to the event dressed as Robespierre. Pleasence plays Bitos and Robespierre with Charles Gray as Maxime and Saint-Just. *Poor Bitos* did a second run in London in 1964 and then moved to the Cort Theatre in New York City for an additional run in which Pleasence received his second Tony nomination for Best Actor in a play. At this time, Pleasence was given a new nickname:

> "He is now as ordinary-looking as everyone else. He is five foot seven inches tall, of slight build, bald, with an alert face

capped by keen grey-blue eyes that he describes as 'duck-egg blue.' At least one of these orbs achieved some fame in England where, as a result of his roles in the *Armchair Mystery Theatre* television series, he became known as "The Man with the Hypnotic Eye." [22]

Photogenically, Pleasence was much more than "ordinary-looking," as noted by photographer Howard Grey, who set up a photo session with Pleasence in 1963 for *Queen* magazine that catered to the younger side of 1960s British society or the swinging "Chelsea Set."

"I remember that my meeting with Donald Pleasence was quite short but intense. He was in the middle of rehearsals for a play in London (*Poor Bitos*) and was at his Datchet home for only an hour or so. My pictures were taken in his walled garden. I sought only to get a full-on, passport style picture of this legendary actor because in doing so I felt that this gaze of his would captivate the editor of the magazine to publish the image to full page.

"For the first few frames, Pleasence just stared into my lens as directed, then I thought I should alter my concept and suggested that slowly he should now look away from the camera. Expecting him to move his face around to his left or right, I was absolutely astounded to experience the great man's interpretation of my direction by him adjusting just his focus, meaning that instead of focusing at say six feet (the distance my camera was to say his nose), he focused on what must have been infinity yet still at the lens. We are all used to people looking at us in daily conversation but not with eyes that you feel are looking straight through your head at a view that is behind you. I am a third-generation portrait photographer and have never experienced such a phenomena through my camera since." [23]

In October of 1963, Pleasence appeared in the popular TV sci-fi program *The Outer Limits* in the episode "The Man with the Power" in which he portrays Harold J. Finley, a mild-mannered and timid college professor who is pushed around by his employer, coworkers, and especially his wife Vera. But Harold is a man with big dreams and wants to be part of a secret government space project. Vera flat out refuses to support him and his boss dean Radcliff refuses to let him out of his contract. But little do they know that Harold is already deeply involved in this secret government project through undergoing a brain operation that implanted a device that allows him to manipulate objects with his mind for use in the mining of asteroids in space. However, the unknown side effect of this operation proves to be much more powerful and dangerous because the device also allows Harold to use it as a weapon against those who anger him. As a character, Harold J. Finley allowed Pleasence to create a sympathetic monster, a person who is truly good but ends up as a freak of science with the power to destroy at will. "The Man with the Power" also provides a great example on Pleasence's ability to use his eyes to convey feelings of menace via a haunted stare that indicates something sinister is going on deep within his subconscious mind.

The next three years saw Pleasence appearing in a number of Hollywood films. One in particular was *Dr. Crippen* in 1964, a film that paved the way for Pleasence to create a niche as a "horror star." Based on the real-life case of Dr. Hawley Harvey Crippen, Pleasence plays the doomed Dr. Crippen, charged with the murder of his wife and then hung in a London prison. Much later in his career, Pleasence related that everything "started with *Dr. Crippen*. Then I got *lots* of horror offers. In fact, I was asked to play Christie in *Ten Rillington Place* which Dickie (Richard) Attenborough played, but I wouldn't do it because I was determined not to be typecast." [24] Roles in *The Greatest Story Ever Told* as Satan and *The Hallelujah Trail* as a drinking mystic rounded out the mid-1960s for Pleasence. But during this time, Pleasence came under the representation of agent Joy Jameson, thus creating a relationship that would endure for the remainder of his career.

As Jameson explains it:

"The year I started looking after Donald would have been around 1960 when I joined the Heyman International Agency which at the time was a very big operation representing Richard Burton, Elizabeth Taylor, Richard Harris, Trevor Howard, and Shirley Bassey; I could go on forever. I had left Richard Hatton Ltd. where we looked after people like Sean Connery, Robert Shaw, and Leo McKern. Donald was with Heyman International when I arrived there, so I didn't poach him from any other agent; that is, not until Heyman International decided to go into producing films and I decided to set up my own business. Donald and Billie Whitelaw (his onetime next-door neighbor) were my first clients." [25]

In 1966, Pleasence provided one of his most powerful performances in Roman Polanski's black comedy thriller *Cul-de-sac* that takes place in a castle on a small island in England. The inhabitants of the castle are the neurotic and cowardly English husband George and his sensual French wife Teresa. One day, Dickie the gangster and his dying partner Albie come to the island while on the run and take George and Teresa hostage. Albie dies and Dickie has to spend the night with George and Teresa while he waits for his boss to come and get him. What results is a four-way character study that is raw, humorous, and quite powerful, especially with Pleasence as the cross-dressing, humiliated owner of the castle. Shot in black and white with glorious landscapes and a wonderful musical score, *Cul-de-sac* presents an almost dreamlike quality. Jameson notes that "I'm not sure how Donald felt about playing the lead in Polanski's *Cul-de-sac* but I know his then wife Josephine threw up outside the cinema after seeing it. I was there!" [26]

As for Pleasence, "I think that was Polanski's best picture. We were very creative together and although we had fights, a lot of the scenes were improvised on the spot." [27]

Even though his father had passed away on May 27, 1966, Donald reveled in how far he had come since his days in local theatre, and with hard won success in the film industry came wealth that allowed him to enjoy his varied interests, such as classic automobiles. His most prized car was his first—a classic Riley with an all leather interior. He later added a black Lincoln Continental from America, an Alfa Romeo, and other classic cars along the way. Donald also possessed a keen interest in art with a great admiration for British painter John Randall Bratby, who developed his own Expressionistic style known as "kitchen sink realism." Donald first noticed Bratby's work in 1966 after reading a newspaper article on a series of paintings he had done of nude portraits of ethnic women with flags as backgrounds. Later that same year, Donald, his wife Josephine, and actress and neighbor Billie Whitelaw attended a private showing of Bratby's work at an Eaton art gallery, where the Pleasences purchased two of Bratby's paintings, one being *Dominican Singer with Zoot Money and his Big Roll Band*. Soon after meeting Donald and his wife, Bratby ended up as a guest at their home and asked to paint both husband and wife. Bratby rendered a portrait of Donald during his filming of *You Only Live Twice* and then later on painted a double portrait of Donald, first in a casual setting and then in his German uniform for the theatre production of *The Man in the Glass Booth*. [28] Eventually, Donald's collection of Bratby originals grew to seven paintings and in 1977, he served as a witness to Bratby's marriage to Patricia Prime. [29]

In 1967, Pleasence appeared in his most iconic film role, that of the villain Ernst Stavro Blofeld opposite spy hero James Bond (Sean Connery) in *You Only Live Twice*. What makes this interesting is that Pleasence was not the first choice to portray the villainous Blofeld (whose face would be revealed for the first time in a Bond picture). Because this was one of the major points of the film, producer Harry Saltzman looked long and hard for a suitable actor and finally settled on Czech actor Jan Werich. But after a week of Werich filming his scenes as Blofeld, the rest of the producers decided that he looked too much like Santa Claus with his beard, definitely not a suitable look for a Bond villain. Needing an actor who could elicit the right amount of menace, the producers turned to Pleasence, who agreed to portray Bond's arch-nemesis.

"I sort of devised Blofeld's facial scar and other little quirks to his character," recalled Pleasence in a June 1995 interview. "The producers liked my style, but didn't find me physically imposing, so the makeup and costuming helped quite a bit. As a matter of fact, some of the shots weren't even me at all; they were just the uniform and what was supposed to be my legs and arms." [30]

Jameson admits that *You Only Live Twice* is her favorite film among Pleasence's output:

"My favorite of Donald's roles was as Blofeld. I think it was about three weeks work and from day one. Donald knew they didn't think he was really right. I received many phone calls from Donald in which he told me, 'They're shooting me in shadow' and 'They're shooting over my shoulder.' Little did anyone know however that Donald's performance was so iconic that people hardly remember another Blofeld. Then of course there is Pleasence's visual influence on the character Dr. Evil in the *Austin Powers* series!" [31]

Pleasence ended the 1960s with some high profile films, including the innovative science fiction epic *Fantastic Voyage*, the political thriller *Night of the Generals*, and the 1968 western *Will Penny*, as well as returning to the theatre which reunited him with Harold Pinter. *Night of the Generals* features Pleasence and Charles Gray who also appeared in *You Only Live Twice* and would go on to play Blofeld in a Bond film. For Pleasence, not being under contract for *Night of the Generals* turned out to be a stroke of luck. As Jameson explains it:

"The first film that Donald did under my new agency was *Night of the Generals* and it was a long shoot, around eighteen weeks. The film also starred Peter O'Toole and Omar Sharif. In a recent biography of producer Sam Spiegel, the author states that as O'Toole and Sharif were under option to Sam, they got £12,000 and Donald got $80,000 as he was not under option to Sam!"[32]

Also in 1967, Pleasence appeared as Gregori Andreanu in *Matchless*, along with Italian-born beauty Ira von Furstenberg who recalls Pleasence as being a "genius actor" and a brilliant craftsman. Off the set, Pleasence was not exactly a "girl charmer, but he was serious and it showed how well-educated he was." Overall, von Furstenberg admits that it was a great honor to work "with such a brilliant actor" as Donald Pleasence.[33]

Pleasence had always wanted to be in a Western and *Will Penny* afforded him the opportunity, playing opposite Hollywood icon Charlton Heston. While filming this excellent American Western, Pleasence discovered that Heston had a good sense of humor—"At the end of the shoot, Heston shoots me with a sawed-off shotgun, knocking me several feet through the air. After we did that scene, Heston said to me "That'll teach you to tangle with the leading man!" [34]

Pleasence also returned to the theatre in 1967 via a reunion of *The Caretaker* of sorts, starring in *The Man in the Glass Booth*, written by his friend Robert Shaw and directed by Harold Pinter. This production first opened at the St. Martin's Theatre in London before relocating to Broadway the following year at the Royale Theatre. Plot-wise, *The Man in the Glass Booth* tells the story of Arthur Goldman, a Jewish concentration camp survivor who becomes a wealthy industrialist in New York. Goldman is then kidnapped by Israeli agents who bring him to Israel, where he is put on trial and charged with being a Nazi war criminal. Reviewers praised both the play and its star with Clive Barnes noting that *The Man in the Glass Booth* "will, justifiably, be talked about. And much of the conversation will, also justifiably, be of Donald Pleasence and his remarkable performance as the paranoiac Jew." Barnes adds that "When I saw the play in London a year or so ago, I was vastly impressed with Mr. Pleasence, and now I am lost in admiration. The portrayal has the intensity of madness. It convinces against one's intellect, and thrills with its sheer, remorseless virtuosity."[35]

Pleasence was nominated for his third Tony Award for his performance in *The Man in the Glass Booth* and won a Drama Desk Award for his outstanding performance. Shortly after completing the play, Pleasence worked with Pinter again on a different type of project called *Pinter People*, a collection of some of Pinter's sketches done as animated shorts with Pleasence and Pinter providing voice-overs. Gerald Potterton, the director of *Pinter People*, shares an amusing anecdote concerning the making of these shorts:

> "We were recording lines for *Pinter People* in a studio up on the west side in New York, and I took time out for lunch at a restaurant with Donald and Pinter. While sitting at a table by a window looking onto the avenue, the face of an old bum (direct from Central Casting) appeared suddenly pressed against the glass. Donald took a look at him and said, 'Oh God, it's one of mine.'"[36]

By the early 1970s, Pleasence had become a well-known character actor for his film roles, theatre performances, and numerous television appearances; he also divorced and then married Meira Shore, his third wife with whom he would have his fifth daughter Miranda Pleasence. Because of his growing family, Pleasence kept himself very busy with work just to make sure his finances were in order, and due to the fact that film roles paid more money, Pleasence accepted some roles beneath his experience, perhaps simply to cash in on playing a villainous character. Pleasence tends to support this by declaring "I just play parts, and bad people are more interesting than good." [37]

Pleasence certainly kept to his word with a rather sinister performance in the realistic western *Soldier Blue*, sporting the somewhat silly name of Isaac Q. Cumber. He then gave a sympathetic portrayal as SEN 5241 in the first feature film by a young filmmaker named George Lucas—*THX 1138*—which relates the story of THX 1138 and LUH 3417 who live in a futuristic big brother society that controls its citizens with drugs and has outlawed sex.

As SRT, one of the disillusioned citizens trying to escape along with Robert Duvall's THX 1138 and Pleasence's SEN 5241, Don Pedro Colley shares his experiences working for Lucas:

"After I was hired to be in the film, my main concern was to provide the best performance possible, but as we got started, the three of us male cast members soon realized that the things that George was proposing as his vision were not going to do what any great story, or play is supposed to do—to draw the audience in and allow them to identify with what the actors have to do to survive their situation in the boundaries of the storyline. George's view called for the actors to stand there and spout their lines, and then use his camera wizardry to complete his vision. The first person to speak up and say to Georges' face that good or great filmmaking cannot be done this way was Sir Donald and Mr. Duvall was right there to back him up. I also was seeing we were on the wrong track and wanted to have my say in the matter, but I was brand new in the business and to start out by being argumentative on my first big break would have been my last break!

"George would wander off mumbling to himself about damn actors! We stood together in explaining how it has to be to make it all work. First, we were real live characters caught in this strange world attempting to survive the consequences of where we were. We must be allowed to show our reaction to these strange and unusual circumstances and deal with what will come next. George could still use his expertise with producing all the rest!" [38]

Following his role in Lucas' science fiction adventure, Pleasence gave a harrowing performance in Ted Kotcheff's 1971 thriller *Wake in Fright* which tells the tale of John Grant, a school teacher who leaves his outback job to go on vacation and gets drawn into the male-dominated drinking society of the town of Bundanyabba. As the alcoholic "Doc" Tydon, Pleseance draws Grant into a world of utter debauchery and is responsible for Grant's slow decent into pure madness.

At this time, Pleasence also appeared in *Kidnapped*, based on Robert Louis Stevenson's novel, with Michael Caine, whom he had worked with a number of times in the past. Pleasence portrays Ebenezer Balfour, the heartless betrayer of his young nephew who ends up kidnapped for service on a ship before being rescued and teaming up with a rebel Scotsman. However, in real life, Pleasence could not have been any nicer toward his film nephew, as actor Lawrence Douglas recalls:

"*Kidnapped* was my first experience in a feature film. Previously, I had worked on stage and television at the time when rehearsals could last up to three weeks, so my confidence was not helped when the film company told me that on *Kidnapped*, I would only have a couple of quick scene run-throughs before taking a long shot and close-ups of the internationally famous actors working on the film. They could then be released and lights and camera reversed for my close-ups as David Balfour though apparently I would be left playing to a blank space and disembodied voices.

"I was also told that my first scenes would be with Donald Pleasence as Uncle Ebenezer Balfour, and because we lived not too far from each other in London, Donald asked if I wouldn't mind sharing his limousine with him for the morning journey down to the studio during his five or six days on the film. I had long admired Donald's work and of course jumped at the chance of getting to know him personally, though given the ominous roles he sometimes plays, I began wondering if this would help my confidence in the studio.

"I needn't have worried though as Donald had a great sense of humor and a high degree of professionalism and was only too keen to go over and over our scenes together en route so that by the time we reached the set I felt much more confident about my performance. Not only that, after he had finished his filming for the day, he would volunteer to work on from behind the camera to help me find a correct playing lever for my close-ups. Donald had done a considerable amount of stage work where this type of approach is not unusual as all the exchanges between actors are under scrutiny from the audience. However, he went well beyond the call of duty in applying it to these circumstances. Donald was not officially called when I started work with Michael Caine, yet he still found his way onto the set to offer his continuing support and I could not have wished for a better introduction to film." [39]

Pleasence's next theatrical performance in James Hammerstein's 1972 production of Simon Gray's *Wise Child* led to a fourth Tony Award nomination, but unfortunately, lukewarm reviews resulted in poor box office receipts and the production closed at the Helen Hayes Theatre on Broadway after only four performances. The culprit for the play's early demise may have been due to its unusual plot involving a cross-dressing criminal played by Pleasence and a boy staying with him who wants him to be his "mother." Also in the play was George Rose who made an excellent murderous partner with Pleasence in *The Flesh and the Fiends* and a young Bud Cort. Although *Wise Child* did not long endure, reviewers praised Pleasence's performance—"Feminine and masculine by turn. What a field day a psychoanalyst would have with this. Mr. Pleasence is both queenly and touching; his comic timing, harsh, tough and pointed, is superlative." [40]

Following *Wise Child*, Pleasence returned to television and films and soon gave one of the finest performances of his career in Gerald Potterton's 1973 film *The Rainbow Boys,* in which Pleasence plays Ralph Logan, an eccentric gold miner living in British Columbia whose simple life is made more adventurous upon meeting a New Yorker named Mazella who teams up with Logan and his friend Gladys to search for gold in Logan's lost Little Lemon mine. According to Potterton:

"I was blown away by Donald's performance as the old tramp in Pinter's *The Caretaker* which I had seen on Broadway. As I subsequently got to known him and Harold when we made my animated/live *Pinter People* special for NBC television, I decided to write a screenplay that would feature a character somewhat like Donald's tramp but in a totally different locale and situation. By the time we got to shooting *The Rainbow Boys* in the wilds of British Columbia, Donald knew his character and the script by heart. His character in the film was also based on a real local gold miner whom I introduced to Donald while filming *The Rainbow Boys*. Being the highly professional person that he was made my work as an inexperienced live feature director that much easier. He was always cheerful, helpful, prepared and ready to roll. Working with him was a pleasure. I later heard this same assessment had been made by other directors in Hollywood and elsewhere." [41]

Pleasence's co-star Don Calfa had this to say about working with Pleasence on *The Rainbow Boys*:

"The cabin that we used for Pleasence's character Ralph Logan was owned by a guy whose real name was Anton Logan, a Scandinavian. Everyone called him Logan like he was Irish. Interestingly, he told us everything in the cabin came out of the river. As a matter of fact, Donald's character mentions it in the movie, so we incorporated that fact in. The cabin had a wood stove and Anton Logan even made a violin out of a cigar box; he was very resourceful. When we filmed the scenes in his cabin, the real Logan sat outside and watched. He also had a good buddy who was a farmer and liked to work on cars. As a result, the guy's shirt looked real tatty with battery acid burns all over it. Donald thought it would be a perfect touch for his character and literally bought the shirt off his back for five dollars. To match the look of the shirt, Donald sanded down the rest of his clothes to give them a real worn look. He also wore his father's hat and World War I puttees or leg wraps that the soldiers wore. I was amazed at how much Donald got into his role. I think that Donald's performance as Ralph Logan was one of his most sympathetic performances. Harold Pinter also saw *The Rainbow Boys* and loved it." [42]

Subsequent films offered Pleasence more choice roles. One was as Inspector Calhoun in the 1973 horror film *Death Line* in which

Pleasence provides a tour-de-force performance filled with comedic flair and bravado. In 1974, Donald got the chance to team up with his daughter Angela, an established actress in her own right, in the Amicus horror anthology *From Beyond the Grave*. In the segment, "An Act of Kindness," Pleasence portrays Jim Underwood, an army veteran peddling wares on the street who befriends Christopher Lowe, an unhappy husband played by Ian Bannen. A relationship develops and it is not long before Jim introduces Lowe to his daughter Emily (Angela Pleasence). Lowe fancies Emily but is not prepared for her other hobby—witchcraft.

As director Kevin Connor relates:

"It was really creepy directing both Donald and Angela. They both have the same piercing blue eyes and when you have those four eyes pin-pointing you and following you around the set, it's unnerving to say the least. But it was my idea to use both Donald and Angela, or perhaps first the casting director and then I jumped on it! You could not have had any other father/daughter team playing those parts! It was a real delight to work with Donald and Angela. I feel that Donald was a brilliant actor and quite versatile and would become his character; you would forget he was Donald Pleasence on the set. He was always word perfect, charming, and helpful. I felt very honored working with Donald since it was my first directing job." [43]

Associate producer John Dark kindly provided the following comments on his involvement in *From Beyond the Grave—*

"My working relationship with Donald actually goes way back to the first picture I ever produced, *The Wind of Change* in 1961. This was a low budget 'B' film in the days of the double bill and Donald played the lead. It was many years later when I was to work with him again on *From Beyond the Grave*. I remember director Kevin Connor suggested that Donald and his daughter Angela should play father and daughter in the film. I knew Angela as for a time her son and my son went to the same school. Donald was a lovely man to work with, a total professional on both productions. During the filming of *The*

*Wind of Change*, Donald was playing in the West End in his marvelous role as Bernard Jenkins in *The Caretaker* at night apart from starring in the film during the day. Sadly, I was not able to work with him ever again after *From Beyond the Grave*. I think Donald gave wonderful performances, my favourite being his role as Blythe 'The Forger' in *The Great Escape*." [44]

Pleasence followed up *From Beyond the Grave* with *The Wolf and the Dove*, known as *The House of the Damned* in the US market, an almost dreamlike film concerning a gold statue that a young girl has hidden away and the efforts of her "family" to try and get her to reveal its whereabouts. Director Gonzalo Suarez recalls some production details and memories of working with Pleasence—

"The main house seen in the film was actually located in an estuary along a strait in Villaviciosa, Spain. The film's original title was *Darkstone* and the first draft of the script was based on an idea from Sam Peckinpah whom I had spent some time with in Austria. This was before Peckinpah made *Straw Dogs* which actually provided some non-credited dialogue to *The Wolf and the Dove*. This type of informal collaboration with Peckinpah continued for years until his death and both Donald and his wife Meira were very interested in the personality of Sam Peckinpah and asked me to tell stories about working with him.

"I remember filming the opening scene with Donald and Jose Jaspe in a cave on the ocean which was difficult and dangerous to shoot as the tide had come in and the water was up to our waistlines. However, Donald was a trooper and never complained. In fact, Donald displayed a generous amount of physical ability in the scenes that required it, an example being when his character Zayas swims from the cave to the house.

"In playing Zayas, Donald was meticulous and suggested ideas on how he could approach the character. He enjoyed the opportunity to play the protagonist, which he did not usually get a chance to do in his repertoire of films. The final scene of Zayas sitting down in a chair to die was Donald's suggestion and I liked it, despite its theatrical nature or perhaps because of it. I got on very well with Donald who was a wonderful, intelligent man with an exceptional sense of humor.

"Off-set, Donald and I used to speak French to each other and we would go to dinner together with our wives, Meira and Helene, after filming was done for the day. We especially liked a small restaurant called Port Bowl in a nearby village and during dinner, we would often grumble about how the producers of the film did not always live up to our requirements. Donald took his role very seriously and gave a lot of intensity to everything he thought about or any subject that we touched upon at dinner. When we had finished the film, Donald sat through the rushes and exclaimed, 'The film looks Japanese!' I agreed. *The Wolf and the Dove* is certainly a Japanese style film." [45]

Pleasence then appeared in *The Mutations*, a rather unconventional film with Pleasence as a mad scientist who creates a mutated hybrid human/plant creature. Much like Tod Browning's *Freaks* (1932), *The Mutations* also featured real circus freaks as cast members. As producer and co-writer of the script, Robert Weinback recalls some anecdotes on Pleasence the man and the actor:

"He was the first choice of myself and director Jack Cardiff to play Professor Nolter. I was on the set everyday and hung out with Donald as well as Tom Baker and Michael Dunn on many occasions. I loved Donald. He was great to work with and a very down to earth person with a terrific sense of humor. I do remember one funny anecdote when Donald was being 'eaten' by the plant monster, he began bellowing forth with the most ungodly shrieks. After the scene was finished, I commented on his performance and the strange, surreal utterances coming from him. His reply was 'What are you talking about? That was some of my best work!'" [46]

In 1975, Pleasence was hired for another unusual genre film called *I Don't Want to be Born*. Unlike his role in *The Mutations*, Donald plays the good doctor involved in a curse that results in a demonized baby, but his efforts as the doctor only end in an untimely demise. Script supervisor Renée Glynne recalls her time working with Pleasence—

"In my role as script supervisor, I did two films with Donald Pleasance, the first in 1973 at Pinewood (Studios) on *Sharon's Baby* (a film of many titles). He played a simpatico doctor and was pleasurable to work with and be with in the bar for awhile at the end of the day with other members of the cast and crew. The second production was *Hanna's War*, filmed during 1987 in Budapest and was such a harrowing subject. He played the main role of the slimy Hungarian fascist captain-torturer of Hanna Senesh, portrayed by Maruschka Detmers. They both came out of character between takes, making the filming bearable. Loved Donald as he was a gentle gentleman." [47]

Also in 1975, Pleasence appeared in the role based on the real-life "B" Western film producer A.J. Neitz in the comedy *Hearts of the West*. Young star Jeff Bridges recalls something that speaks volumes about Pleasence—"As I let my mind reflect, I'm reminded of nothing negative, and a smile comes to mind—gentleness, an intense gentleness." [48]

Pleasence's next film required him to suit up in medieval armor and do battle in another Kevin Connor production, the adventure comedy *Trial by Combat*. David Birney, an American actor making his first film appearance as the protagonist opposite Pleasence's villainous Sir Giles Marley, shares some of his memories on working with Pleasence in *Trial by Combat*:

"I had seen Donald before on stage and was terribly impressed. Donald and I had a lot of 'writing' to do. We were cooped up together in an under-heated room over a stable or garage. He was very down to earth and had an immense repertory of funny stories and incidents. I laughed a lot. There was one funny moment for me during the filming when I watched Donald, all dressed in armor that dwarfed his small figure (his chain mail hood kept slipping over his eyes), gamely taking up this huge broadsword and attempt battle. It was like Alice in Wonderland and very funny." [49]

A bittersweet time for Pleasence occurred in June of 1977 when his mother Alice passed away in Teddington at the age of eighty-nine. Despite this, Pleasence branched out into the writing field with the publication of his children's book *Scouse the Mouse* that revolves around a Liverpool mouse that escapes from captivity and goes on to become a pop singing sensation. *Scouse the Mouse* was also released as a children's album with former Beatle Ringo Starr as Scouse. This album was a family affair with Donald providing the narrative voice, his wife Meira helping to write the lyrics, and daughters Miranda, Polly, and Lucy contributing to the production. As illustrator for the book edition of *Scouse the Mouse*, Gerald Potterton reflects on how everything came about:

> "I once mentioned I had done a book myself for Harper and Row in the 1960s and it had been a nice experience. Donald's *Scouse the Mouse* was a nice and original story and I suggested it would also be suitable for an animation film. We formed a company and a record was made with Ringo Starr, Adam Faith and others. Unfortunately, a few years later, a film came out called *An American Tail*—strangely, a similar story to Donald's. We probably could have sued, but who knows?"[50]

Along with demonstrating his resourcefulness and humor, Pleasence also brought a disciplined approach to his film roles, and every so often would allow aspects of his past history to creep in. Such was the case with the 1978 war drama *Power Play* in which Pleasence portrays the chief of the secret police with a very cruel streak. Director Martyn Burke provides some rather startling reminiscences about Pleasence in relation to *Power Play*:

> "I was doing a film initially called *Coup d'état* that when Hollywood was finished with became *Power Play*. It was the first big Canada-UK co-production and a lot of the Canadians were nervous about working with stars like Donald who came in trailing legendary roles behind him (in those days, Toronto was not the sophisticated film production city it has since become). Peter O'Toole and David Hemmings were also in the film and came in as forces of nature, but Donald showed up so low key that had you not known he was a major international star, you could have mistaken him at first for an extra. But quickly,

that persona faded under the fiercely disciplined approach he took on the set and the impenetrable wall he carried around himself. He showed more authority with his silent looks than other actors could hope for with a month of tirades.

"Donald was both friendly and unknowable. We had many such quasi-social events and Donald was always unfailingly congenial yet intensely private. His wife was with him in Canada but we never met her. He would show up on the set, wearing his oddly incongruous little Greek fisherman's hat, become his character and then leave. He was generally adored by the crew—and a mystery. Donald asked minimal questions about his character. In retrospect, I think it was because he had already plumbed the depths of characters like the one he was playing, an Eichmann-like head of the secret police. I wanted it played in as understated a way as possible, and he outdid my expectations. He was as exciting an actor to watch as I've ever seen.

"One moment from directing Donald sticks in my mind, a strange, almost sad one, and I have wondered if it was due to playing a character he might have encountered similarly when he was held in a POW camp. We were shooting a night scene that had more minor key action than dialogue, yet suddenly, Donald went utterly and uncharacteristically blank. He was mortified that he could not remember his lines. I called a break. He studied his lines and we reshot the scene with the same results. Panic suddenly crossed Donald's face. I went to great lengths to reassure him that we'd get through it together. After another break, we began again and part way through it, he turned to me, nearly in tears saying 'I'm sorry. I simply can't do it.' It was a complete and stunning anomaly in an actor whose work ethic exuded the pride he took in what he did. We had to shut down production for the night. It never happened again."[51]

Every so often during an actor's career, a film project comes along that at first may seem trivial or perhaps beneath the talents of the actor chosen to portray a particular role. In 1978, this is exactly what occurred in the acting career of Donald Pleasence who at the time was already recognized as a talented screen performer. This film project under the direction of a little-known filmmaker named John Carpenter was *Halloween* that in essence catapulted Pleasence into the stratosphere of stardom for a whole new generation of fans.

As a so-called "slasher film," *Halloween* ushered in a new type of horror extravaganza and provided Pleasence with an iconic character that would carry him through the 1980s and into the 1990s. In this cult favorite, Pleasence is Dr. Loomis, a psychiatrist whose patient Michael Myers is the incarnation of pure evil. Plot-wise, Loomis and Myers wage an epic battle of good versus evil as Myers pursues with murderous intent a babysitter named Laurie Strode and Loomis does everything in his power to thwart him.

*Halloween* turned out to be a smash hit with fans and at the box office, resulting in seven sequels (excluding Rob Zombie's remakes). As noted by John Carpenter, Pleasence was not his first choice to play Loomis—"In the spring of 1978, I began to cast *Halloween*. My first choice was Peter Cushing as Dr. Sam Loomis. This was a year after *Star Wars* had been released. We were a tiny little, low budget movie. I was a nobody with a lot of dreams. We offered the script to Cushing and were immediately turned down by his agent." [52] However, although rejected by Cushing and later by Christopher Lee, the bright suggestion of Donald Pleasence for the role of Dr. Loomis created instant karma between actor and director and brought both of them great success. As Carpenter relates:

> "I was an enormous fan of Donald Pleasence before I worked with him. *The Great Escape, Fantastic Voyage, Will Penny,* and numerous other movies made an impression on me. He was one of the great character actors of all time. We decided to offer Donald the part of Dr. Loomis. To my amazement, he accepted the role. I first met him for lunch in Hollywood. He told me he had no idea why he was doing *Halloween* except that his daughter had liked my music for *Assault on Precinct 13.* He absolutely terrified me. Donald was extraordinary with the spooky 'Michael is evil' dialogue, and no one else could have played the ending like he did. He could hypnotize you with his eyes." [53]

Another big event in 1978 for Pleasence was being chosen by Holsten Pils Lager, a major brand in the British lager market since 1952, for their "Odd Lager Campaign" that ran until 1984. As the company's spokesman, Donald appeared in a number of comedic commercials that capitalized on his appearances in unusual films, thus bringing the Holsten Pils brand into the national spotlight. Two memorable commercials feature Pleasence as a magician's volunteer being cut in half and as an eccentric scientist that invents a robot made from Holsten Pils lager cans.

Rounding out the 1970s, Pleasence appeared with his good friend Sir Laurence Olivier in John Badham's *Dracula*, adapted from the popular Broadway play with Frank Langella as the infamous vampire. Apparently, Pleasence had been offered the role of Professor Van Helsing but felt it was too much like his just-complete Dr. Loomis role in *Halloween* and so instead chose the character of Dr. Jack Seward. Also in the cast was Sylvester McCoy as Walter the butler, and during filming, he became good friends with Pleasence. As McCoy recalls—

"Donald Pleasence? Pleasant more like it! He was a lovely witty man. I loved working with him on *Dracula*. He was funny and cheeky in his interpretation of his role. It was a joy to watch him upstaging. In everything he did, he invented a 'Tick,' which he tried to employ in every scene. In *Dracula*, eating was his 'Tick'; in others, it would be dabbing his hanky on the side of the nose or a twitch and many others. I always looked out for them in his films; they gave me such pleasure (that word again).

"He was a great actor. I first saw him on stage in *The Man in the Glass Booth* and he blew me away. That was in the early 1960s as I remember. What a joy to work with him and hang out with him. He invited me to his home and I met and became friends with his daughters, especially Angela and Polly.

"His film work was wide and brilliant. His intensity was captivating and sometimes disturbingly frightening. While on *Dracula* in Cornwall, he and I were on weather cover, so we had to wait till it rained. It became one wonderful glorious week where we sat on a lovely Victorian balcony. The sun shone, the wine flowed, the conversation roamed widely over many funny and interesting topics. He was a great tale teller. We were in Fowey in Cornwall, a beautiful old town with a history of pirates and French frigate invasions. As we sat on this magic balcony of the Fowey Hotel looking at the two guard towers, one on the other side of the mouth to the river, where a chain was pulled up each night between them to keep the French out and the pirates in and safe, a tall ship sailed through with full rigging and compliment of sailors in all their finery. It was a stupendous sight. Donald and I raised our glasses of French wine and cheered all those on the Sailing Ship Churchill as it passed by within hailing distance on its way up the beautiful River Fowey on this beautiful day in the beautiful week with Donald Pleasence."[54]

Pleasence's appearance in the film *Halloween* was the impetus for a working relationship with Carpenter. Their next collaboration was the thriller *Escape from New York* in which Pleasence portrays the President of the United States whose plane is taken over by terrorists after crashing on Manhattan Island, which has been converted into a massive escape-proof prison. The US government resorts to sending in a hardened criminal (Kurt Russell) to save the President. Carpenter reveals that Pleasence brought his own touch to the role of the President—"Donald improvised several scenes in *Escape from New York*. It was his idea to wear a blonde wig while he was being held prisoner. When he machine-guns Isaac Hayes, it was his improv, 'You're the Duke! You're the Duke! You're A number one!'" [55]

Almost back to back, Pleasence reunited with Carpenter again for a second outing of *Halloween*, which begins directly after the conclusion of the first film with Michael Myers still in pursuit of Laurie Strode, who is in the hospital where she is being treated for injuries sustained from Myers' first attack. Oddly enough, this sequel ends with Dr. Loomis apparently being burned alive in an explosion in the hospital, along with Michael Myers, but because of his popularity with *Halloween* fans, Pleasence returned as Dr. Loomis in future sequels but without Carpenter's direction.

In a 1990 interview, Pleasence provided one of the reasons why he so enjoyed working with Carpenter—"The Italians and the French treat everything seriously, while Americans do not. That's the difference between them and I'm sure there are American directors who do the same, but John Carpenter tends to have his tongue in his cheek and so do I."[56]

Stuntman and actor Dick Warlock as Michael Myers in *Halloween II* had this to say about his costar—"Donald was a complete professional. He knew everyone's lines and was always ready to work." [57]

After appearing as Dr. Loomis in the *Halloween* films, Pleasence began to be considered by the viewing public as a full-blown horror actor; however, he did not allow himself to be tied down to horror films and did appear in other genres. One of his better horror films of the 1980s was the thriller *Alone in the Dark* with fellow veteran actors Martin Landau and Jack Palance. In this film, Pleasence appears as Dr. Leo Bain, a hospital psychiatrist (although a total opposite from his turn in *Halloween*) whose psychopathic patients escape during a blackout and go after the new doctor and his family. Actress Annie Korzen, as Dr. Bain's assistant Marissa Hall in *Alone in the Dark,* recalls that the film's art director Henry Shrady "insisted on purchasing a very expensive antique desk for Donald to use. Nobody saw the point of this extravagance but then they all agreed afterwards that the desk was perfectly suited to Donald's character and it added just the right flavor to his scenes." [58]

In 1982, Pleasence gave a stirring performance in the excellent BBC adaptation of *The Barchester Chronicles* that combined Anthony Trollope's novels *The Warden* and *Barchester Towers*. Set in Victorian times, *The Barchester Chronicles* relates the lives of clergymen and their families with Pleasence as Reverend Septimus Harding whose responsible for a charity almshouse that comes under scrutiny concerning its use of funds. This series allowed Pleasence to work once again with his daughter Angela, cast as Harding's screen daughter. With Nigel Hawthorne portraying Harding's son-in-law Archdeacon Grantly, a clash of wills is set up between the two men via their differing views on politics and theology. One particular review of *The Barchester Chronicles* praises Pleasence for his portrayal of the conflicted reverend—"Mr. Pleasence brings to Harding a saintliness that hints of a fine madness. His interpretation is never less than fascinating." [59]

In 1983, Pleasence appeared in *Warrior of the Lost World*, a low-budget science-fiction adventure yarn with Pleasence as Prossor, a sort of Blofeldian dictator in a post-apocalyptic world. The film's director and writer David Worth remembers:

"I was a huge fan of Donald's work in *The Great Escape*, as a Bond villain in *You Only Live Twice*, his performance in

*Cul-de-sac*, and *THX 1138*. He was an amazing presence and always arrived prepared and ready to work. It was a real thrill for me as a very young director to be able to work with an actor of his caliber and experience. I think that Donald was the same type of actor as the great Sir Lawrence Olivier who once they had on the wardrobe, they assumed the character. Pleasence's character Prossor who resembled Blofeld as a modest 'homage' on our part, had some physical disabilities that helped flesh out his character. I specifically remember one scene when Persis Khambatta's character had to spit on Donald's face. He encouraged her to really do it several times as it seemed to give him motivation! Off the set, Donald was very quiet and unassuming. We had dinner one evening in Rome and he was as charming and fun to be with as he could possibly be." [60]

In *The Devonsville Terror*, Pleasence plays yet another doctor diligently fighting a family curse that dates back to a centuries-old witch hunt. Ulli Lommel, the film's director, provides some fascinating memories about Donald Pleasence:

"He was an angel to direct. He was sweet and caring and always so sincere and quiet. His favorite novel was Hermann Hesse's *Siddhartha* and we would discuss it when we were not shooting. And when I asked him where all the great thoughts came from, his ideas as to how to interpret his character or a scene, he would always refer to a sequence in *Siddhartha*—just be quiet and listen to the river. Five years after completing *The Devonsville Terror*, I left for Mescalero, New Mexico, to spend eighteen months with the Apache Nation. I took *Siddhartha* with me and sat on the banks of the Rio Grande and thought about Donald.

"Donald truly lived in the moment and each take was different. Sometimes, he would get very, very quiet; other times, he was suddenly screaming. But it was always very true, very authentic. He was one of the most wonderful actors to work with as opposed to Klaus Kinski who was a terrible ham and a complete idiot in every way, even though he too had his genius moments, but when you work with someone day after day, you want to have a good time with someone that loves his profession, like Donald.

"One amusing memory I have of Donald is when we would drive down Sunset Boulevard to the beach on the weekends and visit the self-realization center near the ocean in Pacific Palisades. And then we would walk around the peaceful pond and visit the gift shop where Yogananda books and memorabilia were for sale. And one day, Donald bought the kind of shirt Yogananda used to wear. It was orange, and he started imitating the famous Yogi and visitors came and thought he was a Yogi from India. And afterwards, when I drove him back to the hotel, he continued playing the role. I think he started buying into it himself. Even next morning, when the driver picked him up for the shoot, Donald was still acting like a guru and it took quite a while for him that day to switch back to the doctor of Devonsville.

"Although a very versatile actor, Donald was also highly enjoyable as the strange villain opposite James Bond in *You Only Live Twice*. No matter whether he played the everyday man or an accountant or a bastard or a vicious villain, Donald was unbeatable. There was always a certain tenderness, some special type of humanity that came shining through." [61]

Pleasence also did his share of war dramas during the 1980s, such as the Italian *First Blood* inspired *Operation Nam* in which Pleasence portrays Father Lenoir, a priest and gunrunner who provides arms to a group of ex-Marines returning to Vietnam to rescue American prisoners of war. Actor Oliver Tobias who had previously worked with Pleasence, recalls his experiences:

"I played the leading role of Berger in the London production of the musical *Hair* in 1968-69. During the run, I took part in my very first film that Donald happened to star in—*Arthur, Arthur!* I got to know him quite well at this time and we got together socially quite a few times for lunches and dinners. A very intelligent, amusing, lively, ambitious man, he was always kind to me as a younger actor and we got on well.

"Over time I lost touch with him until we were in another production together—*Dick Turpin's Greatest Adventure*. He played Ignatius Snake and I played the part of Noll Bridger. By this time, he had become more withdrawn and kept very much to himself.

"Then, many years later and much to my surprise, he turned up on the set in the middle of the godforsaken hot and humid Philippine jungle for *Operation Nam*. The main cast was staying in a hotel in Paksan Han close to the various locations. But not Donald, he had a car with a driver that ferried him back to a five star hotel in Manila. Two hours each way. This was the last time I saw and worked with him.

"It did not matter what role he played or where or for whom, he always gave an exceptionally intense, believable and dramatic performance that when working with him made situations very real. He added a most unusual complex dimension to every character he played. Every time I had the pleasure of working with him, I walked away pleased by the fact that he was such a bloody good actor, a very rare thing nowadays!"[62]

In 1987, Pleasence returned to Australia to appear in *Ground Zero*, one of his best films of the 1980s. For his powerful performance as Prosper Gaffney, Pleasence was nominated for Best Actor in a Supporting Role by the Australian Film Institute, but much like *Wake in Fright*, *Ground Zero* was not widely regarded because of the sensitive nature of the plot. According to Joy Jameson, *Ground Zero* received little or no release in England and she suspects that "it was too much when trials for compensation of aborigines had been going on for ages. Only last year were some of the cases settled." [63]

Co-director Michael Pattinson kindly agreed to provide some relevant background notes on Pleasence and the making of *Ground Zero*—

"The character Prosper Gaffney was himself a victim of the atomic tests and his various disabilities contributed to the whole of the character. Despite the fact that he was in a wheelchair, the role was quite physical because it involved being lifted and crawling, usually assisted by Charlie, played by Burnham Burnham. Rehearsals and pre-production for *Ground Zero* took place in Melbourne before moving to Cooberpedy and the outback. We (my co-director Bruce Myles and myself) introduced Donald to Les Tanner, a very well known Australian cartoonist who used the electrolarynx device. Tanner generously spent time with Donald instructing him on the use of the device and the sound it created is quite spooky which suited the character. The final sound mix is a combination of Donald's real voice and some electronic processing because the truthful sound produced by this device is devoid of inflexion and emotion." [64]

Pattinson also mentions that Pleasence was asked by the moderator of an interview held in the city of Berlin if he had ever been there before. Pleasence's reply was no, but he later "in an aside, confessed to me that he had made airborne visits" during World War II. Pattinson also warmly supports what others have had to say about Pleasence's professionalism and talent—

"Donald was a supreme professional. He was always prepped and ready to work. It is a great joy for a director when an actor adds to one's vision of a role and this was certainly the case with Donald via his imagination, extraordinary talent and experience.

"I recall Bruce Myles and I kicking around some ideas at our first meeting at the Windsor Hotel in Melbourne only hours after Donald's arrival in Australia. He had already made tape recordings of various performance ideas that simply blew us away. One idea of his was to incorporate the 'On Ilkla Moor Baht 'at' song as part of the character's mad delusion and this was a breathtaking idea. He was a perfect gentleman to work with but was also forthright in his views and spoke up when he believed the story was not being told correctly. As a young director, I greatly appreciated his wisdom and contributions." [65]

Pleasence concluded the 1980s with a return to the *Halloween* series, starring in the fourth and fifth sequels, and in 1989 starred in the remake of *Ten Little Indians* in which he portrays the judge with an axe to grind against nine other seemingly innocent strangers. Frank Stallone as the heroic Captain Philip Lombard, recalls working with Pleasence on *Ten Little Indians*—"Donald was a wonderful actor! Of course, I was in my thirties at the time and really did not have that much in common with him, but I remember that he did his job well and did not really mingle too much as he was getting up there in age by that time." [66] The end of the 1980s also marked a very happy moment in Pleasence's life, for he moved on from his divorce from Meira and married Linda Kentwood in Barbados in 1988.

After an eleven-year absence from the theatre, Pleasence returned in full form to reclaim one of his most famous roles as the tramp in Harold Pinter's *The Caretaker*. Directed by its creator, this version also featured Peter Howitt as Mick and future Oscar winner Colin Firth as Davis. After touring local theatres, this revival of *The Caretaker* officially opened on June 20, 1991 at the Comedy Theatre in London. Pleasence had first played Pinter's disheveled tramp back in 1960, a full thirty plus years that neatly bookmarked his long and distinguished career. Pleasence was quite happy to be working with his good friend Pinter once again and noted, "It's interesting to come back and work on it with Harold Pinter because he didn't direct it before and because I'm now the right age." [67] In a collaborative attempt, Pinter and Pleasence worked closely together to help flesh out the character of the tramp, which might explain why Pleasence's performance still influences actors today.

Of course, the critics could not help but compare Pleasence's different performances (two theatre productions and one film) but reacted in a positive manner on his last take on the tramp—"Donald Pleasence, who created the role of the tramp Davies at the Arts Theatre in 1960, adds the insights of the intervening years to season a performance of depth, subtlety and sly wit." [68] As Joy Jameson reminds us, "To be honest, I still think Donald felt more about the stage roles, certainly *The Caretaker* which he did twice in London, and *The Man in the Glass Booth*, written by one of his good friends Robert Shaw. In fact, for a time Pinter/Shaw/Pleasence were like the Three Musketeers." [69]

In 1991, Pleasence was featured in two interesting film roles. One showcased him in a funny tribute to Woody Allen's black comedy

*Shadows and Fog* in which Pleasence portrays the doctor of Woody Allen's character who spouts his philosophies on the nature of evil, a sort of send-up for his Dr. Loomis character in the *Halloween* series. Sharp-eyed viewers will notice a nod to one of Pleasence's most memorable films on a wall during his character's death scene—the realistic war drama *Dien Bien Phu*, which tells the story of the defeat of the French and their withdrawal from Vietnam in the late 1950s through the eyes of an American reporter. In this film, Pleasence plays real-life US correspondent Howard R. Simpson who wrote numerous books about the Vietnam War era. Pleasence once remarked that his role in *Dien Bien Phu* was "a marvelous part, but it was very exhausting making it." [70] Perhaps part of the reason for Pleasence's exhaustion was the total lack of hygiene in the jungles of Vietnam where portions of *Dien Bien Phu* were filmed and where Pleasence contracted a virus that placed a strain on his heart, which eventually necessitated surgery. [71]

1994 brought great honor for Pleasence when he was appointed an O.B.E. (Officer of the British Empire) by Queen Elizabeth II for his services to theatre and film. Pleasence attended the ceremony at Buckingham Palace with his wife Linda and his family and later proudly posed for photos. Certainly, for a young boy who once dreamed of becoming an actor, receiving the O.B.E. fully exemplified Pleasence's dedication to the craft that he so dearly loved.

During this same year, Pleasence appeared in his last theatre performance as Captain Shotover in *Heartbreak House* with production taking place at His Majesty's Theatre in Perth, Australia. Pleasence also worked with his daughter Polly who plays his character's daughter. Fellow cast member Donald MacDonald kindly shares his memories of Pleasence—

"Donald seemed to be very frail at the time we did the Shaw play in Perth, but he was very happy to work with his daughter Polly and his son-in-law as the director. I felt that I was in the presence of a great actor and used to watch him from the wings. Some of his moments were spectacularly good as if dragged up by force from his soul and his weakened body. Offstage, he spent the days alone to rest, though I did sometimes go back to his hotel after the show to see him and his wife. Donald told some Hollywood stories that were very funny but too wicked to repeat, I am afraid. Overall he was very generous and respectful of the other actors." [72]

In 1995, Pleasence appeared in his final film—*Halloween: The Curse of Michael Myers*, which concluded the "Man in Black" storyline and explained Myers' grisly penchant for murder. Pleasence returned as the now-retired Dr. Loomis, but through a plea from Jamie, Michael's niece, Loomis is driven back into action against his murderous former patient and a former colleague. As Michael Myers in this *Halloween* finale, George Wilbur recounts his experiences working with Pleasence:

"On *Halloween 6*, we traveled to and from the sets in the same van and Donald seemed to have a cold during the filming. We would only talk briefly during those encounters. He did tell me that as long as the producers kept handing him these *Halloween* scripts, he would keeping appearing in the films. He did seem to love playing the Dr. Loomis character. I was privileged to work with him on the two Halloween movies. I was a fan of his and I always watched his movies. I admired him as an actor and it was a privilege being on the same production together. In terms of his acting, he was very precise and professional. He was very believable as an actor."[73]

After completing principal shooting on the last *Halloween*, Pleasence was slated to star in a production of *King Lear* with his daughters Polly Jo and Miranda, but just before Christmas, he was admitted to the hospital for a necessary heart valve replacement. Following the operation, Pleasence, then seventy-five years old, returned to his home in France with his wife Linda to recuperate; unfortunately, complications related to the heart valve replacement led to his passing from heart failure on February 2, 1995.

A memorial service for Pleasence was held at the Comedy Theatre, where he had performed his last turn as the tramp in Harold Pinter's 1991 revival of *The Caretaker*. Besides his immediate family members, Pleasence's friends and colleagues came to honor him, including Harold Pinter, John Mortimer, Alan Bates, Gerald Potterton, Don Calfa, Joanna Lumley, Ian McShane, Bill Wyman, and Joy Jameson. Peter Vaughan, Donald's best friend, provided a touching eulogy, as did John Mortimer. The service ended with the Beatles song *All You Need is Love*. [74] As Don Calfa recalls—

"Donald was a dear friend. Gerry (Gerald Potterton) and I went to his funeral. It was very emotional. Harold Pinter spoke at the funeral as did Peter Vaughan who gave the most eloquent eulogy. There was a reception at Donald's house afterwards given by Linda. I always knew Donald was a big art collector but was amazed to see his paintings by John Bratby and Francis Bacon." [75]

In the words of Gerald Potterton, "Donald was the most generous of men, and even if he jumped up and down and yelled his head off occasionally over some mishap or such, one knew under the mask there was a true and gentle giant. Of course, he could play the worst kind of monsters on screen, but it was all an act. With Donald, there was never a dull moment." [76]

Joy Jameson added, "Donald was a great actor and a very generous man. He was an excellent parent. A *bon viveur* too. He is very much missed and no one has come along to replace him." [77]

Lastly, John Carpenter thoughtfully relates, "I loved Donald and he became a close friend. He always brought something unique to every role. He was versatile, yes, but he had the quality of any great movie star. He was Donald Pleasence." [78]

In essence, whether portraying a villain, a doctor, a military officer, a psychiatrist, a lowly tramp, or a madman, Donald Pleasence always provided interesting and fascinating characterizations that drew the audience in and then pleasantly rewarded them with an excellent stage, television, or screen performance. For this, Donald Pleasence will forever be remembered in the hearts and minds of his fans around the world.

# THE FILMS

## *The Beachcomber* (1954)

**Cast:** Glynis Johns (Martha Jones), Robert Newton (Edward "Honorable Ted" Wilson), Donald Sinden (Ewart Gray), Paul Rogers (Reverend Owen Jones), Donald Pleasence (Tromp), Walter Crisham (Vederala), Michael Hordern (The Headman), Auric Lorand (Alfred, Major Domo), Tony Quinn (Ship Captain). Directed by Muriel Box.

**Synopsis:** Ewart Gray is the new Resident in Charge of the Welcome Islands in the Indian Ocean. Once at his new location, Gray is introduced to his staff by Tromp (Donald Pleasence), his personal adjutant. The only other Europeans on the island are the Reverend Owen Jones, his physician sister Martha, and the perpetual drunk and ne'er-do-well Edward Wilson, known as "Honorable Ted" by the locals. Jones and Martha make it known to Gray that Ted is not to be trusted and they accuse him of corrupting a village girl to steal money from the collection box. At first, Gray tries to give Ted the benefit of the doubt, but when he causes an out of control bar fight, Gray sentences him to three months hard labor on a nearby island. During that time, Martha travels to the islands to operate on the village chief, but winds up also doing unexpected surgery on an elephant following a crocodile attack. When Ted is released from his punishment, he immediately returns to his old ways, forcing Gray to decide that Ted must be deported to Australia. But when a cholera outbreak occurs on the islands, Martha asks for Ted to accompany her for protection as she travels to some of the islands to try and help the natives. Ted reluctantly agrees and they travel to the islands to nurse the sick and disinfect the water. Some of

the villagers believe that the white man's medicine is actually causing the disease and when the chief's daughter dies from it, Martha
and Ted are tied up to be killed. However, luck is on their side when
the elephant sent to crush them turns out to be the same one Martha
treated, thus sparing their lives. Back on the island, Gray is comforted
about the cholera outbreak by Tromp who explains how they saved
many lives. Gray then realizes that they did do well and is pleasantly
surprised to hear that Martha and Ted, now a changed man, are getting
married and together will help out the villagers.

**Commentary:** *The Beachcomber* is a well-done love story set in an exotic locale. The real stars of the film are Glynis Johns as the good-hearted
Martha and Robert Newton as "Honorable Ted," the black sheep of the
family outcast to the islands and a true diamond in the rough. Newton,
well known for his portrayal as the pirate Long John Silver, was sadly a
case of life imitating art in *The Beachcomber*. His career suffered numerous problems, due to his drinking, and died at the age of fifty in 1956,
but his performance in *The Beachcomber* is certainly very well-acted and
the eventual romance between his character and Martha is made all the
more believable because of it. Another unexpected star of this film is the
elephant as part of a graphic battle with a crocodile that later proves that
elephants truly never forget.

In his very first film role, Pleasence plays Tromp, an Indian assistant
to the new Resident in Charge. While Pleasence is a British actor playing an Indian which was standard practice at this time in British films, he
actually does quite a good job and his role albeit a minor one is featured
throughout the storyline. Pleasence even received recognition in a *New
York Times* review, "Donald Pleasence is properly authentic in a native
role." [79] Dressed in a white British imperial uniform and wearing spec-
tacles, Tromp is clearly the go-between for the natives and their British
masters. All communications with the natives goes through him and he
seemingly must announce all visitors to Gray, but his best part comes toward the conclusion when Tromp explains to Gray that even though cholera took the lives of 1,200 people, they saved many more through their
efforts. Tromp's speech explaining how he lost his whole family because of
an earlier cholera outbreak and how things are now better is quite moving
and is certainly an excellent beginning in film for Donald Pleasence.

# *Orders are Orders* (1954)

**Cast:** Brian Reece (Captain Harper), Margot Grahame (Wanda Sinclair), Raymond Huntley (Colonel Bellamy), Sid James (Ed Waggermeyer), Tony Handcock (Lieutenant Wilfred Cartroad), Peter Sellers (Private Goffin), Clive Morton (General Sir Cuthbert Grahame-Foxe), June Thorburn (Veronica Bellamy), Maureen Swanson (Joanne Delamere), Donald Pleasence (Corporal Martin), Eric Sykes (Private Waterhouse), Bill Fraser (Private Slee). Directed by David Paltenghi.

**Synopsis:** Hollywood director Ed Waggermeyer convinces Captain Harper of the British army to allow his crew to use some barracks to shoot his new low-budget science fiction film involving an alien invasion and lots of pretty women. Harper secretly hopes that by allowing the filming, he will impress aspiring actress Joanne Delamere to whom he is greatly attracted. But when Waggermeyer arrives, all-out chaos ensues because his pretty actresses are a constant distraction for the soldiers. Colonel Bellamy finds out but is smoothed over by Waggermeyer's partner Wanda Sinclair who promises him a role in the film. Soon enough, Waggermeyer's film crew takes over the barracks' gym and the soldiers work for him as helpers and extras. Adding to the chaos is that Bellamy's daughter Veronica likes Harper which inspires privates Goffin and Slee to attempt to sabotage Harper's advances toward Joanne since they are loyal to the colonel and his daughter. Everything comes to a head when General Sir Cuthbert Grahame-Foxe shows up for an unannounced inspection amid all of the shenanigans. In order to get him off the base, the general convinces Waggermeyer to use his cousin's supposed haunted house for filming while Harper convinces Joanne that she is his one true love. Once the base is cleared of the outsiders, the general tells everyone to return to work—orders are orders.

**Commentary:** As a remake of the 1934 film version, *Orders are Orders* is not a great film by any means but does provide some laughs, mostly because of a standout performance by a young Peter Sellers. As private Goffin, Sellers is a bit of a goofball whose attempts to become an extra in the film and defend Veronica Bellamy's honor at the expense of Captain Harper are quite funny. More laughs are provided by Sid James as the fast-talking American director Ed Waggermeyer who seems to be able to fool everyone except the general. An interesting note is that *Orders are Orders* also features the film debut of Tony Handcock as Lieutenant Wilfred Cartroad, the director of music whose band keeps interrupting Waggermeyer's filming. During the same year that *Orders are Orders* was released, Sid James teamed up with Tony Handcock for a BBC radio comedy series entitled *Handcock's Half Hour* which proved so successful that it branched off into a television series.

Pleasence appears as Corporal Martin in only one scene when the soldiers bring film props into the gym where Waggermeyer plans on shooting his science fiction film. Corporal Martin is in charge of some of the officers and announces to his superior that they have just delivered ray guns and space suits before discussing the use of an alien mind control device. This particular role is smaller than Pleasence's first in *The Beachcomber*, but as Pleasence was a struggling actor in 1954, he was forced to take whatever he could get.

# *Value for Money* (1955)

**Cast:** John Gregson (Chayley Broadbent), Diana Dors (Ruthine West), Susan Stephen (Ethel), Derek Farr (Duke Popplewell), Frank Pettingell (Mayor Higgins), Charles Victor (Lumm), Ernest Thesiger (Lord Dewsbury), Donald Pleasence (Limpy), Hal Osmond (Mr. Hall), Jill Adams (Joy), Joan Hickson (Mrs. Perkins), John Glyn-Jones (Arkwright), Ferdy Mayne (Waiter). Directed by Ken Annakin.

**Synopsis:** Chayley Broadbent's father passes away, leaving him a large sum of money from the family rag mill. Being a chip off the old block, Chayley penny pinches whenever spending and imagines that his father speaks to him from beyond the grave with advice about money. Engaged to Ethel, a town reporter, Chayley proposes they get married under the premise that he would be saving money on a housekeeper which drives Ethel away in frustration. Chayley's friends convince him to go to London with them to watch the football game and catch a show afterwards. All goes well, in fact very well for Chayley who falls head over heels in love at the revue for the gorgeous blonde actress Ruthine "Ruthy" West. He takes her to dinner but fails to make an impression when Chayley tells her about his family business and she witnesses firsthand his penny pinching ways. At their second dinner, Chayley proposes to Ruthy but she turns him down. Returning home alone, Chayley decides to change his life around to attract Ruthy, so he becomes a member of the town council after donating a large parcel of land for a recreational center for children. Chayley then convinces Ruthy to come and supply some glamour for the official opening of the center which she does reluctantly. However, when Ruthy finds out that Chayley inherited a considerable sum of money, she quickly warms up to him and is soon shopping for an engagement ring much to the disappointment of Ethel. But being engaged to an actress does not turn out as Chayley expected as his money starts disappearing quickly. When Ruthy picks out a fancy house, Chayley can take no more and walks away from her, but when Ruthy meets Ethel who has come for an interview, they have a heart to heart discussion and devise a plan to set Chayley straight in his ways. Under the threat of being exposed for having proposed to two different women, the mayor calls him in to marry one girl and pay off the other. Realizing the errors of his ways, Chayley proposes again to Ethel who accepts, but as Ruthy is about to leave, she meets up with one of Chayley's friends, resulting in a double wedding.

**Commentary:** *Value for Money,* a phrase used by Chayley's friends concerning their trip to London and the show, is a nicely done romantic comedy and truly captures the working class look and feel of the town with Batley, England substituting for the fictional Barfield. The story on how Chayley Broadbent is finally able to step out of the shadow of his father involves pitting Londoners against country folk is quite amusing, mostly because of the presence of Diana Dors as the sexy blonde bombshell, a role that Dors perfected throughout her career. Considered as the British counterpart of Marilyn Monroe, Dors was not only a beautiful woman but also an accomplished actress and she would later appear in two other Donald Pleasence films—*The Pied Piper* and *From Beyond the Grave*. In *Value for Money*, Dors' character of Ruthine "Ruthy" West possesses more than enough looks and charms to entice Chayley to relentlessly pursue her; the scene in which she is presented to the town of Barfield at the new swimming pool is a comical delight.

*Value for Money* marks Pleasence's first appearance in a color film. His portrayal as Limpy, aptly named due to a limp, projects with great effect an old timer with his hair all grayed out and sporting a bushy mustache. As a character, Limpy was previously employed by old Mr. Broadbent at the rag mill and thus has the respect of Chayley who asks him for advice. Although Pleasence's role is a secondary character and does not have much screen time, he still manages to invest life into Limpy by making it appear that he has been through it all at the family business and deserves respect from those around him.

# *1984* (1956)

**Cast:** Edmond O'Brien (Winston Smith), Michael Redgrave (General O'Connor), Jan Sterling (Julia), David Kossoff (Charrington), Mervyn Johns (Jones), Donald Pleasence (R. Parsons), Carol Wolveridge (Selina Parsons), Ernest Clark (Outer Party Announcer), Patrick Allen (Inner Party Official), Ronan O'Casey (Rutherford), Michael Ripper (Outer Party Orator), Ewen Solon (Outer Party Orator), Kenneth Griffith (prisoner). Directed by Michael Anderson.

**Synopsis:** In the immediate future of a nuclear war, three great police states rise up and divide the world. Although atomic weapons have been abolished, continuous warfare between the states keeps absolute power in the hands of the governments. In London, the capital of one of the states known as Oceania, lives Winston Smith, a worker who translates history into New Speak for the government. Smith becomes fed up with the ever-watchful eye of "Big Brother," due to witnessing first-hand the injustice of the government in accusing and condemning the innocent. While at work, Smith becomes infatuated with a fellow female worker named Julia, but because "Big Brother" has outlawed the intermingling of the sexes, Smith and Julia secretly make plans to meet out in a field, free of the government's watchful eyes. There, they find themselves committing the crime of falling in love and continue to do so in clandestine rendezvous before finding an empty apartment above an antique store. Wanting desperately to break free of "Big Brother," Smith joins an underground movement and confides to his boss General O'Connor, due to sensing that he is a secret member of the movement. However, Smith and Julia are tricked by O'Connor who uses their trust to track them to their apartment where they are arrested and tortured in order to convert them into "'useful" citizens for "Big Brother" once again. Smith and Julia are eventually released when Big Brother deems them as "cursed" with their once blossoming love being no more.

**Commentary:** George Orwell's horrifying look at the future and the intrusive power of government was previously filmed by the BBC in 1954 as a teleplay that adhered close to Orwell's original novel. This 1956 version of the film (with the title as numbers instead of spelled out), strays from the original source in some respects and as a result is an inferior version. However, the performances in Michael Anderson's *1984* are well acted and convey quite well the paranoia, dreams, and fears of Orwell's dystopic novel. Particularly chilling is Michael Redgrave's performance as the cool and calculating Inner Party Chief O'Connor. With an obviously bigger budget than the earlier BBC teleplay, *1984* features a number of futuristic gadgets that in 1956 were still years away.

Pleasence had the unique distinction of being in both the 1954 and 1956 versions of *1984*. In the original, Pleasence plays Syme, a fellow government worker of Winston Smith who is truly loyal to the government but is "turned in" for being a traitor and suffers a nervous breakdown. In the 1956 film version, Pleasence portrays R. Parsons, a character based on Syme, who is also a fellow government worker of Winston Smith but is much more fleshed out. Parsons is also Smith's neighbor and lives with his daughter Selina who is even more loyal to the government. In many ways, Selina expresses the attitude and loyalty of a member of the Hitler Youth during World War II. Parsons does his bit for the government by going around and collecting contributions for "Hate Week" when political prisoners are paraded in front of the enraged citizens of Oceania. However, Parsons, like Syme, is eventually reported to "Big Brother" for disloyalty by none other than Selina. The scene in which Pleasence is thrown down a staircase by a guard and begs to be "saved" by "Big Brother" is truly a sympathetic performance, even more so than Edmond O'Brien's Winston Smith; in fact, Pleasence actually improved upon his performance from the 1954 version. An interesting side note is that Carol Wolveridge as Parson's daughter Selina would years later appear in Pleasence's popular television program *Armchair Mystery Theatre*.

## *The Black Tent* (1956)

**Cast:** Donald Sinden (Colonel Sir Charles Holland), Anthony Steel (Captain David Holland), Anna-Maria Sandri (Mabrouka ben Yussef), Andre Morell (Shiek Salem ben Yussef), Terence Sharkey (Daoud Holland), Donald Pleasence (Ali), Ralph Truman (Major Croft), Anthony Bushell (Ambassador Baring), Michael Craig (Shiek Faris), Anton Diffring (Senior Nazi Officer), Frederick Jaeger (Junior Nazi officer). Directed by Brian Desmond Hurst.

**Synopsis:** Captain David Holland, the owner of a large estate in England, disappears during a desert campaign in Libya during World War II and is presumed missing or dead. As a result, his brother and heir to his estate, Colonel Sir Charles Holland, is called down by the local military command because of receiving a note for a military bond written in David's handwriting only two weeks before his disappearance. Curious as to what happened to his brother, Charles travels to Libya and with his guide Ali (Donald Pleasence) travels to the black tents of the Bedouins from where the bond was originally sent. Once there, Charles's questions to Sheik Salem ben Yussef fall on deaf ears; he then sees a boy who closely resembles his brother among the tribe that leads to the boy's mother giving Charles his brother's diary. According to the diary, David was wounded during an attack by Nazi forces and was rescued by Mabrouka ben Yussef, the daughter of the sheik, who nursed him back to health and in the process fell in love with him. However, Mabrouka was already promised to Sheik Faris who was jealous of David being so near to his betrothed. Wishing to rejoin his troops, David sought out the help of the sheik to ambush some Nazi soldiers in order to steal their jeep. This mission was successful but the body of Faris who had provided the camp locations ended up among the Nazis. Back at the camp, David professed his love for Mabrouka and with the sheik's blessing were married, but their happiness was interrupted with news that the Germans are on the run with David once again enlisting the sheik's help to assist British troops. But this time the mission failed and

David was killed saving the sheik. After reading the diary, Charles inquires about the last pages and discovers that the boy Daoud is the real heir to David's estate. But Daoud does not wish to leave his mother or give up his culture, so he burns the page as his answer.

**Commentary:** *The Black Tent* is an average film that crams in much material—World War II battles, Nazi soldiers, a family mystery, and a love story. The results are mostly good, although the love angle is a bit weak, due to the less than stellar acting of Anna-Maria Sandri as Mabrouka (apparently her English was so bad that screenwriter Bryan Forbes had his wife dub her voice), plus the fact that other main native roles are played by British actors with Andre Morrell and Donald Pleasence both providing great performances. The scenery is breathtaking as are the Roman ruins and the war scenes. Another plus is Anton Diffring as the senior Nazi officer (a role he perfected during his career), and the debut of Frederick Jaeger as the junior Nazi officer.

Two years after playing the servant to Donald Sinden's character in *The Beachcomber*, Pleasence once again found himself in a similar though this time larger role. Like his previous character of Tromp, Pleasence's skin has been darkened in order to play Ali, a happy-go-lucky Syrian who knows his way around and how to make a quick buck. One great scene that occurs not long after their journey has begun has Ali boasting to Charles that he can arrange women for a price. But Charles, being more concerned about finding his brother, refuses which prompts Ali to innocently ask, "What can be more important than girls, colonel?" After getting to know Charles, Ali reveals that he has been westernized via complaining about the Bedouin tents and declaring that he prefers clean living, education, and Coca-Cola.

# *The Man in the Sky* (1957)

**Cast:** Jack Hawkins (John Mitchell), Elizabeth Sellars (Mary Mitchell), Jeremy Bodkin (Nicholas Mitchell), Gerard Lohan (Philip Mitchell), Walter Fitzgerald (Reginald Conway), John Stratton (Peter Hook), Eddie Byrne (Ashmore), Lionel Jeffries (Keith), Donald Pleasence (Crabtree). Directed by Charles Crichton.

**Synopsis:** Test pilot John Mitchell is experiencing some financial difficulties and only wishes to make a better life for his wife Mary and their two children. At Conway Aero-Manufacturing Company where he works, Mitchell has just been assigned to take the company's pride and joy, a new rocket powered prototype transport plane, for a test flight. Also onboard are government ministry official Crabtree (Donald Pleasence) and Ashmore, a buyer's representative. Before take-off, Conway, Mitchell's boss, tells him that if Ashmore does not give his recommendation to buy the plane, the company will go out of business because every cent is tied up in the project. Mitchell realizes that he too will be out of work if Ashmore's recommendation fails to result in a contract. While in flight, the plane's engine catches fire, and although it is quickly extinguished, the plane's navigation is affected, forcing Conway to order the passengers and crew to parachute from the plane, leaving only Mitchell who decides to ignore Conway and try to safely land the aircraft. After flying until most of the fuel has run out, Mitchell finally lands the plane safely, saving both the company and his job.

**Commentary:** Much like *No Highway in the Sky* (1951), *The Sound Barrier* (1952) and *Cone of Silence* (1960), *The Man in the Sky*, a.k.a. *Decision Against Time*, features a heroic pilot and lends itself to a lot of tension which of course makes for great cinema. Jack Hawkins plays the lead role with dignity and loyalty as the everyman who simply wishes to provide for his family and satisfy his boss. There is some fine drama between Mitchell and his wife Mary while arguing over the purchase of a new house and Mitchell's decision to try and save the prototype plane is a noble effort and keeps the audience rooting for his success against insurmountable odds. The rest of the cast, including Pleasence in a small role as government minister Crabtree and Eddie Byrne as the would-be plane purchaser, provides solid acting that helps drive the storyline. Pleasence's role is typical of his first few films, but he still manages to invest his talent and abilities to make his character believable. Although *The Man in the Sky* is a drama, it is interesting to note is that it was made by Ealing Studios, mostly known for its well-crafted comedies like *The Ladykillers* (1955) and later *Barnacle Bill* that also provided a small role for Pleasence.

# *Manuela* (1957)

**Cast:** Trevor Howard (James Prothero), Elsa Martinelli (Manuela Hunt), Pedro Armendariz (Mario Constanza), Donald Pleasence (Evans), Warren Mitchell (Moss), Jack MacGowran (Tommy), Harcourt Curacao (Wellington Jones), Barry Lowe (Murphy). Directed by Guy Hamilton.

**Synopsis:** James Prothero is the captain of an old steamship that docks in South America to drop off the body of their recently deceased chief engineer. While on leave, crew member Mario Constanza meets the beautifully captivating Manuela Hunt who is desperate to get to England. Constanza is instantly attracted to her and agrees to sneak her aboard ship hoping to make her his future wife when they return home. But when he tries to make romantic advances once they are aboard, Manuela cries out which attracts the attention of Prothero who promptly has Constanza locked up. Upset at having a woman aboard, Prothero decides to stop at the nearest port to get rid of both Constanza and Manuela, but along the way, Prothero finds himself falling for Manuela's charms and soon enough can think of nothing else but marrying and spending the rest of his life with her. Constanza is eventually released to return to work in the engine room, where he notices some of the stored coal has caught on fire and alerts Evans (Donald Pleasence), Prothero's first mate. Evans does what he can but his efforts to get Prothero to come and evaluate the problem falls on deaf ears because the captain has holed himself up with Manuela in his quarters. The fire soon spreads out of control and everyone is forced to evacuate by lifeboat. On the way back to shore, Evans promises Prothero that he will turn him over to the authorities for his negligence, but Constanza throws Evans overboard. Realizing the dangers that Manuela has caused, Prothero sends Constanza to the inn where Manuela is waiting to tell her that Evans has died.

**Commentary:** *Manuela*, a.k.a. *Stowaway Girl*, is a well-made drama on how a woman brings about total disaster for a ship and its crew. In fact, Manuela should have been the poster girl for why women were not allowed on ships in the past. In the title role is Elsa Martinelli in one of her early film appearances. An Italian by birth, Martinelli started her career after being discovered working as a barmaid and by the 1960s was acting in a number of films opposite Hollywood stars like John Wayne in *Hatari!* (1962) and Robert Mitchum in *Rampage* (1963). Trevor Howard as the crusty sea captain Prothero also provides a strong performance as a man who at first is cold to the world but opens his heart to a beautiful girl, ends up spurned for his advances and then reverts back to his old self.

After small roles in his first six films, Pleasence was finally allowed to shine in *Manuela*, his first big break. His character of Evans is featured throughout and acts as the conscious of the ship. While the crew as well as the captain is head over heels in love with Manuela, it is Evans who maintains his composure and tries to keep the ship on course to their destination. Apparently, Evans' relationship with the captain is somewhat shaky which is understandable as Evans is an up-and-coming by the book man while Prothero is a hard drinking, melancholy captain facing the end of his career. Here in his first major role, Pleasence utilizes an acting cue that he would rely on throughout his career—his eyes. For example, when Evans goes to Prothero's cabin to fetch him, the captain come to the door in his robe with Manuela's legs in view on the bed. Pleasence's eyes go from shock to disapproval in a bit of ocular acting. Evans is also revealed to be the minister of the ship, saying prayers in his first scene for the departed engineer and then praying in the lifeboat for God to show them the way. Unfortunately for Evans, Prothero and Constanza do not share the same views which leads to Evan's death. One interesting note is that *Manuela* is the first film in which Pleasence's lack of hair is truly revealed. Also, the credits misspell Pleasence as Pleasance, an error that occured a number of times during his career.

# *Barnacle Bill* (1957)

**Cast:** Alec Guinness (Captain William Horatio Ambrose), Irene Browne (Mrs. Barrington), Maurice Denham (Crowley), Percy Herbert (Tommy), Victor Maddern (Figg), Allan Cuthbertson (Chailey), Harold Goodwin (Duckworth), Donald Pleasence (Cashier), Lloyd Lamble (Superintendent Browning), Harry Locke (Reporter). Directed by Charles Frend.

**Synopsis:** William Horatio Ambrose comes from a long line of seafaring ancestors, but his own entry into the profession does not go smoothly because Ambrose is prone to bouts of sea sickness. After spending the war years doing secret trials for the British Navy testing antidotes for seasickness, Ambrose is promoted to captain and purchases a run-down amusement park on the water called Sandcastle Pier. But the pier is more run down than Ambrose expected; he also has to deal with lazy sailors and Mrs. Barrington, the town councilwoman who deems his amusement games as a form of gambling. Not to be deterred, Ambrose runs the pier like a vessel, making his sailors ship up, clean up the boardwalk, and even convince the local authorities to allow Ambrose to keep the amusement games. But at every turn, Mrs. Barrington is there, trying to prevent improvements and additions that Ambrose plans for the pier. When the mayor and his supporters decide to demolish the pier to make way for a new marine front, Mrs. Barrington at first is very pleased until she discovers that her bathing huts are also going to be razed. With no one to turn to for help, Mrs. Barrington is surprised to find Ambrose offering to assist her that makes her see the error of her ways. Together, they combine their ideas and make the pier their own pleasure craft called the Arabella. With the bathing huts combined with the pier and its amusements and music, the Arabella becomes a tremendous success, drawing in large crowds of visitors. Of course, the mayor and his supporters are not happy about the success of the Arabella, due to standing to make a lot of money from its demolition and the rebuilding of the marine front. This sets up a confrontation between the mayor, his cronies and his lawyers and Ambrose and Mrs. Barrington who are more than capable of taking on the corrupt town counsel.

**Commentary:** *Barnacle Bill*, a.k.a. *All at Sea*, the US title and a reference to the Ambrose family motto, is a delightful comedy from famed Ealing Studios that began turning out comedies in 1947 with writer T.E.B. Clarke at the helm via his first comedy called *Hue and Cry*. *Barnacle Bill* would be the last of the Ealing Studios comedies and was also written by Clarke. What really makes this film such a success is its lead star Alec Guinness who first became noticed through his various hit comedies for the studio like *Kind Hearts and the Coronets*, *The Lavender Hill Mob*, and *The Ladykillers*. Guinness possessed not only a flair for witty and slapstick comedy but was also a master of the physical aspect of comedy. Scenes with Guinness dancing in the pier's new dancehall and trying to pace back and forth in his quarters (a converted funhouse) are classic bits that highlight his varied comedic skills.

Donald Pleasence has a very small role in *Barnacle Bill* with only one line of dialog, not counting him singing along with the rest of the bankers at the conclusion. Playing a cashier at a bank, Pleasence's scene is opposite Alec Guinness and is quite amusing. Ambrose marches into the bank with a canister of rum and a reporter writing his story in tow. Marching up to the cashier, Ambrose demands cups for the rum. Pleasence's incredulous look is great when he tries to point out that they are in a bank, only to have Ambrose force him to hand over a cup from a first aid kit and a vase after emptying it of water and flowers which Ambrose leaves behind in the dumbfounded cashier's hands.

# *A Tale of Two Cities* (1958)

**Cast:** Dirk Bogarde (Sydney Carton), Dorothy Tutin (Lucie Manette), Cecil Parker (Jarvis Lorry), Stephen Murray (Dr. Manette), Paul Guers (Charles Darnay), Christopher Lee (Marquis St. Evremonde), Donald Pleasence (Barsad). Directed by Ralph Thomas.

**Synopsis:** As the French Revolution begins to unfold, Dr. Manette is freed from the Bastille. His daughter Lucie travels by coach to bring him home and along the way finds herself falling for fellow passenger Charles Darnay. After collecting her father, Lucie appears in court to support Darnay, falsely accused of treason in a set-up orchestrated by his cousin the Marquis St. Evremonde and his spy Barsad (Donald Pleasence). British barrister Sydney Carton wins Darnay's freedom, but is it bittersweet because he loves Lucie and knows that it will be unrequited because she only loves Darnay. Darnay eventually marries Lucie, but his membership in the St. Evremonde clan gets him arrested while in France with the threat of death by the guillotine unless Carton can somehow prove his love and save the day.

**Commentary:** Charles Dickens' classic tale of love set amid the French Revolution has been filmed numerous times, with the best known example being the 1935 production with Ronald Colman. However, this adaptation has strong performances from the supporting cast and sticks more closely to the novel. Bogarde provides a believable Sydney Carton, the British barrister who has wasted a good portion of his life drinking only to finally find his true love who does not think of him in the same way. Also on hand is Christopher Lee who was just beginning to make a name for himself with Hammer films as the villainous Marquis St. Evremonde whose cruel demeanor and callous actions draw the wrath of the citizens of Paris, resulting in his murder and Charles Darnay's death sentence.

*A Tale of Two Cities* provided Pleasence with the first important role in his early career, and he certainly took advantage of the opportunity. His character of John Barsad is indeed treacherous as a henchman for the Marquis St. Evremonde, spying on the Marquis' cousin Charles Darnay and then setting him up for a charge of treason. But when this fails, Darnay is warned by Sydney Carton that Barsad will not give up and is a very dangerous fellow. True to this description, Barsad fakes his own death, due to being exposed in court which provides a neat connection to Pleasence's role in *The Flesh and the Fiends* as William Hare, the wily and immoral grave robber. Starting over as a "friend" of the revolutionary cause, Barsad then goes by the name of John Solomon and shows up at the trial of Darnay whom he was previously unsuccessful in framing. Sydney Carton recognizes Barsad and after cornering and threatening to expose him, forces him to help free Darnay in a swap before his execution. This is Pleasence's highlight as his character reaches a turning point when he finally realizes that Carton intends to sacrifice himself to save Darnay and offers his hand in admiration and respect. Carton does not shake his hand but rather touches Barsad's shoulder as a sign of forgiveness for his crimes. Later seen while Carton is being led to the guillotine, Barsad shouts at a zealous citizen to be quiet so as not to upset Carton. Certainly, Barsad was the first of many well-developed characters that later on would become a sort of trademark for Pleasence the actor.

# *Heart of a Child* (1958)

**Cast:** Jean Anderson (Maria), Donald Pleasence (Herman Spiel), Richard Williams (Karl Spiel), Maureen Pryor (Frau Spiel), Norman Macowan (Heiss), John Glyn-Jones (Priest), Willoughby Goddard (Stott), Andrew Keir (Constable), John Boxer (Breuer), Carla Challoner (Elsa), Raymond Adamson (Hans Heiss), Charles Gray (Frtiz Heiss). Directed by Clive Donner.

**Synopsis:** Karl Spiel is a young boy living with his family on a farm in Austria during World War I. His beloved dog Rudy is always with him, ready to help with his chores for his overbearing father Herman Spiel (Donald Pleasence). Karl is often torn between family duties and his education and religion by the village priest, but the only person who lends Karl a sympathetic ear is Maria, one of the village women. One day, Karl's father catches a butcher trying to poach animals off his land to sell as meat in his shop and after a discussion, they settle on selling Rudy instead for meat. When Karl hears of this plan from his sister Elsa, he immediately goes to Maria for help who hatches a plan to hide Rudy and then have Karl take him to Innsbruck where she knows a veterinarian who will take the dog in. After hiding Rudy and narrowly escaping from getting caught by his father, Karl goes to church to pray for money for the trip to Innsbruck, but ends up taking money from the church collection box. In Innsbruck, Herr Breuer the vet takes in Rudy and Karl returns home, where he is met by his father who savagely beats him over the missing dog. The priest and the villagers intervene on Karl's behalf, and when Karl sees Maria again, he is told that Rudy was sold to the English Red Cross. Horrified that they may harm his dog, Karl once again travels to Innsbruck and steals Rudy back to hide in a mountain pass. When a big snowstorm strands Karl on a cliff, Rudy runs back home for help and the villagers rescue Karl. Karl's father, after seeing a second chance to reconnect with his son, then allows Karl to keep Rudy.

**Commentary:** *Heart of a Child* is an enjoyable drama set in the beautiful English countryside that substitutes for Austria. There are some similarities to the classic *Lassie*, but Rudy is instead a Saint Bernard, a more rugged and suitable canine for life in the Alps. Richard Williams, who plays the young Karl Spiel, is quite sympathetic as the traditional boy devoted to his dog; the Saint Bernard as Rudy is also a pretty good "actor," especially during the finale when Karl needs to be rescued. An interesting note is that Carla Challoner who portrays Pleasence's daughter would also play the daughter of his character in *Circus of Horrors*; eagle-eyed viewers will also spot Charles Gray as one of the villagers. Both Pleasence and Gray would later appear as the villainous Ernest Blofeld in the ever-popular James Bond 007 action thrillers.

Pleasence plays Herman Spiel, a man who would give Darth Vader a run for his money as one of the cruelest fathers ever depicted in the cinema. Spiel certainly cares for his valuable livestock, but when the butcher suggests buying Karl's dog Rudy to turn into sausage meat, a light goes on in Spiel's head and he readily agrees. Other undesirable actions by Spiel includes forcing his son Karl to skip school and religion to do manual labor, and later beating him bloody with a large stick until the villagers step in and stop him. But Spiel's worst offense is refusing to look after Karl when told that he is lost and relying on the villagers to rescue him. When Karl is eventually returned, Spiel seems to care more about his lost lamb that Karl had almost died from saving. But all is not lost, and like Darth Vader, there is some good in Spiel, such as when he gives a moving speech to Maria that he wants to be liked and loved but does not know how. Pleasence does a great job using his eyes to convey lost emotions and confusion, and in the end, it is clear that Spiel will try to repair his relationship with his son.

## *The Wind Cannot Read* (1958)

**Cast:** Dirk Bogarde (Flight Lieutenant Michael Quinn), Yoko Tani (Sabbi), Ronald Lewis (Lieutenant Fenwick), John Fraser (Lieutenant Peter Munroe), Anthony Bushell (Brigadier), Donald Pleasence (Doctor). Directed by Ralph Thomas.

**Synopsis:** As a Flight Lieutenant in the British Royal Air Force stationed in India during World War II, Michael Quinn is informed by fellow lieutenant and friend Peter Munroe that they have been selected to enter a training program to learn Japanese in order to interrogate prisoners of war. While in the program, Quinn finds himself falling in love with the instructor, a beautiful Japanese woman named Sabbi whose family left Japan before the war, and as they get to know one another, Sabbi ends up falling in love with Quinn. They eventually marry on a secret holiday getaway to India, but back at base, their relationship is exposed although the brigadier allows them to live off base in his former home. Quinn is later sent into service in Japan but gets captured by the Japanese army along with Lieutenant Fenwick. In the enemy camp, Fenwick reveals that Sabbi has a life threatening condition that she kept hidden from Quinn. Desperate to see Sabbi again, Quinn escapes from the camp with the help of Fenwick and makes it back to the British camp, where he discovers that a doctor (Donald Pleasence) has operated on Sabbi. Quinn visits her and they make plans for the future, but as he walks away, Sabbi dies.

**Commentary:** Derived from the title of a Japanese poem that explicates the uselessness in trying to restrict nature, *The Wind Cannot Read* is a dramatic romance set amid World War II and while Dirk Bogarde is fine as the romantic lead, the plot itself is rather sappy and the speed at which Quinn and the other soldiers learn to speak fluent Japanese is a tad bit unbelievable. Pleasence appears as the doctor who operates on Sabbi toward the conclusion of the film. He only appears in one scene in which he discusses the operation with Quinn and Sabbi's chances for survival which he unfortunately overestimates. Looking rather dapper in a suit and twirling a stethoscope, Pleasence looks the part but is not given much to do.

# *The Man Inside* (1958)

**Cast:** Jack Palance (Milo March), Anita Ekberg (Trudie Hall), Nigel Patrick (Sam Carter), Anthony Newley (Ernesto), Sid James (Franklin), Donald Pleasence (Organ Grinder). Directed by John Gilling.

**Synopsis:** For many years, Sam Carter, a low-level clerk working for a jeweler, has dreamed of making the "big heist" that would allow him to live the good life. Eventually, Carter gets the opportunity when he travels to New York City, where he steals a priceless diamond out of a store and escapes. The police are clueless as to who may have taken the diamond, so private investigator Milo March is called in to try and track down the diamond. March picks up Carter's trail as he jet sets around Europe and doggedly pursues him. Also in pursuit of Carter is the voluptuous Trudi Hall, who has decided to use her ample charms to obtain Carter's newfound wealth. Desperate chases, twists, and betrayals all take place before the case comes to an end.

**Commentary:** As a "B" picture, *The Man Inside* manages to deliver the goods as a crime thriller. Produced by Albert Broccoli before he gained fame with the James Bond series and directed by John Gilling who would later become involved in a number of Hammer horror films during the 1960s, *The Man Inside* involves a fast moving pursuit storyline supported by various actors like Anthony Newley as a Spanish taxi driver and Sid James as a New York City police officer. In order to appeal to the US market, American actor Jack Palance was brought in to play investigator Milo March and due to his usual intensity, Palance is a good foil for the always on the move Sam Carter. Cast in a small role as a Spanish organ grinder, Pleasence portrays the man with the information and gets to share some scenes with Palance. Although quite stereotypical, Pleasence as the organ grinder wears a droopy mustache and a ratty hat and must contend with a Capuchin monkey on his shoulder while playing his hurdy-gurdy.

## *The Two-Headed Spy* (1958)

**Cast:** Jack Hawkins (General Alex Schottland), Gia Scala (Lili Geyr), Erik Schumann (Lieutenant Reinisch), Alexander Knox (Gestapo Leader Muller), Felix Aylmer (Cornaz), Walter Hudd (Administrator Canaris), Edward Underdown (Kaltenbrunner), Laurence Naismith (General Hauser), Geoffrey Bayldon (Dietz), Kenneth Griffith (Adolf Hitler), Donald Pleasence (General Hardt), Michael Caine (Gestapo Agent), Martin Benson (General Wagner), Richard Grey (Field Marshal Keitel). Directed by Andre De Toth.

**Synopsis:** Alex Schottland is a British agent who has achieved what many deemed as impossible—infiltrating the Nazi Party in Germany. After achieving success for the Nazis in their Polish campaign, Schottland is promoted to a general, giving him greater access to top secret files. While at a party to celebrate his promotion, Schottland is introduced to the beautiful singer Lili Geyr, and although attracted to her, Schottland avoids getting close for fear of being exposed to the Nazis. He has good reason, as Lieutenant Reinisch sees him as a suspicious person and a bit too perfect. Schottland then slips away from the party to meet Cornaz, an antique store owner and his major contact in Nazi Germany. Using the cover that Schottland is a clock collector, information on Nazi maneuvers is sent through Cornaz to the Allied troops, but when the Nazis get too close for comfort, Cornaz gives Schottland explicit instructions on how to find his new contact should anything happen to him. Not long afterwards, Schottland is called to headquarters where he nervously watches Cornaz tortured to death without revealing any information to the Nazis. Schottland immediately begins to search for a new contact that will be revealed through a newspaper advertisement selling a Nuremberg egg. Schottland then comes face to face with his new contact Lili Geyr and together they devise a plan to make the Gestapo think they are having a love affair as a way of concealing their exchange of information. All goes well with Schottland providing information on Nazi troop movements to Lili who in turn sends the information to Allied forces through codes that she writes in her songs. But when the Nazis pull Lili off the air just before revealing the latest troop movements, Schottland comes to believe that the Nazis may suspect Lili, so he attempts to take the message to the front lines to broadcast it. But his plans fall apart when a German soldier spots him, forcing him to shoot the soldier and his backup regiment so he can escape. After regrouping, Schottland decides to send Lili to the front lines with the message so she can escape while he remains in Berlin, but along the way, Lili is intercepted by Reinisch who shoots her and takes the message. Reinisch then corners Schottland in his quarters and the two men fight to the death with Schottland walking away. Upon making his way into Hitler's bunker, Schottland piques the interest of the Fuhrer by telling him that defeatists are within his army and then offers a solution by volunteering to convince the sole remaining German military unit to defend Berlin. Escaping by the skin of his teeth, Schottland finally makes his way to the Allied troops and then back home to England.

**Commentary:** *The Two-Headed Spy* is based on the real life of Lieutenant Colonel Alexander Scotland, a British intelligence agent in World War I and II, who after successfully convincing the Germans that he was defecting to their side (using the name Alex Schottland), rose up in the ranks to general which provided him with access to sensitive information on Nazi maneuvers during the Second World War. It was Scotland that alerted Allied forces on the German plan to invade Russia and after World War II was involved in the questioning of suspected war criminals including those who killed forty-one Allied soldiers that had escaped from Stalag Luft III of which *The Great Escape* was based on. *The Two-Headed Spy* relates Scotland's story quite well but with some creative changes, such as the romantic angle with Lili Geyr. There is also an abundance of nail biting tension throughout the film, one good example being when Schottland must stand by nonchalantly while his contact Cornaz is tortured in front of him to reveal the mole in the Nazi ranks. Another interesting point is that *The Two-Headed Spy* is supposedly the first film produced after World War II to feature Adolf Hitler as a character.

Donald Pleasence (credited as Donald Pleasance) plays General Hardt, a true to the bone military man who eventually decides he would rather save his own skin than go down with a sinking ship. He first appears in a scene with Hitler furiously demanding his generals to come up with plans to stop the advancing Allies. Standing next to Schottland, Hardt steps up when Hitler wants to know if anyone has ideas to which Hardt states that he supports the importance of having a steady stream of supplies from Schottland. Near the conclusion of the film as Schottland enters Hitler's underground bunker, he comes across Hardt again who speaks for a number of other generals lined up behind him. Pleasence masterfully uses his eyes and a cigarette to convey his desperation and all but begs Schottland to speak to Hitler on their behalf so they can escape. But there would be no escape for Hardt and the other generals as Schottland makes a point of telling Hitler they are all defeatists who will be dealt with accordingly.

# *Look Back in Anger* (1959)

**Cast:** Richard Burton (Jimmy Porter), Claire Bloom (Helena Charles), Mary Ure (Alison Porter), Edith Evans (Mrs. Tanner), Gary Raymond (Cliff Lewis), Glen Byam Shaw (Colonel Redfern), Phyllis Neilson-Terry (Mrs. Redfern), Donald Pleasence (Hurst), Jane Eccles (Miss Drury). Directed by Tony Richardson.

**Synopsis:** Hothead Jimmy Porter shares an apartment with his wife Alison and his best friend and coworker Cliff Lewis. Porter and Lewis operate a sweets stand in the local market, where Porter rages on against injustices in the world and the overbearing commissioner of the district counsel who patrols the stands. Things are no different at the apartment with Porter going off on what everyone is doing wrong, including his long-suffering wife Alison. The only pleasures that Porter seems to have in his life are seeing Mrs. Tanner, his former landlord who helped him start his business, and playing the trumpet. Alison, who is afraid of Porter, knows she is pregnant with his child but does not tell him, and when she goes to ask about an abortion, her doctor dissuades her. Knowing that she will need help, Alison calls her friend Helena who is acting in a play nearby. This complicates measures even more as Porter seemingly has a hatred for Helena and when Alison tells Lewis, he knows that trouble will ensue. As expected, when Porter returns home from work and sees Helena, he goes into a tirade against her and Alison. His antics to embarrass them goes on until Alison decides to finally leave and stay with her father during her pregnancy. This situation leaves Porter and Helena alone, and the mutual attraction between them is instant. After seeing Porter with Helena, Lewis decides that he would rather leave and start over somewhere else. The love affair between Porter and Helena continues until Alison returns, having lost her baby and now more broken than ever. When Helena leaves, not wanting to get in the way any further, Porter goes to Alison and after confessing their problems ends up back together.

**Commentary:** Based on the popular British theatre production by playwright John Osborne, *Look Back in Anger* captures the look, feeling, and despair of the young discontented 1950s generation. One of the film's strong points is its director Tony Richardson who also directed the stage play. Osborne had to fight to get Richardson the job as he had never directed a feature film before, but Richardson's results are outstanding, due to expertly capturing the essence of a lower class neighborhood and the ensuing tension that inhabits it. As one reviewer noted, "Mr. Richardson does provide us with a sense of the dismal atmosphere, the prevalence of social stagnation, which helps to frustrate" the character of Jimmy Porter. [80] Another strong point is the inclusion of a jazz soundtrack which draws in Porter's use of the trumpet to "shout" back at society. One criticism pointed out by many of the critics is that Richard Burton seemed a bit too old to play the young disillusioned Porter, but his performances is pure bravado and carries the film effortlessly. Thus, the viewer tinges with trepidation at what Porter might do next because he is wholly unpredictable, much like a bad car accident that one cannot seem to look away from.

In the small role of Hurst, Pleasence, the overseer of the market where Porter works, does his finest to breathe life into an otherwise ordinary character. Featured in only three scenes, Pleasence's performance shows a man that revels in his authority and relishes every opportunity he gets to use it. His character is a true opposite of Porter and the two bang heads on a couple of issues. As one critic noted, "The piteousness of (Burton's) occupation as the keeper of a candy stall is conveyed in a stinging little drama of discord" with Pleasence as the market superintendent. [81] The big confrontation between Hurst and Porter involves Kapoor, a new Indian merchant at the market who sells his wares at a cheap price. This immediately draws suspicion from Hurst who visually quasi-interrogates Kapoor before giving him a selling license. Porter rushes to Kapoor's defense later when Hurst is ready to pull his license because of a complaint from a woman, but Porter's quick thinking proves that the woman did not buy any damaged goods from Kapoor which buys him a reprieve. However, Hurst eventually does take Kapoor's license and boots him from the market, but Porter is powerless this time around to help because his fellow merchants have made a complaint about unfair competition. Porter tries to get Kapoor to rally back against Hurst like he would himself, but his friend gives up. Once again, Pleasence demonstrates how well he could act with his face when a huge Cheshire cat grin appears on his face as he basks in his win over Porter in a pub.

# *Killers of Kilimanjaro* (1959)

**Cast:** Robert Taylor (Robert Adamson), Anthony Newley (Hooky Hook), Anne Aubrey (Jane Carlton), Gregoire Aslan (Ben Ahmed), Allen Cuthbertson (Sexton), Martin Benson (Ali), Orlando Martins (Chief), Donald Pleasence (Captain), John Dimech (Pasha), Martin Boddey (Gunther). Directed by Richard Thorpe.

**Synopsis:** Robert Adamson is an engineer sent by the Mombasa engineering company to complete the first East African railway. Along with him comes Jane Carlton whose fiancé and father were also engineers on the project before disappearing in the jungle. Upon arriving by ship, Adamson manages to set up a meeting to ask for workers with Ben Ahmed, an Arab slaver, since Adamson befriended Ahmed's young son Pasha on the trip over from England. However, Ahmed already has a partner for a new railroad and he is not pleased with Adamson's attempts. Adamson then resorts to hiring recently released criminals to use as porters and soon are making their way deep into the treacherous Warusha country, known for its wild native people. They eventually find the railroad company's camp but Jane is upset to discover that her father has died and his fiancé has gone quite mad from the isolation and lack of water. Moving on to try and complete the railroad, Adamson's group encounters many dangers and end up captured by the Warusha tribe. Adamson then applies his skills and bravery to convince the Warusha chief to allow him to build the railway through their territory. Ahmed, who is desperate to stop his competition, allows Gunther to set up an ambush for Adamson that results in a drawn-out battle. The fighting ends with Gunther and Ahmed shot and the dying slave trader telling Pasha not to follow his ways. Marching on, Adamson, Jane, Pasha, and the surviving porters finally reach their destination.

**Commentary:** Made by Warwick Films which later would become Eon Films, best known for their James Bond series with Albert R. Broccoli producing, *Killers of Kilimanjaro* is a well done adventure feature, thanks to the cinematography of Ted Moore and close-up scenes of native animals in the wild, making this film seem almost like a documentary. Hollywood veteran Robert Taylor is more than suitable in the lead role of Robert Adamson, the charismatic and no-nonsense leader of the operation; however, his romantic entanglements with Jane Carlton are a bit stretched. Also on hand providing some comic relief is Anthony Newley as Adamson's underpaid assistant, who manages to steal a few scenes, such as when some Warusha women prepare to give him an impromptu shower.

Pleasence's role in *Killers of Kilimanjaro* is quite brief as the Captain transporting Adamson and Jane to Africa to begin their survey of the land. Sporting a full beard and dressed in a spiffy white captain's uniform, Pleasence certainly looks the part and exchanges a few lines with Robert Taylor about the horrors of the slave trade. One in particular has Adamson spotting a slave ship dumping Africans overboard as it attempts to flee a British vessel. Wanting to do whatever he can to help save them, Adamson is told by the Captain that sadly, it is too late because the African slaves cannot swim, thus relegating them to drowning.

## *The Battle of the Sexes* (1959)

**Cast:** Peter Sellers (Mr. Martin), Robert Morley (Robert Macpherson), Constance Cummings (Angela Barrows), Jameson Clark (Andrew Darling), Ernest Thesiger (Old Macpherson), Donald Pleasence (Irwin Hoffman), Moultrie Kelsall (Graham), Alex Mackenzie (Robertson), Roddy McMillan (Macleod), Michael Goodliffe (Detective). Directed by Charles Crichton.

**Synopsis:** Angela Barrows is an American business consultant who is not afraid to speak her mind, and for this reason, the firm she works for ships her off to Scotland for an "export survey." Once there, her partner Irwin Hoffman (Donald Pleasence) leaves her unexpectedly, so she allows a certain Robert Macpherson to stay in the empty train bunk. With the death of his father, Macpherson is now the head of a family operated tweed business in Scotland and due to being impressed with Angela's knowledge and his obvious physical attraction to her, he hires Angela as the company's new industrial consult, much to the shock and dismay of the all-male staff at the firm. Once the staff realizes that their world as they know it may be changed forever, mild-mannered business manager Mr. Martin attempts to deal with the problem. After failing to get Angela fired, Martin decides on a more drastic approach by plotting her murder, but when Martin finally goes to Angela's apartment ready to do the deed, everything that possibly can go wrong does and it is only through sheer luck that he escapes unnoticed with the arrival of Macpherson. The next day at work, Angela accuses Martin of being homicidal but because Macpherson only sees his trusted employee as a quiet non-violent man, he calls in a doctor to take Angela away for what he deems as too much stress.

**Commentary:** *Battle of the Sexes* is a cleverly done comedy that still holds up well today; the premise itself is humorous and well carried out by the entire cast, although the film clearly belongs to its star Peter Sellers. Made up to look twenty years older than his real age, Sellers excels as the meek and soft-spoken Mr. Martin, but his appearance is only a façade as Martin is obviously a little more devious than he appears. His cunning approach to setting up Angela to fail almost does the trick, but when she still is not fired, Martin and the *Battle of the Sexes* goes full swing. After viewing a mystery film that details how the killer carefully planned everything out, Martin decides to copycat the plot in Angela's apartment with an unplanned hysterical outcome. The climax highlights Seller's comic brilliance and although *Battle of the Sexes* was overshadowed by another great comedy Sellers made the same year, *The Mouse That Roared*, it is a must see film.

Pleasence's role in *Battle of the Sexes* is small but amusing. He plays Irwin Hoffman, one of the employees at the American firm where Angela Barrows is driving the men nuts. Hoffman gets a dressing down by Angela at the end of a meeting when she adjusts his tie right in front of all his coworkers, and when his boss decides to ship Angela off to Scotland, Hoffman is overjoyed until he finds out that he will be accompanying her. Pleasence's last scene is played out in the train while heading for Scotland as Hoffman turns up late and clearly inebriated. His lame excuse? "I've been dressing up on my Scottish" to which Angela retorts "You've been dressing up on your scotch!" Hoffman then bails on Angela though not before giving Pleasence a funny role in a very funny film. *Battle of the Sexes* also marks the first time that Pleasence's last name was spelled incorrectly (as Donald Pleasance) in the credits which occurred a few times during his long career.

# *The Shakedown* (1960)

**Cast:** Terence Morgan (Augie Cortona), Hazel Court (Mildred Eyde), Donald Pleasence (Jessel Brown), Bill Owen (David Spettigue), Robert Beatty (Chief Inspector Bob Jarvis), Harry H. Corbett (Gollar), Gene Anderson (Zena), Eddie Byrne (George), John Salew (John Arnold), Dorinda Stevens (Grace). Directed by John Lemont.

**Synopsis:** Augie Cortona, a notorious crime boss, has just been released from prison, but before he leaves is warned to stay clean by Chief Inspector Bob Jarvis. Once out, Augie tracks down Zena, his old girlfriend/prostitute, who is now working for Gollar, another boss who has taken over his territory. Chased out by Gollar's thugs, Augie moves on and soon ends up in a diner where he comes to the aid of Jessel Brown (Donald Pleasence), an out of work photographer who has a run in with one of the customers. Augie tells Jessel that he will finance a new studio for him and work together as partners. Augie then proceeds to rob Gollar's thugs of Zena's cash to pay for the studio. After finding a location, Augie explains to Jessel that the new photography studio will also house a training school for models to bring in more income, but what Augie fails to tell the unsuspecting Jessel is that he is using the studio as a front for an amateur nude photo market. The studio quickly becomes a success on both ends of the business, attracting many hopeful models, including the beautiful Mildred Eyde whom Augie falls for. Meanwhile, Augie also begins to blackmail John Arnold, one of his amateur photographer clients and a prominent banker. Augie also hires his old prison mate Spettigue to act as backup when he suspects there is a rat in his organization. Together, they discover a woman secretly working for Gollar which turns out to be Mildred, an undercover police officer working for Jarvis. She secretly observes Augie taking a payment from Arnold so he can get the negatives that Augie is using to blackmail him. When Augie calls Arnold again to blackmail him for more negatives, Spettigue learns that Mildred is a cop and they trap her in the studio, but before any harm comes to her, Jarvis and his men break into the studio, forcing Augie to flee but only to be shot dead by Arnold who is waiting for him outside.

**Commentary:** *The Shakedown* is a slick crime thriller with a jazzy soundtrack that delivers the goods associated with the genre—tough cops, tougher criminals, and of course beautiful women. *The Shakedown* has an overall gritty feel to it and Terence Morgan really knocks it out of the park as the sly as a fox crime boss Augie Cortona. Augie's battles with his competitor Gollar gets bigger and more complex as the film progresses; also, there are some parallels between Augie and true-to-life criminal John Dillinger, such as Augie's bloated ego, personality, notoriety, and the fact that women brought both men to their demise. Mildred Eyde, the woman who does in Augie, is played with style by Hazel Court who later became known for her horror films with Hammer studios.

Pleasence has a plum role as a down on his luck photographer who happens to be in the right place at the wrong time. At first appearing quite shabby and desperate, Pleasence as Jessel Brown is quite timid but kind who does not want any trouble when a loudmouth customer breaks his tripod. When Augie gets the customer to pay up and then questions Jessel about his job, Jessel explains that he once was a successful photographer but the pressure drove him to drink, costing him his business. Just trying to get by and now drinking sodas, Jessel is drawn in by Augie's charm and promises to start up a new studio, but by the time Jessel finds out about the illegal side of the business, it is too late. In response, Jessel protests and threatens to turn Augie in to the police, but knowing that he would be out of work if the business ends up being investigated, Jessel decides to keep quiet and starts drinking again.

## *The Flesh and the Fiends* (1960)

**Cast:** Peter Cushing (Dr. Robert Knox), Donald Pleasence (Willie Hare), June Laverick (Martha), Dermot Walsh (Dr. Mitchell), Renee Houston (Helen Burke), George Rose (Willie Burke), Billie Whitelaw (Mary Paterson), John Cairney (Chris Jackson), Melvyn Hayes (Daft Jamie), June Powell (Maggie O'Hara), Andrew Faulds (Inspector McCulloch), Philip Leaver (Dr. Elliott), George Woodbridge (Dr. Ferguson), Garard Green (Dr. Andrews), Esma Cannon (Aggie). Directed by John Gilling.

**Synopsis:** In Scotland, 1828, the medical field faces a dilemma—there are not enough cadavers for medical students to practice on and learn about the human body. This need gives rise to a new illegal business known as grave robbing or "body snatching." At the Academy of Dr. Knox in Edinburgh, students are enthralled by the teachings of Knox, a brilliant surgeon and leader in the medical field. In order to procure enough cadavers for his students and further his research, Knox takes to paying grave robbers for their services. During this time, Knox's niece Martha returns to the Academy from school in France and becomes smitten with Knox's assistant, Dr. Mitchell who cares for her in return. Meanwhile, in a tavern in town, local ne'er-do-wells William Hare (Donald Pleasence) and Willie Burke are lamenting about their current lack of money when they see the wealth obtained by a local pair of grave robbers employed by Knox. They then follow Knox's medical student, Chris Jackson who just paid the grave robbers, out of the tavern where they attempt to mug him before being scared off by Mary Paterson, a local prostitute. Upon returning to a room and board Burke runs with his wife Helen, Burke and Hare sense a golden opportunity when they find out that one of the tenants died overnight. In response, they bring the dead man's body to Dr. Knox who is delighted with the freshness of the corpse. He then pays Burke and Hare and they soon are enjoying their newly-found wealth by celebrating in a local tavern. But when the money is spent, Burke and Hare decide they can make a steady income by committing murder and bringing the bodies directly to Knox. Dr. Mitchell, however, is concerned that a vengeful medical board will end Knox's career if they find out about his dealings with Burke and Hare, but Knox is content to look the other way as long as fresh bodies keep arriving. Eventually, Burke and Hare draw too much suspicion to themselves by murdering Mary Paterson and a local boy and are arrested for their crimes. Hare turns King's witness against Burke who is convicted and hanged. After being let go by the police, Hare is attacked by locals who burn his eyes out. Knox is brought up on charges by the medical board but exonerated after Dr. Mitchell defends him. Realizing the error of his ways, Knox returns to teaching at the Academy and soon implores his students to consider the Hippocratic Oath of their profession.

**Commentary:** *Flesh and the Fiends* is truly a "horror film" in that it is based on real events. This film of course exploits the events and even starts with the caption "We make no apologies to the dead… It is all true" which only increases the audience's thrills. A popular but lurid story known as the West Port murders had already been filmed as Robert Wise' *The Body Snatcher* (1945), and subsequent versions have been released up until the current day. Writer-director John Gilling hit pay dirt with his adaptation of the real-life murderous duo of Burke and Hare who terrorized the city of Edinburgh from November 1827 until October 31, 1828. This film actually follows very close to the actual facts and includes the real-life characters of Dr. Knox, William Hare, Willie Burke, Helen McDougal (Burke's mistress), Mary Patterson, and some of the victims including James Wilson, a.k.a. "Daft Jamie."

Perhaps to make Pleasence's character of Willie Hare more of a brutal monster, *The Flesh and the Fiends* lets the viewer know that Hare did in fact have a wife and child, and although Gilling's script tones down the number of killings that occurred in reality, Burke and Hare managed to kill sixteen people, unlike the six depicted in the film. To give a bit more justice to the evil Willie Hare, his eyes are burned out, but this is only based on unconfirmed rumors. By most accounts, Hare was never punished for his horrendous crimes and eventually died a pauper in London in 1858. [82] Ironically, Burke's body was donated to science and is still on display at the University of Edinburgh School of Medicine. Dr. Knox, who redeems himself in the film, did not do so in real life, for he continued to employ body snatchers for his research until the passage of the Anatomy Act in 1832. Not surprisingly, his popularity waned among his students.

Although it does cut down on the number of victims, *The Flesh and the Fiends* certainly pulls no punches by starting out with a shocking opening scene of a man's body being ripped from the grave and flopping around on the ground in a state of rigor mortis. Burke and Hare's method for smothering their victims is horrendous and eventually gave rise to the term "Burking" or to "murder, as by suffocation, so as to leave no or few marks of violence." [83] While many dead bodies, smothering deaths, and stabbings may be more commonplace in films of today, in 1959, such things on the screen were truly shocking for audiences. Another shocking part, at least for those who saw the film in Europe, are scenes of nude prostitutes and additional violence. These so-called "continental" versions were not that uncommon, as Europeans were considered more permissive concerning explicit scenes. In addition, the film features quite a bit of dark humor, one example being when Knox examines a dead drunk woman whom Burke and Hare just delivered and exclaims that he would rather have the bodies pickled externally because this one is liable to explode.

Although Pleasence had been acting in films since 1954, *Flesh and the Fiends* is truly the first in which he practically steals the whole film, due to his tour-de-force performance. Pleasence was given second billing after Peter Cushing who had by 1960 gained a reputation as a "horror" star, something that Pleasence would also experience later in his career. Producers Robert S. Baker and Monty Berman formed Triad Productions with John Gilling in order to make *Flesh and the Fiends* which marked the first instance of a company "borrowing" Peter Cushing from Hammer Films, where he had been starring in a number of remakes like *The Curse of Frankenstein* (1957) and *Horror of Dracula* (1958), both of which ushered in a new wave in horror cinema. Pleasence had acted with Cushing in an earlier horrific tale—George Orwell's *Nineteen Eighty-four* which the BBC adapted in 1954. Perhaps as a nod to that production, Pleasence's character has a deathly fear of rats just like Cushing's character of Winston Smith in *Nineteen Eighty-Four*.

As William Hare, Pleasence creates a character that serves as the real brains behind the murderous operation. He is especially unnerving in that he apparently lacks a conscience and is willing to take advantage of everyone, including Burke, his good friend and partner in crime. You can almost see the wheels turning inside Hare's mind when he sees one of Burke's recently deceased tenants and begins thinking of capital investment. Perhaps the most telling scene related to Hare's personality is when he gives the signal to Burke to smother an elderly woman and then dances mockingly in front of her as she dies. George Rose and Pleasence, Burke and Hare respectively in the film, would team up again many years later in the English comedy-drama theatre production of *Wise Child* (1971) by Simon Gray.

As a film character, William Hare is a hypocritical psychopath who will stop at nothing to get his way and despite getting paid rather handsomely for selling the bodies of his victims, Hare is also a sadist who finds it enjoyable to force Burke to do all of the dirty work. Melvyn Hayes as "Daft Jamie" who ends up as one of Burke and Hare's victims, said of Pleasence and Rose, "Working with them was great! Nice people if you're going to get murdered in a pigsty." [84]

# *Hell is a City* (1960)

**Cast:** Stanley Baker (Inspector Harry Martineau), John Crawford (Don Starling), Donald Pleasence (Gus Hawkins), Maxine Audley (Julia Martineau), Billie Whitelaw (Chloe Hawkins), Joseph Tomelty (Furnisher Steele), George A. Cooper (Doug Savage), Geoffrey Frederick (Devery), Vanda Godsell (Lucky Lusk). Directed by Val Guest.

**Synopsis:** Notorious career criminal Don Starling has just busted out of jail and returns to his old haunts in Manchester. To set himself up with necessary money, Starling plans a robbery with some old cronies. Hot on his trail is Inspector Harry Martineau who went to school with Starling and has locked him up many times in the past. One of the best cops on the beat, Martineau is a relentless worker which takes a toll on his home life with his wife Julia who is tired of being alone. Martineau is drawn deeper into the case after Starling and his gang rob prominent banker Gus Hawkins (Donald Pleasence) and kidnap a young woman that works for him. During the getaway, Starling kills the girl and dumps her body by the side of the road. On top of this comes news that the warden Starling attacked during his jail break has died, making him a wanted man for first degree murder which makes him more desperate and dangerous than ever. Needing a place to stay, Starling goes to the home of Hawkins whose wife he had an affair with. Hawkins returns home earlier than expected and later after hearing noises in the attic, climbs up the attic ladder, only to be knocked unconscious by Starling from his hiding spot. After interviewing Hawkins, Martineau becomes suspicious and forces his wife to reveal that Starling was in the house and is looking for other places to stay. Following a lead on the location of one of the robbery suspects in Starling's gang, Martineau arrests Doug Savage in a betting ring and after interrogating him begins to bring in each partner until only Starling is left. With nowhere left to hide, Starling breaks into the house of a former partner to recover hidden money, but gets surprised by the former partner's deaf and mute daughter. Starling then shoots her but not before she alerts the people in the neighborhood—including a watchful Martineau. A chase ensues between the two men until Martineau finally corners Starling, resulting in a shoot-out. But Martineau manages to get the upper hand and finally arrests Starling in order to bring him to justice.

**Commentary:** For a British actor known at least in the latter half of his career for his horror roles, one might assume that Donald Pleasence would have appeared in at least one film for the famed Hammer Studios, well-known for their horror films with stars like Christopher Lee and Peter Cushing. This assumption would be correct, although the Hammer film was instead the tense crime drama *Hell is a City*, one of many crimes films produced by Hammer Studios and undoubtedly the best of the lot. With quick pacing by veteran British director Val Guest, the viewer is slowly drawn into Martineau's pursuit of the fugitive Darling through the city's urban jungle. Lead actor Stanley Baker, no stranger to the heroic policeman as evidenced by his previous roles for *Violent Playground* (1958) and *Chance Meeting* (1959), presents himself in this film as a hard-nosed inspector willing to do whatever it takes to get his man, even at his own expense. The scenes between Martineau and his wife Julia are top notch, exploring the toll his work takes on his home life. He is committed to his job and wants to have a family, but his wife wants to spend more time with her husband and does not want children. The dynamics played out are quite powerful and support an underlying tension as Martineau tries to hunt down a killer.

As the bank manager at the heart of the robbery, Pleasence seems to be a simple background character, but he develops his role as Gus Hawkins into much more. Constantly blowing his nose (a trait that Pleasence would use in other roles such as in *Death Line*) and snapping at everyone including the police, Hawkins appears as a gruff and easily agitated man, but at the same time, he melts like butter at any sign of affection from his wife Chloe, played by Billie Whitelaw. This takes on even more significance when it is revealed that Chloe cheated on her husband, currently and also in the past with Starling. One great suspenseful scene has Hawkins hearing a noise up in the attic and then climbing up not knowing that Starling is hiding above. After being hit about the head and knocked unconscious, Hawkins later tells Martineau that "I thought we had another starling trapped in there; you know, a bird." The performances by Pleasence and Whitelaw were duly noted—"Billie Whitelaw and Donald Pleasence do well as an oddly mated couple."[85] An interesting fact concerning Pleasence and Whitelaw was revealed by Pleasence's agent Joy Jameson—"Donald and Billie Whitelaw, who was his one-time next door neighbor, were my first clients when I started my own agency."[86]

# *Circus of Horrors* (1960)

**Cast:** Dr. Schuler/Rossiter (Anton Diffring), Erika Remberg (Elissa Caro), Yvonne Monlaur (Nicole Vanet), Donald Pleasence (Vanet), Jane Hylton (Angela), Kenneth Griffith (Martin), Conrad Phillips (Inspector Arthur Ames), Jack Gwillim (Superintendent Andrews), Vanda Hudson (Magda von Meck), Yvonne Romain (Melina), Colette Wilde (Evelyn Morley Finsbury). Directed by Sidney Hayers.

**Synopsis:** In 1947 England, plastic surgeon Dr. Rossiter has disfigured the face of Evelyn Morley in an operation gone horribly wrong. Rossiter flees the house and runs down a police officer with his car before veering off a cliff and crashing to avoid a fallen tree blocking the road. Mangled with his face all cut up, Rossiter makes it back to his house, where his assistants Angela and Martin operate on his disfigured face. Rossiter then assumes the new identity of Dr. Schuler and takes Angela and Martin with him to France, where he hopes to start over with his work. While in France, Schuler meets a disfigured girl named Nicole on the roadway and after seeing her father Vanet (Donald Pleasence) who operates a run-down circus, Schuler decides to offer his services as a surgeon to operate on the girl's face and remove all of the scars. A successful surgery delights Vanet who then signs over his circus to Schuler as a way of thanking him. Vanet then proceeds to get drunk and mistakenly frightens a dancing bear that mauls him to death as Schuler stands by and does nothing. Now as the sole owner of the circus, Schuler decides to incorporate it with thieves and murderers who need his services in order to hide from the law, figuring they would never turn him in to the police. Ten years later, Schuler's circus is one of the top draws in Europe. Schuler's success goes to his head and he rules over his performers with an iron fist. Not content with just continuing his operations, Schuler becomes obsessed with creating the perfect example of beauty and keeping her for himself. The female performers who refuse Schuler's advances or simply wish to leave the circus meet with "accidental" deaths, courtesy of Schuler with Martin doing all of the dirty work. As a result of these "accidents," Schuler's production becomes known as a jinxed circus and soon attracts the attention of the authorities. After learning of the latest death of one of Schuler's beautiful performers, Inspector Ames goes undercover as Arthur Desmond, a freelance crime reporter writing a story on Schuler's "Circus of Horrors." His investigation is aided by Nicole who innocently betrays some facts about Schuler's past which then allows Desmond to makes the Rossiter/Schuler connection with the help of Evelyn Morley who lived through her botched surgery helping to positively identify Dr. Rossiter. Now on the run again, Schuler attacks his two assistants, fends them off with a rampaging gorilla, and proceeds to elude the police, only to be run down and killed by the vengeful Evelyn Morley.

**Commentary:** *Circus of Horrors* is a colorful and entertaining horror film. It flows along quickly from beginning to end and holds the suspense of the audience as to what Schuler will attempt next. As Dr. Rossiter/Schuler, Anton Diffring makes a great villain. With his charismatic manner, he smooth talks the women, but can turn into a raging murderous fiend. A perfect example is when Schuler convinces Angela that he will marry her if she and her brother Martin help out with his plastic surgery front. But she is rewarded by watching the man she loves seduce prostitutes whom Schuler turns into objects of beauty. When Angela and Martin finally confront Schuler and tell him that they are leaving, he assaults Martin and stabs Angela. Career-wise, Diffring became typecast by playing similar villains and especially Nazis, due to his German background and aristocratic manner.

Circus of Horrors also boasts a bevy of beauties like Erika Remberg, Yvonne Monlaur, Vanda Hudson, and Yvonne Romain. Dr. Schuler certainly was not starting out with any ugly ducklings for his operations. The best of the female performances goes to Erika Remberg who portrays a former prostitute and murderer for whom success must be measured at the top of the circus's billing at any cost. An amusing storyline has Inspector Ames making out with one of the women so he can detect her previous facial surgery, and then later, he becomes romantically attached to Nicole as he questions her. Here's a man that certainly goes all out for his job.

As Vanet, Pleasence has only a small role in *Circus of Horror*, but he does make the most of it by expressing the concerns of a father for his daughter's well-being and happiness. The happiness on Vanet's face when Nicole's bandages are removed is also quite touching. But Vanet is not a simpleton, for he quickly realizes that Schuler must be in some kind of trouble with the law to want to remain with the circus. Pleasence also adds some subtle touches to his character by speaking bits of French, venting his frustrations about the ruinous effects of World War II, and even lisping when drinking too much wine. For this effort, Pleasence was singled out with some other actors in *Circus of Horrors* for a *New York Times* review for giving such a good performance. But Pleasence's most impressive acting in this film might have been convincing audiences that his character was actually in danger from a very unconvincing man in a bear suit masquerading as Bosco the bear.

*Circus of Horrors* is made a bit more credible through the use of the real Billy Smart's Circus, a popular attraction in England at the time. Intercut footage shows acrobatic trapeze acts, clowns, and animals which helps the overall look of the film. Other producers must have been impressed with this because some of the same footage was later used in *Circus of Fear* (1966). Unfortunately, Bosco the bear's attack on Vanet and a similar attack by a man in a gorilla suit on Schuler leaves a lot to be desired. *Circus of Horrors* also features the hit song "Look for a Star," written by Tony Hatch under the pseudonym of Mark Anthony and as sung by Garry Mills made its way up the charts in England. Released shortly after the horror juggernaut that was Alfred Hitchcock's *Psycho*, *Circus of Horrors* still managed to do well and garnered some favorable reviews. As Howard Thompson writes, "*Circus of Horrors* turns out to be the crispest, handsomest and most stylish shocker in a long time." [87]

## *Sons and Lovers* (1960)

**Cast:** Trevor Howard (Walter Morel), Dean Stockwell (Paul Morel), Wendy Hiller (Mrs. Morel), Mary Ure (Clara Dawes), Heather Sears (Miriam), William Lucas (William Morel), Conrad Phillips (Baxter Dawes), Ernest Thesiger (Mr. Hadlock), Donald Pleasence (Pappleworth), Rosalie Crutchley (Mrs. Leivers), Sean Barrett (Arthur Morel), Elizabeth Begley (Mrs. Radford). Directed by Jack Cardiff.

**Synopsis:** In the small mining town of Nottinghamshire, Paul Morel lives at home and plans to pursue a career in art. His mother nurtures yet smothers him, while his father does not understand why his son has chosen not to work in the mines like he does. However, a mining accident takes the life of Paul's brother Arthur, thus changing the dynamics in the Morel household for the worse. Mr. Morel harbors anger toward his wife for looking down on him and often goes on drinking sprees; in turn, Mrs. Morel becomes more controlling over Paul, especially regarding his love life. No woman that Paul has met pleases his mother, least of all the farmer's daughter Miriam whom Paul has been seeing. Due to his mother's biased views, Paul constantly wonders about love and passion, his only examples being his constantly embroiled parents and his other brother William who has recently married. Feeling that Miriam is not physically compatible with him, Paul ends their relationship and begins an affair with Clara Dawes, a married woman employed at Jarrod's. Although there is instant physical attraction between them, Clara is not convinced that Paul is totally committed to her and she goes back to her husband. In order to help his parents out financially, Paul goes to work at Jarrod's, a women's clothing store, but complications set in when Paul's mother has a heart attack and passes away. Paul sees Miriam again, but is afraid she will smother him just like his mother, and so goes off on his own to finally be free.

**Commentary:** *Sons and Lovers* is a beautifully shot film and showcases the feelings that a black and white film can produce. As a testament to this, cinematographer Freddie Francis won an Oscar for his work on *Son and Lovers*. Jack Cardiff, often referred to as one of the best cinematographers to come out of Hollywood, claimed that this film was among his career favorites. One reviewer noted that "Jack Cardiff, camera man turned director, has filled the film with picture poetry." [88] As an adaptation of D.H. Lawrence's classic tale, *Sons and Lovers* certainly garnered a lot of praise with many nominations and awards for the lead actors as well as for Francis and Cardiff. Dean Stockwell, who started out as a successful child actor, proves here that his acting talent matured as he got older, for his Paul Morel is a tortured, free-thinking youth, due mostly to his mother's controlling interference in his life. Like the previous Pleasence film *Look Back in Anger*, *Sons and Lovers* fits well into the British new wave genre that dealt with the hardships that youths of the 1950s were forced to confront; in fact, an interesting connection is Mary Ure who plays similarly jilted women in both of these films stuck in abusive relationships.

Pleasence is practically wasted in *Sons and Lovers* as the owner of Jarrod's, for he is not given much to do and appears in only a single scene. One day, and looking quite dapper in his suit, Pappleworth walks into the factory to find Paul holding a woman's brassier and quickly becomes the brunt of a joke by Pappleworth. The best interaction occurs between Pappleworth and Clara Dawes, the overseer of Jarrod's, who besides being one of Paul's love interests is also an outspoken suffragette. The two exchange some heated words and go head to head before Pappleworth, after probably realizing that he cannot win an argument with Clara, relents with a joke and lets her go on to train Paul. An interesting note is that *Sons and Lovers* was filmed on location in Nottinghamshire, the birthplace of Donald Pleasence.

# *The Big Day* (1960)

**Cast:** Donald Pleasence (Victor Partridge), Andree Melly (Nina Wentworth), Colin Gordon (George Baker), Harry H. Corbett (Harry Jackson), William Franklyn (Mr. T. Selkirk), Susan Shaw (Phyllis Selkirk), Freda Bamford (Betty Partridge). Directed by Peter Graham Scott.

**Synopsis:** Mr. George Baker is the manager of a small but progressive company in England and decides to appoint a new director from among his own staff and has narrowed the field down to three choices. The first candidate is Victor Partridge (Donald Pleasence), a company accountant who although quiet and a worrier, is willing to take risks. The second candidate is Harry Jackson, the company's transport manager who feels entitled to the position due to being married to Mr. Baker's sister. The third candidate is Tom Selkirk, the company's sales manager and the youngest of the three who wants to grow his career with the company. Mr. Baker then interviews the three candidates and tells them he will make his final decision within a week, but during the time before the announcement, the lives of the three candidates become very stressful. Partridge, sensing that he will not be chosen as the new director, becomes increasingly nervous as the week drags on and starts making mistakes with company sales figures. Selkirk also makes an error which Jackson notices and tries to take advantage of, but Selkirk evens the odds by discovering an underhanded practice that Jackson was conducting in his transport department. Fearing he may lose the coveted spot, Jackson openly reveals that Partridge, a married man with children, is having an affair with Nina, his nineteen year-old secretary. When the big day finally arrives, Mr. Baker chooses a greatly surprised Partridge on the condition that he immediately dismiss Nina.

**Commentary:** *The Big Day* is one of a handful of Pleasence films that never received proper release and has unfortunately faded into obscurity with the exception of an occasional TV airing and a 16mm showing at the British NFT season of films. Categorized as a "B" film or "quota quickie," *The Big Day* served as a filler before big budget Hollywood films. Pleasence obtained an early lead role which makes it more unfortunate because the film has rarely been shown. As an effective office drama, *The Big Day* reveals the desires and desperation related to climbing up the office work ladder to success, and as Victor Partridge, Pleasence portrays the dual-sided man, a role that he perfected during his career. At first glance, Partridge appears to be a quiet and unassuming accountant with a family, except for his daring office romance with a girl half his age. As more is revealed, it becomes evident that Partridge is a man in despair, due to falling behind in both his finances and family life. The announcement of the director position within the company only adds more stress for Partridge who finds it difficult to cope and can barely answer questions during his interview with Mr. Baker. His only happiness is with Nina that turns bittersweet when Partridge is rewarded and punished at the same time. Thematically, *The Big Day* provides a realistic look at the nature of sex and office politics, something that similar films have either shied away from or have opted to present a happy outlook.

# *Suspect* (1960)

**Cast:** Peter Cushing (Professor Sewell), Tony Britton (Dr. Bob Marriot), Virginia Maskell (Dr. Lucy Byrne), Ian Bannen (Alan Andrews), Kenneth Griffith (Dr. Shole), Thorley Walters (Special Agent Prince), Donald Pleasence (Bill Brown), Spike Milligan (Arthur), Raymond Huntley (Sir George Gatting, Minister of Defense). Directed by John Boulting and Roy Boulting.

**Synopsis:** At the Haughten Research Laboratory, a number of scientists under the direction of Professor Sewell are finalizing their study on cures for plagues. While most of the researchers are excited, Lucy is upset because everything is repetitive and takes too long to achieve results. Her partner, Dr. Bob Marriot is worried that Lucy is stressed out and offers to take her to the movies. However, their evening is cut short when Lucy tells Bob that she must return home immediately. The next day, Bob asks Lucy why she had to leave so quickly, and she explains that she must care for Alan Andrews, a man who used to be her fiancée but was injured in the Korean War and now stays with her. Alan, who lost both his arms due to friendly fire, has learned of Bob and is fiercely jealous of him and is extremely angry that he cannot be the man that Lucy deserves. Meanwhile, Sewell contacts his superiors for permission to publish the research team's findings but is shocked and dismayed to learn that the Ministry of Defense under Sir Gatting has decided that the information could be used by a hostile group to actually cause a plague. With their work on the official secrets list, everyone at the lab is upset and subject to security by Special Agent Prince. Bob's anger at being censored comes to the attention of Alan who then notices a way to set him up and get back at his country for his injuries. Alan puts Bob in touch with Bill Brown (Donald Pleasence) who claims he is in the publishing business and can put the research team's information into the hands of the scientific community. Bob agrees to bring the information to Brown, but is unaware that one of Prince's men is watching them. Prince begins to question the research team and Lucy confirms that Bob may be planning something, but before Bob can steal away with the project information, Sewell catches him and with the help of Prince, they hatch a plan to catch Brown and his employers. Bob then meets up with Brown who takes him to his employer to copy the plans. Once there, Bob hands over a fake set of plans as Prince quickly moves in and arrests Brown and his employer.

**Commentary:** Based on the novel and screenplay by Nigel Balchin, *Suspect*, a.k.a. *The Risk*, was previously adapted for the BBC teleplay *Number Three*. In this film version under the direction of Roy Boulting and produced by his brother John, the story is basically the same but with slight variations. The plot is intelligent and there is also a fair amount of humor injected throughout, some of which comes courtesy of Goon Squad co-creator Spike Milligan who has some amusing scenes opposite a chimpanzee. More than just science-fiction, *Suspect* is also a tense drama filled with suspense that builds towards a satisfying conclusion. Reviews were mostly in favor of the film—"An unusual sort of spy drama which is crisply and grippingly unraveled in a neat little British film," [89] says *The New York Times*. Taking a break from his Hammer horror films, Peter Cushing plays the lead as Professor Sewell, the head chemist of the research team. But some of the best scenes belong to Ian Bannen who portrays Alan Andrews, a tortured soul and traitor to his own country. Left without arms following a battle in the Korean War, Alan feels that he cannot marry Lucy, his fiancée, and because he is unable to support himself, he ends up living in an apartment with her as his nurse-in-waiting. But when she starts dating Bob, Alan's dreams are crushed. His biting, sarcastic remarks directed at those around him reveals a disturbed man, but one can almost not blame him for his actions. A subtle touch throughout *Suspect* is the use of piano pieces by Chopin, perhaps because Alan was set to become a pianist before losing both of his arms in the Korean War.

As Bill Brown, alias Evans, alias Parsons, Donald Pleasence plays a shifty underworld character looking to make some quick money even if it means selling out his country. A *New York Times* review points out that "Donald Pleasence is weird and weaselly as an ambulating spy," [90] and apparently had turned up before, causing problems for Great Britain and resulting in Prince commenting numerous times that "We don't like Brown, do we? We don't like him at all." Although not a large role, Pleasence makes the most of it, slowly luring Bob into his trap to sell the secret plans. Pleasence uses his eyes to great effect, especially in the climax when he hears Prince outside the door and goes from relaxing with a bottle of liquor to a frozen state of terror.

## *The Hands of Orlac* (1960)

**Cast:** Mel Ferrer (Stephen Orlac), Christopher Lee (Nero the Magician), Dany Carrel (Li-Lang), Lucile Saint-Simon (Louise Cochrane Orlac), Felix Aylmer (Dr. Francis Cochrane), Peter Reynolds (Mr. Felix), Donald Wolfit (Professor Volchett), Donald Pleasence (Graham Coates). Directed by Edmond T. Greville.

**Synopsis:** Classical concert pianist Stephen Orlac is on a plane to his next engagement that soon encounters thick fog and crashes on a runway. Orlac survives but his hands have been horribly burned and mutilated. Rushed to a nearby hospital, Orlac is seen by Professor Volchett, known for his ground-breaking surgeries, who grafts new hands onto Orlac from Louis Vasseur "The Strangler," a recently executed criminal. As Orlac recovers from the operation, he begins to experience visions and feelings that his new hands have a dangerous feel to them. At a villa in the country with his wife Louise, Orlac tries to strangle her in bed and quickly runs away for fear of her safety. Winding up at a cheap hotel, Orlac registers under a fake name to try and escape from any publicity until he can figure out his problem. While performing at the hotel, Nero the Magician soon notices Orlac's money and plans to blackmail him. Nero's assistant Li-Lang then attempts to seduce Orlac to discover his secret and when she eventually does, Orlac is constantly hounded by Nero who psychologically tortures him over having the hands of a strangler. Eager to help her husband, Louise asks her uncle to go to Scotland Yard, where Inspector Henderson takes up the case. Henderson ultimately discovers that Vasseur has been proven innocent of the murders and Nero is arrested after killing Li-Lang who was about to turn him over to the authorities.

**Commentary:** Maurice Renard's classic novel *Les Mains d'Orlac* has been adapted for film three different times—*Orlacs Hande* (1924), *Mad Love* (1935), and *The Hands of Orlac* (1962). *Mad Love* turned out to be the best of the three, mostly because of a bravado performance by Peter Lorre as Dr. Gogol. The 1962 version was a big English/French co-production; however, the results were less than spectacular and rather slow moving. In this version, Mel Ferrer does an adequate job as Orlac, but the film really belongs to a young Christopher Lee, fresh from appearing in several horror films by Hammer Studios that made him an instant star. Lee turns in an unbelievably nasty and slimy performance as a magician who preys upon unsuspecting strangers and has all of the best scenes, such as when he shows up in Orlac's home dressed as Vasseur to scare him out of bed, complete with hooked hands and a sewn-on head.

Pleasence's role in *The Hands of Orlac* is quite small; in fact, he is billed as a guest star along with Donald Wolfit. Playing an eccentric artist named Graham Coates, Pleasence interacts quite well with Fer-rer's Stephen Orlac and at one point wishes to use Orlac's new hands as a model for his latest work of art. It is not much of a role that was typical at this stage in Pleasence's acting career. For those fans wishing to check out Pleasence's performance in *The Hands of Orlac*, avoid the English version known as *Hands of the Strangler* because Pleasence's role is completely cut out.

## *No Love for Johnnie* (1961)

**Cast:** Peter Finch (Johnnie Byrne), Stanley Holloway (Fred Andrews), Mary Peach (Pauline), Donald Pleasence (Roger Renfrew), Billie Whitelaw (Mary), Hugh Burden (Tim Maxwell), Rosalie Crutchley (Alice), Michael Goodliffe (Dr. West), Geoffrey Keen (The Prime Minister), Dennis Price (Flagg). Directed by Ralph Thomas.

**Synopsis:** Johnnie Byrne is a lifelong politician who has just been overwhelmingly reelected by his constituents to represent the Labour Party in Parliament. While his political stature is on the rise, his love life is falling apart with his wife Alice leaving him upon returning home. Mary, Johnnie's neighbor in the apartment complex, is smit-ten with him, but the timing always seems off for them. Meanwhile, unhappy that the Prime Minister failed to chose him for a higher po-sition, Johnnie joins a group of Labour "back benchers" led by Roger Renfrew (Donald Pleasence) with plans to stir up the pot in Parlia-ment. At a local party that he attends with Mary, Johnnie meets a beautiful young blonde named Pauline who shows an interest in him, and after getting to know one another over a series of dates, Johnnie falls madly in love and later skips out on an important debate with the Prime Minister related to Renfrew's plan. The consequences back at Parliament are that Johnnie is seen as a traitor by his group and Roger almost has him removed from office with a vote of no confidence. Meanwhile, Pauline leaves Johnnie because of concerns over their dif-ferences in age and her desire for a family that she feels will not work out. Despondent, Johnnie returns home, only to find Alice waiting for him hoping for reconciliation. Even more uplifting is when the Prime Minister calls Johnnie and offers him the position of Assistant Postmaster General. Apparently, Johnnie was originally passed over for this position because Alice is a member of the communist party. Searching his inner soul, Johnnie has one more major decision to make.

**Commentary:** As a political drama, *No Love for Johnnie* actually takes a deep look at the underside of politics where careers are more important than families and wives and all politicians seems to have a hidden agenda. In the title role is Peter Finch who does a marvelous job as a man with deep personal issues who almost turns his life around after a series of unsettling events. His political and love lives travel in opposite directions which makes for fascinating drama and many viewers may find themselves rooting for Johnnie and may even feel suckered in at the end. Also in a strong role is Billie Whitelaw as Johnnie's neighbor Mary, obviously the right woman for him, but because of a series of awkward and clumsy encounters, they never get together. Toward the end, Mary seems fed up with Johnnie and tells him she is getting married, but she calls him again and sounds somewhat disappointed when he reveals that Alice has come back home. Sharp-eyed viewers will also spot a very young Oliver Reed at a party that Johnnie attends.

Pleasence plays Roger Renfrew, a schemer in every sense of the word. First seen lurking in the background of Parliament with his wire-rimmed glasses and bowtie, Roger comes out of the shadows when he calls a meeting with some fellow politicians concerning how to counteract the Prime Minister's policies. Roger quickly decides to form a Labour Party splinter group to "attack" the Prime Minister on an important issue that will make him look bad and provide them with generous publicity in the newspapers. It is Roger who nominates Johnnie to be the chairman of the group and also gives him prepared notes for his speech at Parliament, but when Johnnie chooses love over politics, Roger shows his true colors by ominously threatening him. Last seen speaking secretly in a phone booth, Roger almost has his revenge on Johnnie in a way that would hurt him the most—his political life. An interesting note is that in real life, Pleasence was an avid supporter of the British Labour Party.

# *Wind of Change* (1961)

**Cast:** Donald Pleasence ("Pop" Marley), Johnny Briggs (Frank Marley), Ann Lynn (Josie Marley), Hilda Fenemore (Gladys), Glyn Houston (Detective Parker), Norman Gunn (Ron), Bunny May (Smithy), David Hemmings (Ginger). Directed by Vernon Sewell.

**Synopsis:** Frank Marley is a disenchanted youth who spends most of his time hanging out with his friends in a café. One night, he spots a black teenager talking with a white waitress. This enrages him and he confronts and threatens the black teenager before he and his friends chase him out of the café and down the street. Convinced that something must be done to stop the influx of black people coming into his neighborhood, Frank and his friends go out the following night with the expressed purpose of sending a "message." When they finally corner a black teenager with his white girlfriend in a dimly lit alleyway, they severely beat him before being chased off by the police. Frank then runs home and hides a bicycle chain used in the beating. Soon after, Frank's parents begin to question him about his stay-out late sister Josie when a detective suddenly shows up at the house and explains that Gladys was the victim of an attack that put her new boyfriend in the hospital. Josie then arrives home and heads for her bedroom as Frank and his parents discuss the impact of the attack on Josie. As Frank's true feelings about black people begin to come out, his father "Pop" Marley (Donald Pleasence) clashes with him while his mother defends him. Eventually, they realize that Frank was the one who attacked his sister and was involved in the beating of her boyfriend who dies in the hospital from his wounds. Gladys overhears what transpired in the house and calls the police who come and arrest Frank.

**Commentary:** Like *Sons and Lovers* and *Look Back in Anger*, *Wind of Change* fits well into the early 1960s British new wave genre that tackled the issue of disenfranchised youths. However, *Wind of Change* goes one step further by delving into the issue of racism and its harmful effects on society and does not shy away or dance around the issue. Frank Marley is clearly a racist with an axe to grind, especially against young black men with a penchant for white women. Frank, played with a fiery intensity by Johnny Briggs, is a powder keg ready to explode and when he finally does fails to realize that his own sister was a victim of his violence. Also in the cast is a young

David Hemmings as Ginger, a member of Frank's inner circle of friends. Hemmings displays noticeable talent that would rise to the surface later in his career.

Pleasence received top billing in *Wind of Change* and exhibits a conflicted character. At first, Pleasence's turn as "Pop" Marley seems a bit comical because he is always fussing around with his pet rabbits that he houses by the garage. But like his son Frank, "Pop" is also a racist, such as when he refers to his black rabbit with a derogatory term. His son then is an extension of his beliefs except that Frank is willing to go one step further to act upon his violent beliefs. There is a turn around moment for Pop when he realizes how Frank's beliefs have led to his daughter's disfigurement, resulting in a major confrontation. The two physically come to blows when Frank berates his sister and Pop steps in to defend her. Pop also argues with his wife who wants to hide the bicycle chain and let Frank escape from the police, but when the police eventually arrive, Pop is seen holding his black rabbit outside of his house and looking quite dazed before calling the rabbit by its derogatory name once again. As a result, *Wind of Change* provides one of Pleasence's most powerful emotional performances early in his career.

# *A Story of David: The Hunted* (1961)

**Cast:** Jeff Chandler (David), Basil Sydney (King Saul), Peter Arne (Doeg), David Knight (Jonathan), Barbara Shelley (Abigail), Donald Pleasence (Nabal), Richard O'Sullivan (Abiathar). Directed by Bob McNaught.

**Synopsis:** The legend of David slaying the mighty Goliath had long spread throughout the kingdom of Israel, bringing David fame and the love of the Israelites. One person that is not happy about David's success is King Saul of Israel who wants all the attention for himself. Under the advice of Doeg, his royal Edomite counselor, King Saul plots to have David killed; however, Jonathan, the son of King Saul, is close friends with David and alerts him of the plot on his life. David becomes confused and at first refuses to go against King Saul because he pledged his loyalty to him. But Jonathan leads David into the light and decides to assist him in a fight against his own father.

**Commentary:** *A Story of David: The Hunted* was originally intended as a television feature but the producers decided to release it as a theatrical film. Unlike earlier Biblical epics, *A Story of David* stays fairly close to the original depiction of David's life as recounted in I Samuels in the Holy Bible before he became King of Israel. In the title role of David, actor Jeff Chandler, born Ira Grossel and always proud of his Jewish heritage, does a remarkable job as the heroic and loyal David who committed no crime yet was forced to confront the greedy and jealous King Saul. Pleasence portrays Nabal, a wealthy Calebite who owes David a favor for providing protection to his shepherds in the town of Carmel which was under his control. When David sends his men to ask Nabal for supplies in order to rise up against King Saul, Nabal stubbornly refuses that results in David preparing to go after him only to be stopped by Nabal's wife Abigail, played by Barbara Shelley, who ends the quarrel and later marries David after Nabal justifiably dies of a heart attack. For Pleasence, *A Story of David* was his first biblical epic and later on appeared in *The Greatest Story Ever Told* as a much more devious character, namely the Devil. An interesting anecdote is that *A Story of David* was the first biblical film to actually be made in Israel.

## *Spare the Rod* (1961)

**Cast:** Max Bygraves (John Saunders), Geoffrey Keen (Arthur Gregory), Donald Pleasence (Mr. Jenkins), Betty McDowall (Ann Collins), Peter Reynolds (Alec Murray), Jean Anderson (Mrs. Pond), Mary Merrall (Miss Fogg), Richard O'Sullivan (Fred Harkness), Jeremy Bullock (Angel). Directed by Leslie Norman.

**Synopsis:** John Saunders has just been hired as the new teacher at the Worrell Street School, and although he lacks real teaching experience, Mr. Jenkins (Donald Pleasence), the headmaster of the school, hires him, due to his background in the British Navy which he believes might make a difference, as the students at the inner city school are quite unruly and cause major problems. Mr. Jenkins and the other teachers, especially Arthur Gregory, deal with student misbehavior by meting out punishment through canning which shocks Saunders. The class that Saunders ends up with has some of the worst behaving students, including Fred Harkness and Angel, but through persistence and fairness, Saunders begins to earn their respect. Harkness responds to Saunders efforts and soon becomes his favorite student, but their relationship is threatened when Saunders regretfully finally breaks down and canes him, only to find out that Harkness was innocent. As a result, Harkness acts up and gets in trouble with the police, but Saunders convinces Jenkins to speak on the boy's defense. Thankful for Saunders's assistance, Harkness tells him that he will be leaving school to join an architectural firm as an apprentice. On his last day at school, Harkness gets incorrectly blamed by Gregory for locking him in the bathroom. Gregory then canes Harkness, but Saunders steps in to stop him, resulting in all out chaos with the students trashing the school. Because of this event, Saunders gets transferred to another school by Jenkins and although upset, Saunders realizes that he really loves teaching after all of his students come to thank him.

**Commentary:** *Spare the Rod* is quite an effective drama that deals with a pervasive issue in education, being how to deal with students who do not want to learn. In the lead role is Max Bygraves, mostly known for his comedy but here, he provides a fine performance as a young liberal teacher who wants to make a difference in the lives of his students. John Saunders is clearly a salmon swimming upstream against the tide of teachers who scorn their students and regularly cane them, especially the sadistic Arthur Gregory, played with great zest by Geoffrey Keen. Like many young teachers entering the profession, Saunders is full of enthusiasm and new ideas but is thrown into one of the most difficult classes in the school. The fact that he continues to try and reach out to his students even to the point of resignation speaks volumes in this uplifting story. An interesting note is that Angel, one of the mischievous students in *Spare the Rod*, is played by a young Jeremy Bullock who would later go on to play another trouble maker later in his career, the bounty hunter Boba Fett in the original *Star Wars* series.

Pleasence portrays Jenkins, a former teacher and now headmaster with a downbeat, realistic perspective on his school's clientele. His very first words to Saunders upon arriving at the school are to never leave his office door open because the students are all thieves. Jenkins also provides Saunders with his canning rod and gives him a very specific demonstration on how to use it when administering punishment. Pleasence's character also displays a hacking, out of control cough whenever he gets agitated, brought on by chain smoking cigarettes throughout the film. Even though Jenkins seems at first to be an enemy, it becomes clear over time that he is simply frustrated but is very willing to accept new and successful ways, including those advocated by Saunders. At the end of the film, Jenkins proudly tells a shocked Gregory that he believes Saunders will make an excellent teacher.

## *No Place Like Homicide!* (1961)

**Cast:** Sid James (Sid Butler), Kenneth Connor (Ernie Broughton), Shirley Eaton (Linda Dickson), Donald Pleasence (Everett Sloane), Dennis Price (Guy Broughton), Michael Gough (Fisk), Valerie Taylor (Janet Broughton), Esma Cannon (Aunt Emily), George Woodbridge (Dr. Edward Broughton), Michael Gwynn (Malcolm Broughton), Philip O'Flynn (Arkwright/Gabriel Broughton), Adam Faith (himself). Directed by Pat Jackson.

**Synopsis:** Ernie Broughton is a nervous proofreader of horror novels who shares an apartment with his good friend Sid Butler. One night, Ernie is surprised by the sudden appearance of solicitor Everett Sloane (Donald Pleasence) who tells him that his uncle Gabriel has passed away and that he was named as a beneficiary and must attend the reading of the will at Blackshaw Towers. Ernie and Sid travel to the castle where they meet the sinister, clubfooted butler Fisk, the beautiful blonde nurse Linda Dickson, and the rest of Ernie's family—the constantly drunk cousin Guy, his scheming sister Janet and father Dr. Edward Broughton, the dotty aunt Emily, and the quite mad cousin Malcolm. Sloane gathers all the relatives together for the reading of the will and delivers the shocking news that uncle Gabriel has left them nothing. As they prepare to leave the castle, the lights go out and after splitting up, Ernie and Sid find Dr. Broughton lying dead on the lawn. Suspicions begin to fester and boil over to a climax when Malcolm and Janet also end up dead. Aunt Emily's claim that she spoke to the deceased uncle Gabriel sparks a search of his tomb which reveals Malcolm's body wearing a mask. Inspector Arkwright, summoned by Sloane, soon arrives at Blackshaw, but Ernie and Sid find Sloane lying dead by a fountain and Guy dead in a liquor cabinet. Ernie and Sid then discover a secret passage and find that aunt Emily and Linda have been captured by a gun-toting Arkwright who reveals himself to be none other than uncle Gabriel. Due to being upset with his greedy relatives, uncle Gabriel faked his own death in order to lure everyone to his castle where he could do away with them one by one. He then locks them in a room with a pack of starved dogs and goes to burn down the castle, only to be done in by Fisk who dropped a trick chandelier on him. Fisk releases Ernie, Sid, aunt Emily, and Linda and explains that he has been feeding the dogs all along.

**Commentary:** *No Place Like Homicide!*, a.k.a. *What a Carve Up!*, is an excellent thriller spoof supported by a talented cast. What really makes this film stand out is the talented comedic pairing of Sid James and Kenneth Connor set against a backdrop of Gothic monstrosity with a castle complete with hidden passages and a creepy, dead-looking butler played by Michael Gough who later gained fame for playing another butler—Alfred in the *Batman* film series. James and Connor worked together before this film and following *No Place Like Homicide!* appeared in the popular *Carry On* film series that spoofed every genre imaginable. Producers Baker and Berman who knew a good product when they saw one, made *No Place Like Homicide!* very similar to a *Carry On* film, the same way they made *The Flesh and the Fiends* similar to a Hammer film. This film also features a good deal of low-ball humor and gags and does it quite successfully. One of the most amusing scenes involves Ernie and Sid trying to share a bed with an unwelcome black cat.

*No Place Like Homicide!* was Pleasence's second film for producers Baker and Berman, and perhaps his standout performance in *The Flesh and the Fiends* convinced them to hire Pleasence again for another somewhat sinister role. There is even a quick reference to the grave digging aspects of *The Flesh and the Fiends* when uncle Gabriel's body disappears and Ernie proclaims that its Burke and Hare all over again. Relegated to playing a red herring, Pleasence does his job well with a stone dead look and monotone voice that scares the wits out of an already nervous Ernie. There is a great gag scene in which Ernie proclaims to Sid that Sloane, described as a horrible-looking zombie guy, does not scare him as he opens the apartment door to come face to face with Sloane, holding a scarf in a quite menacing manner.

# *Lisa* (1962)

**Cast:** Stephen Boyd (Peter Jongman), Dolores Hart (Lisa Held), Leo McKern (Brandt), Hugh Griffith (Van der Pink), Donald Pleasence (Sergeant Wolters), Harry Andrews (Avoob), Robert Stephens (Dickens), Marius Goring (Thorens), Finlay Currie (De Kool), Neil McCallum (Browne), Geoffrey Keen (Commissioner Bartels), Jean Anderson (Mrs. Jongman), Michael David (Captain Berger). Directed by Philip Dunne.

**Synopsis:** In Holland, 1946, Sergeants Peter Jongman and his partner Wolters (Donald Pleasence) are on the trail of a suspected Nazi slave smuggler who has brought a young woman with him on the way to England. Jongman travels to Scotland Yard, where he explains to the superintendent that the woman is Lisa Held, a survivor of the Nazi concentration camps, and the man is Thorens, known for smuggling young women into slavery rings in South America. Although sympathetic, the superintendent tells Jongman that he is powerless to do anything because immigration raised no objections. Not willing to accept Scotland Yard's answer, Jongman tracks down Thorens to his apartment and confronts him, resulting in a fight with Thorens being knocked unconscious. Jongman leaves the apartment and finds Lisa nearby. She tells him she just wants to get to Palestine and he promises to help her out, but their journey gets sidelined when Jongman is called into his boss's office and told that Thorens was murdered and that he and the girl are wanted back in England for questioning. Jongman grabs Lisa and using his connections gets both of them aboard a barge as assistants to Captain Brandt who runs illegal cargo to Tangiers. Once there, Jongman meets with another smuggler named Van der Pink who demands that Jongman work for him for a year in exchange for smuggling Lisa to Palestine. Jongman then tries Mr. Browne, an

American known for helping victims of the Holocaust, and as per his request, Browne has Lisa inspected by a doctor before her journey which forces her to reveal that she was experimented on at the medical research block at Auschwitz. As a result, Browne refuses to allow Lisa to enter Palestine because he wants her to instead testify at the war crimes tribunal in Nuremberg. Adding to their troubles is that Dickens, an agent with British naval forces, has been sent to watch and prevent them from reaching Jerusalem. With options and time running out, Jongman goes back to Van der Pink and agrees to his deal. Jongman and Lisa are then sent out on a boat toward Palestine, but when Jongman discovers the boat is smuggling weapons, Van der Pink has his contract torn up, making him a free man. North African gunrunners almost prematurely end their journey by injuring Lisa when the British Navy intercedes and chases them off. Finally reaching the shores of Palestine, Jongman gets Lisa to the Palestinian army for medical care, while he returns to the beach to be taken back to England by the British Navy.

**Commentary:** *Lisa*, a.k.a. *The Inspector*, is a well-made dramatic love story set in the post World War II period, and with scenic visual locales and a tense race to get Lisa to her destination, the film draws in viewers and holds their attention. Jongman, played with strong conviction by Stephen Boyd, clearly is trying to help Lisa make amends for letting his former fiancée be taken away to the camps by the Nazis. Not unexpectedly, during their harrowing journey, Jongman falls in love with the beautiful and mysterious Lisa which only increases the stakes in getting to Jerusalem. Played with a perfect understated performance by Dolores Hart who one year after filming would quit the film industry to become a nun, Lisa is an independent spirit who wishes to start anew. The rest of the cast is also good in supportive roles, especially Leo McKern as the cantankerous but good-hearted Captain Brandt and Hugh Griffith as the sly and underhanded Van der Pink. This film also projects one of the most challenging issues that developed after World War II—how best to help the survivors of the war to move on.

Acting as Jongman's partner Sergeant Wolters, Pleasence plays an early pivotal role, and while Jongman is more hotheaded and ready to chase Thorens to his next destination, Wolters is a practical by-the-book man who does not sweat the issue and sends a cable ahead to alert the authorities. As an actor, Pleasence could use props to his advantage via displaying the traits of a character, such as using a cigarette to highlight his calm and cool demeanor. When he later turns up in the Amsterdam office when Jongman is informed of Thorens' death, he uses his policing skills to provide an accurate description of Lisa Held. But Wolter's biggest impact on the storyline occurs when he arrives at the dockside with other policemen to search for Jongman and Lisa. After realizing that his partner will not give himself up, Wolters decides to help them by concealing their hiding spot on Brandt's barge and cunningly letting Brandt know that he let Jongman and Lisa go free. Wolters is last seen watching the barge pull away, muttering to himself, "Good luck inspector. Good luck you stupid…" which is cut off by the horn of a waiting car.

## *The Great Escape* (1963)

**Cast:** Steve McQueen (Captain Hilts), James Garner (Flight Lieutenant Hendley), Richard Attenborough (Squadron Leader Roger Bartlett), James Donald (Group Captain Ramsey), Charles Bronson (Flight Lieutenant Danny Velinski), Donald Pleasence (Flight Lieutenant Colin Blythe), James Coburn (Flying Officer Louis Sedgwick), Hannes Messemer (Kommandant von Luger), David McCallum (Lieutenant Commander Eric Ashley-Pitt), Gordon Jackson (Flight Lieutenant Sandy MacDonald), John Leyton (Flight Lieutenant William Dickes), Angus Lennie (Flying Officer Archibald Ives), Nigel Stock (Flight Lieutenant Denys Cavendish), Robert Graf (Werner). Directed by John Sturges.

**Synopsis:** Fed up with captured Allied soldiers constantly escaping from their prison camps, the Nazis create a new camp especially built to house the worst offenders. Kommandant von Luger explains this to Allied Group Captain Ramsey with the understanding that he should pass on the message that escape will be impossible from this special camp. But contrary to the Kommandant's wishes, the fact that the Germans have placed "All the rotten eggs in one basket" serves as the impetus for the prisoners to plot out a major escape in order to disrupt the system and force the Nazis to spend their time and resources tracking them down instead of fighting the war. Squadron Leader Roger Bartlett, the ringleader of many former Allied escapes, immediately puts into place a plan to have two hundred and fifty escape at the same time, the most ever attempted. While planning this escape, the British officers also keep an eye on Captain Hilts, an American officer known for his daring escapes. While diggings tunnels under the camp to attain their freedom, various prisoners with special talents like Lieutenant Colin Blythe, "the forger" (Donald Pleasence) who prepares all of the necessary papers, clothes, and equipment the men will need once they make their escape. On the night of the escape, an Allied bombing raid near the camp provides a timely distraction as Bartlett and his men escape through tunnels dug beneath their living quarters. With the Germans in hot pursuit, the escapees scatter throughout Germany; unfortunately, most end up being captured or killed, yet a few manage to escape to Allied-friendly countries. Once back in camp, the former escapees grudgingly accept the sacrifices of those who died with perseverance.

**Commentary:** Based on the real-life account of Allied soldiers that escaped from Stalag Luft III in former P.O.W. Paul Brickhill's book of the same name, *The Great Escape* became a Hollywood blockbuster and is now considered as a classic war film under the direction of veteran filmmaker John Sturges. Part of this film's success was due to the casting of such powerhouse film stars like Steve McQueen, Richard Attenborough, James Garner, James Coburn, and Charles Bronson, among others. The rousing score by Elmer Bernstein highlights the prisoners' sense of duty and is today remembered with great fondness. The tension is well-paced as the prisoners dig their tunnels to freedom and the characters, although somewhat exaggerated, have compelling back stories. The only issue that bugged the critics (Pleasence himself mentioned it to Sturges) is the open-faced boldness of the prisoners toward their armed to the teeth German guards. A *New York Times* reviewer declared that "nobody is going to convince me into believing that the spirit of defiance in any prisoner-of-war camp anywhere was as arrogant, romantic, and Rover Boyish as it is made to appear in this film." [91]

With an acting career spanning over forty years and a hundred and thirty-eight films, Pleasence's role as Flight Lieutenant Colin Blythe certainly ranks as his top performance, and although Pleasence gave many other memorable performances, his role as Blythe tapped into his own personal past to create a character in which humor, duty, sympathy, and humanity all show brightly. Pleasence was the only actor in the cast to have actually been a World War II prisoner-of-war after his plane was shot down over France and then marched back by the Germans to be held at Stalag Luft I which Pleasence once remarked was eerily similar to the camp built for the film. [92]

*The Great Escape* was Pleasence's first big Hollywood film and his performance opened the door to other roles in big films, as well as to working with director John Sturges two additional times. Pleasence's character, based on fellow real-life P.O.W. Tim Walen, is finely-detailed, not only as a lieutenant and forger of documents, but also as an avid bird watcher and connoisseur of tea which is perfectly played out when Blythe exclaims that it is uncivilized to drink tea without milk. Blythe's relationship with "the scrounger" Lieutenant Hendley, played by James Garner, is particularly moving, especially when it becomes evident that Attenborough's Bartlett considers Blythe's loss of vision as a hindrance to the mission. A highlight of Pleasence's performance is when he places a pin on the floor of his quarters to try and convince Bartlett that he can still see. He then tries to prove it by walking across the room to bend down and retrieve the pin on the floor which he had placed there earlier on, but Bartlett stretches out a leg and trips Blythe, sending him to the floor.

As Hendley pleads with Bartlett to let Blythe join the escape, the viewer is treated to the crushed look of despair on Pleasence's face as he listens. Pleasence's eventual fate is also quite sympathetic and his performance is easily the most realistic of all the fine actors in *The Great Escape*. Pleasence would also hold the distinction of being the only actor from the original *The Great Escape* to also appear in the 1988 television sequel, *The Great Escape II: The Untold Story*—though this time as a member of the SS.

# *The Caretaker* (1963)

**Cast:** Alan Bates (Mick), Donald Pleasence (Mac Davies/Bernard Jenkins), Robert Shaw (Aston). Director: Clive Donner.

**Synopsis:** Aston, a kind but reserved man, rescues a homeless man named Bernard Jenkins (Donald Pleasence) after he is kicked out of a café late one cold winter night. After making their way back to Aston's apartment on the top of an abandoned house in London and feeling sorry for Jenkins, Aston offers to let him stay the night in the apartment to keep warm. The next morning, Aston is out of the apartment and his brother Mick arrives and proceeds to frighten and harass Jenkins who does not know what to expect. Aston then returns to the apartment with a bag filled with necessities to replace those that Jenkins lost at the café. As Aston gets to know Jenkins better, he offers him the job of caretaker of the house. Jenkins gladly accepts the offer but does not realize that he must also put up with Aston's brother Mick who has a sadistic streak in him and makes the job quite difficult. Mick convinces Jenkins that Aston is not in his right mind and that he in fact will be taking over the house and will offer him a job as caretaker as long as he can provide references. This leads to much confusion for Jenkins who at one point tries to pit the brothers against each other but ultimately fails, resulting in being thrown out of the house only to return to the streets.

**Commentary:** As a marvelous adaptation of the award-winning stage play by playwright Howard Pinter, *The Caretaker* (titled *The Guest* for American markets) could be described as a low budget, British new wave feature with most of its financial support coming from the likes of Elizabeth Taylor, Richard Burton, Peter Sellers, and Noel Coward. This film captures the claustrophobic feel of the apartment which was one of the main features of the stage production. Only a few scenes take place outside of the house that allows the audience to sense the closeness of the three leads as they discuss and bicker over everything and anything in a power struggle for the house. However, the exterior scenes provide a good linking connection to London's lower class district, something that the stage production could not portray. The real gem of this film is Pinter's writing that highlights the casual conversations between Aston and Mick and an outsider which makes for fascinating viewing. Even the silent moments are utilized to a great effect via lots of tension and the dialogue is at times darkly comic, touching and profound. Donald Pleasence, Robert Shaw, and Alan Bates clearly crafted their characters to the point of perfection after so many performances on the stage and it is difficult to see other actors in revival performances without think-ing of Pleasence, Bates, and Shaw. *The Caretaker* was entered into the Berlin International Film Festival upon release and its director Clive Donner won the Silver Berlin Bear award.

Pleasence plays one of his best and well-known roles as Bernard Jenkins whose promised the job as the title character but in a cruel twist of fate winds up involved in a psychological tug of war between Aston and Mick before being put right back where he started—on the streets. Jenkins is a fast-talking, self-described man of the world and is cunning enough to survive on the streets and take advantage of any opportunity that comes his way. Pleasence truly disappears into his character of the tramp as an angry, paranoid, and sly bigot who simply wishes to survive. This is a role in which Pleasence proved he could create real and believ-able characters outside of portraying the hero or the villain as in numer-ous thrillers that came about later in his career. When Jenkins reveals his shady past to Aston, the audience learns that he left his wife and dropped his real name of Mac Davies for the assumed name of Bernard Jenkins for unexplained reasons. However, despite Jenkins' issues, it is those between Aston and Mick that truly puts Jenkins to the test. In one memorable scene, Mick offers Jenkins a ride to Sidcup to get his iden-tification papers. Happy to get a ride, Jenkins hops in Mick's van, only to be driven around the block and immediately dropped off because as Mick puts it, the van is too high to go under the bridges. The interaction between Jenkins and Mick is dynamite with the two men clashing back and forth in a power struggle while the quiet Aston provides a calming effect over them. For Donald Pleasence fans, *The Caretaker* is a must see film as one of the top five performances of his long career.

## *Dr. Crippen* (1964)

**Cast:** Donald Pleasence (Dr. Hawley Harvey Crippen), Coral Browne (Belle Crippen), Samantha Eggar (Ethel Le Neve), Donald Wolfit (R.D. Muir), James Robertson Justice (Captain McKenzie), John Arnatt (In-spector Dew). Directed by Robert Lynn.

**Synopsis:** Dr. Hawley Harvey Crippen (Donald Pleasence) is unhap-pily married to an American singer named Belle. Over the years, they have grown apart and now fight constantly over Belle's flirting with other men and Harvey's inability to express his love. Eventually, Harvey finds affection from Ethel Le Neve, his secretary at work, and the two begin a love affair that drives Belle mad as she constantly berates Harvey and finally forces him to make a choice—either her or Ethel, or else risk being exposed as a philanderer. Desperate not to lose his one true love, Harvey purchases a powerful sedative that he secretly administers to Belle at night to calm her and prevent more fighting. But one night, Belle dies from an accidental overdose and Harvey in a panic hides her body in the basement. But he continues with his relationship with Ethel, even giving her his dead wife's fancy clothes and jewelry. When the police begin to investigate Belle's disappearance, the disguised Harvey and Ethel attempt to flee to America on a ship. The captain, however, notices them and after alerting Scotland Yard, Harvey and Ethel end up arrested and are brought back to London to be placed on trial. Harvey is found guilty and after being executed by hanging, Ethel walks away into the distance.

**Commentary:** *Dr. Crippen* stands as a fine film dramatization of the infamous 1910 murder case that gripped Great Britain and made plenty of headlines. After the execution of Dr. Crippen, a number of theatre productions and films adapted parts of the case, but *Dr. Crippen* was the first major British film to cover it and follows the case fairly closely through flashbacks and a few dramatic changes. One example shows Dr. Crippen and his mistress Ethel Le Neve on trial together, although in real life their trials were separate. The case of Dr. Crippen, accused of murdering his wife, hiding her body, and trying to escape with his mistress in disguise fascinated England via all of its lurid and shocking details. Another interesting fact that is played out in the film is that Dr. Crippen was the first criminal to be captured through the use of wireless technology, due to the captain of the ship contacting Scotland Yard to relay his suspicions about two of his passengers.

Pleasence's perfectly understated performance as the title character proves that he was quite able to carry a film on his own. When Pleasence is first seen being led by the police to the court, a woman bystander spits in his face as a way of reminding him of the viciousness of his crime. Looking much like the actual Dr. Crippen, Pleasence's hair is neatly combed over and sports a long, bushy mustache and a pair of wire rimmed glasses. His lack of emotion toward his overbearing wife Belle indicates a time bomb ticking away inside of him that is later set off when Belle attempts to force him to end his affair with Ethel or risk public humiliation. His real emotions are saved for Ethel that makes one wonder if he could have had true happiness had he met and married her first. The film also plays up the theory that Dr. Crippen accidentally killed his wife and in a panic hid her body. Pleasence portrays this panic masterfully, helped along by his desperate plan to take Ethel to America to escape the authorities while explaining to her that Belle is still alive and has set the whole thing up against him. Dr. Crippen's scenes with Ethel aboard the ship are touching but it is a doomed romance with Dr. Crippen begging his lawyer to make certain that Ethel changes her name and never mentions their relationship again.

# *The Greatest Story Ever Told* (1965)

**Cast:** Max von Sydow (Jesus), Charlton Heston (John the Baptist), Telly Savalas (Pontius Pilate), Donald Pleasence (Satan), Dorothy McGuire (The Virgin Mary), Roddy McDowall (Matthew), Claude Rains (King Herod). Directed by George Stevens.

**Synopsis:** The life of Jesus Christ, from his birth to his beginnings with the Apostles, his conflict with the Roman government, and his crucifixion and resurrection.

**Commentary:** In every sense of the word, *The Greatest Story Ever Told* is a true epic with massive sets, lots of film stars, and hundreds of extras. Director George Stevens began to hone his craft at making large-scale popular films with *Gunga Din* (1939), followed by *Shane* (1953), and *Giant* (1956). The plot of *The Greatest Story Ever Told* adheres fairly close to the life of Jesus as written in the New Testament and the cinematography and film score are certainly first-class. One of the few let downs in an otherwise fine film is Stevens' inclusion of many Hollywood stars for mostly walk-on cameos. While Max Von Sydow brings an authoritarian angle to Jesus, Charlton Heston provides religious zeal to John the Baptist, but Telly Savalas as Pontius Pilate almost steals the film. Also, it is distracting to see Hollywood stars pop up all over the place which draws the viewer's interest away from the story and creates a spot them if you can game, an example being John Wayne as a Roman soldier.

In a most underrated sinister performance, Pleasence portrays Satan in *The Greatest Story Ever Told*, but unlike the overblown image of the devil in films like *Legend* (1985), Pleasence appears as an old hermit who lives in a cave and moves among the shadows and darkness. His hair is dyed white and the addition of a beard completes the look of an old man with an ancient quality. His first scene occurs with Jesus climbing a mountain and coming upon Satan's cave. With brilliant moonlit shining into the cave, Jesus enters and is met by Satan while enjoying his meal by a fire. After striking up a casual friendship, Satan offers Jesus some food and then something much more precious—ultimate power and glory but only if Jesus promises to pay him homage. Jesus refuses and Satan follows him outside, where he sits in silhouette against the moon and tries to goad him into performing a miracle by jumping off the cliff to prove his divinity. Satan later turns up in a crowd of onlookers watching Jesus perform his first miracle and later on in the darkness watching Judas whom he knows will betray Jesus. In effect, Pleasence creates a most uneasy character through his unique portrayal of Satan, one that speaks volumes even when saying nothing at all.

# *The Hallelujah Trail* (1965)

**Cast:** Colonel Thaddeus Gearhart (Burt Lancaster), Cora Templeton Massingale (Lee Remick), Captain Paul Slater (Jim Hutton), Louise Gearhart (Pamela Tiffin), "Oracle" Jones (Donald Pleasence), Frank Wallingham (Brian Keith), Chief Walks-Stooped-Over (Martin Landau), Sergeant Buell (John Anderson), Kevin O'Flaherty (Tom Stern). Produced and directed by John Sturges.

**Synopsis:** In the promising but dangerous west of Denver, Colorado in 1867, a group of miners call a meeting to discuss their latest crisis—the town's supply of whiskey is all but depleted and winter is fast approaching. The miners go to the only man who can help them, an oracle named Jones (Donald Pleasence) who has great visions of the future as long as he's drinking whiskey. Much to the delight of the miners, Jones declares that he sees a whole wagon train full of the much-valued whiskey on its way to them from Julesberg; however, Frank Wallingham who is shipping the whiskey, is unhappy to see Jones' vision printed in a gazette for all to see, thus making him a target for robbery. In order to guard his precious cargo, Wallingham enlists the aid of Colonel Gearhart and his troops from Fort Russell under the pretext that he is a taxpayer and a good Republican. But as Gearhart readies his troops to meet the wagon train, a problem arises in the person of Cora Massingale, a prominent leader of the women's temperance movement who has practically taken over Fort Russell with her guile and gumption. Complicating matters for Gearhart is that his daughter Louise has joined Cora's movement and decides to accompany her as they attempt to stop the delivery of the whiskey. With Gearhart and his troops and Cora and her women heading for the wagon train, the miners under the guidance of Jones also take off after the precious cargo. Then a fourth party jumps into the fray—a group of thirsty Sioux Indians. Of course, full-blown chaos breaks out when the four groups encounter each other during a dust storm. The peace treaty that follows is hampered by misunderstandings and Gearhart finds himself having to rescue the women while at the same time, Cora must outwit the miners to prevent them from getting the whiskey.

**Commentary:** *The Hallelujah Trail* marks the second time Donald Pleasence worked for director John Sturges which paid off with yet another wonderful role. Sturges, who masterfully directed some of the greatest Hollywood westerns of all time, such as *Gunfight at the O.K. Corral* (1957) and *The Magnificent Seven* (1960), pokes fun at the genre in a grand scale with a large cast and breathtaking locations. Although *The Hallelujah Trail* includes Indian characters like Chief Walks-Stooped-Over, it is obviously politically incorrect, yet it is also quite enjoyable if taken at face value. The comedy flows freely throughout the film, thanks in part to various stereotypes like the Indians, the women's rights supporters, and the working Irishmen, and the tongue-in-cheek narration by actor John Dehner. Another plus is the interaction between Burt Lancaster and Lee Remick which is captivating and charming and greatly benefits the film. The only issue that does distract from the film is its length at way over two hours.

As for Pleasence, *The Hallelujah Trail* offered him one of his best comedic roles as "Oracle" Jones. With his beard dyed blonde and sporting a deep tan, Pleasence looks quite unique as the oracle that informs the miners about the load of whiskey. Jones is quite an amusing character and knows his importance but plays it cool, biding his time playing solitaire in the back of a saloon. He knows ahead of time why the miners wish to seek him out, but stops in mid-vision until given "lubrication" in the form of whiskey. The look on Pleasence's face when he becomes enlightened by the whiskey is truly a sight to behold. Other funny bits are when Jones calls the Indian chief a "real boozer" and when he steals whiskey from the unmanned wagons. Jones is also very important related to the storyline, due to providing the film's title in a vision and setting up the whole premise, wherein the four different groups compete for the precious cargo in Wallingham's wagon train.

## *Cul-de-sac* (1966)

**Cast:** Donald Pleasence (George), Francoise Dorleac (Teresa), Lionel Stander (Richard), Jack MacGowran (Albie), Iain Quarrier (Christopher), Robert Dorning (Philip Fairweather), Marie Kean (Marion Fairweather), William Franklyn (Cecil), Jacqueline Bisset (Jacqueline). Directed by Roman Polanski.

**Synopsis:** After escaping a botched job, criminals Richard "Dicky" and Albie, find themselves marooned near a castle on a beach. Dicky leaves the injured Albie in the car to see if he can make a phone call to their boss from the castle. What he finds surprises him—a sensual French woman named Teresa and her submissive British husband George (Donald Pleasence). Realizing that he has the upper hand, Dicky holds George and Teresa hostage and forces them to help bring Albie back to the castle. Dicky also places a call to his boss Mr. Katelbach and is told to wait for a car to arrive for them. While waiting for their boss, Dicky torments George and Teresa who begin fighting with one another, but the tide turns when George's friends, not Dicky's boss, show up unexpectedly and force Dicky to play the role of a butler. Teresa uses the opportunity to humiliate Dicky at every turn while George gets nervous about Dicky's expected boss and starts an argument to get his guests to leave. Alone again, Dicky calls for his boss, only to find that he has been abandoned. Taking George's car and preparing to leave by himself, Dicky is confronted by George who now has his gun, courtesy of Teresa stealing it. In the chaos, George clumsily shoots Dicky that causes his car to explode. When a guest from the party returns to get his gun, Teresa leaves with him and George is left alone on the beach.

**Commentary:** Polish filmmaker Roman Polanski used the proceeds from his successful 1966 thriller *Repulsion* to help fund his black comedy *Cul-de-sac*. Filmed in black and white, Polanski chose the picturesque Lindisfarne Castle to stage his examination into the lives of his subjects via their isolation that heightens the interaction between them. Polanski also decided to feature Francoise Dorleac for *Cul-de-sac*, perhaps because her younger sister Catherine Deneuve had starred in *Repulsion*. Dorleac, who died in an auto accident not long after making *Cul-de-sac*, proved to be an enigmatic beauty who brought true sensuality to her character. Another standout is Lionel Stander as the gruff, gravely-voiced Richard who certainly is no genius but is smart enough to know that George will offer no resistance, at least at first. In effect, *Cul-de-sac* with an art house feel, provides a fascinating character study of George, Teresa, and Dicky as their personalities clash and try to survive one another.

The role of George in *Cul-de-sac* allowed Pleasence to give one of his most unique and unforgettable performances during his long career. First seen walking back to the beach with a large kite, George is a happy newly-married man who dumped all of his savings into the purchase of the castle on the beach for his fantasy life with Teresa. However, his relationship with his wife is most unconventional, for Teresa is flirtatious and outgoing and is also carrying on an affair with the neighbor's son Christopher who is timid and shy but opens up with Teresa. Their relationship seems precariously like a fragile eggshell that ends up broken through the intervention of Dicky, thus destroying their fantasy life. Watching George trying to convince Teresa of his bravery only to cow down to Dicky's every demand elicits much sympathy, even when George gets his eventual revenge but winds up losing. Pleasence was rightly praised for his strong performance in *Cul-de-sac*—"His shrill and erratic contortions, his towering displays of cowardice in the face of the menacing instructions of the ambiguously canny thug, his virtually epileptic tantrums when his wife or guests get under his skin are so absolutely amazing they're either funny or downright frightening."[93]

# *Eye of the Devil* (1967)

**Cast:** Deborah Kerr (Catherine de Montfaucon), David Niven (Philippe de Montfaucon), Donald Pleasence (Pere Dominic), Edward Mulhare (Jean-Claude Ibert), Flora Robson (Countess Estell), Emlyn Williams (Alain de Montfaucon), Sharon Tate (Odile de Caray), David Hemmings (Christian de Caray), Michael Miller (Grandec), Donald Bisset (Rennard). Directed by J. Lee Thompson.

**Synopsis:** Philippe de Montfaucon is a wealthy nobleman living in Paris with his wife Catherine and their two children, Jacques and Antoinette. Word comes from Philippe's hometown of Gendarmerie where he owns the castle Bellenac that the vineyards are failing again and that he is urgently needed. Although Philippe does not want Catherine to come to Bellenac, she takes the children anyway and drives there the next day. Upon arrival, Catherine is shocked to see a local youth named Christian shooting a dove in front of them with an arrow. At night, Catherine sees people coming into the courtyard. She snoops around the castle and spots Christian along with his sister Odile holding the dead dove on a plate for some sort of ceremony with hooded figures being supervised by the town priest. The next day, Catherine questions Philippe about Christian and the ceremony, but he only makes excuses and is dismissive. Talks with the priest (Donald Pleasence) are also unsuccessful as he warns her not to stay. The lack of answers from Philippe and further incidents with Christian and Odile scare Catherine enough to call Philippe's former schoolmate Jean-Claude. Together, they research the Montfaucon family history at the castle and discover that all of Philippe's ancestors died under mysterious circumstances. Further questioning of Philippe's relatives finally brings out the horrible truth—Philippe is actually part of a pagan cult that practices the Black Mass and as the chosen 13th member of the order, Phillipe must be sacrificed in order to save the crops. Although the villagers try to stop her, Catherine runs to find Philippe but is not in time to stop the ceremony. She sadly goes to leave Bellenac with Jean-Claude the next day, though not before Jacques runs back to the castle to retrieve his watch.

**Commentary:** Although not as well-known as the similarly themed *The Wicker Man* (1973), *Eye of the Devil* is a first-rate tale of the occult and the supernatural. Beautifully shot in black and white and featuring a truly magnificent French castle, *Eye of the Devil* oozes with style and atmosphere. Deborah Kerr excels in the role of the worried wife who wants to save her husband and protect her children. Interestingly, Kerr was a last minute replacement for Kim Novak who had already filmed most of her scenes as Catherine before having a bad fall from a horse, thus making it necessary to re-shoot all of the scenes with Kerr. Each of the actors adds to the film's overall mystery and menace, particularly Sharon Tate in her first credited film role and David Hemmings who appeared in his breakout role the same year in Michelangelo Antonioni's *Blow-Up*. However, critics at the time were not impressed with the film's complex plot; one commented that "In order to bring his vines back to condition, Niven must allow himself to be destroyed by a silver arrow shot through his heart which is enough to mystify anybody." [94]

As Pere Dominic who appears kindly but harbors a terrible secret, Pleasence portrays a complex character. Not much is revealed about Dominic, but he obviously is a central figure in the pagan beliefs and rituals occurring at Bellenac. Although the villagers look to Philippe for authority, Philippe himself turns to Dominic who harbors their secrets and who seems to have a calming effect on Philippe as he resigns himself to his terrible fate. One powerful scene has Dominic berating Odile who almost sends Catherine off the ledge of the castle roof— "I told you to frighten her, not to kill her, child. Where is your conscience?" Without giving away the ending, the last scene in *Eye of the Devil* features a truly chilling conversation between Pere Dominic and the young Jacques de Montfaucon.

## *Fantastic Voyage* (1966)

**Cast:** Stephen Boyd (Grant), Raquel Welch (Cora), Edmond O'Brien (General Carter), Donald Pleasence (Dr. Michaels), Arthur O'Connell (Colonel Donald Reid), William Redfield (Captain Bill Owens), Arthur

Kennedy (Dr. Duval), Jean Del Val (Jan Benes), James Brolin (Technician), Barry Coe (Communications Aide), Ken Scott (Shelby Grant), Nurse (Mrs. Denton). Directed by Richard Fleischer.

**Synopsis:** While in route to share important information concerning the top-secret miniaturization program run by the U.S. government, scientist Jan Benes is seriously injured in an attempt by a rival nation to assassinate him. The U.S. government comes up with a plan to save Benes' life by miniaturizing a special team of scientists and injecting them into his bloodstream so they can travel via a submarine to the site of a deadly blood clot and remove it. Making up the team are Captain Grant, Dr. Michaels (Donald Pleasence), Dr. Peter Duval, his assistant Cora, and Captain Bill Owens, the designer of the miniaturized submarine. Instructions are given that they must complete their mission within sixty minutes because the miniaturization effect will wear off, not to mention being attacked by Benes' antibodies as they grow larger. Another underlying threat is the possibility of sabotage from within their team. Although the mission is well-planned, the team is immediately placed in peril as their submarine, the Proteus, becomes drawn into Benes' jugular vein through a fissure caused by the assassination attempt. Now off-course deep inside Benes' body, the team manages to guide the Proteus through Benes' heart, stop by the lungs to refill their air pressure, and then via his ear canal to the site of the clot, all the while contending with things going wrong courtesy of a saboteur. After reaching the site of the clot, Dr. Duval attempts to dissolve it while Dr. Michaels who reveals himself to be the saboteur, tries to stop the team from completing its mission as time swiftly runs out.

**Commentary:** *Fantastic Voyage* certainly lives up to its name with great performances and amazing effects for 1966. The miniaturization effects and the voyage through Benes' body in no way seems cheap. The first time we get to see the red and blue corpuscles as the Proteus enters Benes' bloodstream is a sight to behold and from this point on, viewers are taken on an otherworldly journey through an ocean of life. *Fantastic Voyage* is also notable for featuring screen legend Raquel Welch in her first major film role. Edmond O'Brian, here playing General Carter, previously worked with Pleasence in the 1956 film version of Orwell's *1984*. At the time of its release, *Fantastic Voyage* garnered praise from the critics for its unique vision—"Yes sir, for straight science fiction, this is quite a film, the most colorful and imaginative since *Destination Moon*" [95] in 1950. For a film produced some forty-five years ago, *Fantastic Voyage* still stands up well today; incidentally, a 3-D remake by producer James Cameron has just been announced.

By 1966, Pleasence was in the thick of a run of big Hollywood films and *Fantastic Voyage* would stand out as one of his best. Besides the effects, part of the fun of this film is the guessing game on which member of the miniaturized team is really working for the "other side" and plans to derail the mission. Pleasence does not disappoint in this regard and it is not really evident to viewers that Dr. Michaels is the real threat until he finally shows his cards. As a result, Pleasence creates a complex character that plays both sides of the fence as the chief of the medical operation on whom the team depends for guidance, and the saboteur that threatens to derail the operation at every turn. Dr. Michaels' claustrophobia, due to being buried alive after an air raid during World War II, gives him more depth; also, this sense of fear is compounded by his assignment as the saboteur as the team gets closer to completing its "fantastic" mission. Dr. Michaels' eventual fate is suitably nasty for his character and is certainly a unique way to go.

## *Night of the Generals* (1967)

**Cast:** Peter O'Toole (General Tanz), Omar Sharif (Major Grau), Tom Courtenay (Corporal Harmann), Donald Pleasence (General Kahlenberge), Joanna Pettet (Ulrike), Philippe Noiret (Inspector Morand), Charles Gray (General von Seidlitz-Gabler), Coral Browne (Eleanore von Seidlitz-Gabler), John Gregson (Colonel Sandauer), Nigel Stock (Otto), Christopher Plummer (Field Marshal Rommel). Directed by Anatole Litvak.

**Synopsis:** During the 1942 occupation of Poland by the Nazis, a prostitute that just happens to be a German agent, ends up murdered. Major Grau is then called in to investigate and after questioning the single witness narrows down the field of suspects to three generals—Kahlenberge (Donald Pleasence), Gabler, and Tanz. As expected, all three avoid or brush off Grau, but as he persists in his investigation, Kahlenberge eventually promotes and transfers him to France. Two years later, Germany has seized France and Kahlenberge, Gabler, and Tanz are all in Paris where Grau is head of German intelligence. Kahlenberge, who is worried that Tanz will disrupt his secret plans with Gabler, has Corporal Harmann escort Tanz around Paris to keep him occupied and out of their way. During a late night out, Tanz takes a prostitute back to his apartment and murders her, framing Harmann and forcing him to flee to avoid capture and arrest. Meanwhile, Grau teams up with French Inspector Morand to dig into the history of the three generals which reveals that Kahlenberge is behind a plot to kill Hitler and build a new German Republic. When Grau hears about the murder of a second prostitute, he back tracks on the steps and then concludes that Tanz must somehow be involved. During this time, the plot to kill Hitler is executed and Kahlenberge, told prematurely that it was successful, orders the arrest of Tanze, but Grau reaches Tanz ahead of time and wants to arrest him but then comes news that Hitler survived the assassination attempt, whereby Tanz shoots Grau dead, labeling him as a traitor. Twenty-three years after the first murder and long after World War II, a third prostitute is murdered, but this time in Hamburg, Germany. Morand, now with Interpol, takes up the case to fulfill Grau's attempt at justice, and after questioning all of the parties around during the murders and finding Harmann, Morand confronts Tanz at an event to honor his war heroics. Not wanting to be exposed to his admirers, Tanz opts to commit suicide.

**Commentary:** *Night of the Generals* is a powerful political thriller with great performances by some top-notch actors. At the top is Peter O'Toole as the mentally unhinged war hero General Tanz, a strict military disciplinarian that is loved by Hitler but hated by his fellow generals for his brutal methods for achieving results. One powerful scene that showcases this brutality is when Tanz orders his troops to completely obliterate a section of Poland in his quest to root out French resistance. Also providing a great performance is Omar Sharif as the justice-seeking Major Grau whose search for the truth exposes the rotten side of the Nazi Party and leads to his own death. In addition, *Night of the Generals* offers an interesting angle that compares the mass murder committed during wartime to murders committed by one person. The idea of what is right and acceptable is also brought up which raises some interesting points.

As General Kahlenberge, Pleasence is basically the red herring for the first half of the film with Major Grau focusing upon him because of his secretive nature. However, later on, Kahlenberge is revealed to be a heroic character of sorts who wishes to dispose of Hitler and his mad dream for conquest and possibly the downfall of Germany. General Gabler, one of his fellow accomplices in the plot, is not as willing as Kahlenberge to stick his neck out for the cause and provides a contrast to all of the risks Kahlenberge must take on. Kahlenberge is also a stickler for authority but knows how to get the best use out of his men. One prime example comes when Corporal Harmann arrives and does not want to be promoted for fear of being killed in combat. Kahlenberge deadpans, "What is the point of being a general when corporals prefer to be corporals?" After hearing the young man's explanation, Kahlenberge decides to put him to work playing a piano at a ceremony in honor of Tanz and later uses him as his eyes on the fiery general. An interesting fact is that three of the actors who portray German soldiers (Pleasence, Nigel Stock, and Gordon Jackson) previously played British prisoners of war in *The Great Escape*.

## *You Only Live Twice* (1967)

**Cast:** Sean Connery (James Bond), Donald Pleasence (Ernst Stavro Blofeld), Bernard Lee (M), Desmond Llewelyn (Q), Charles Gray (Henderson), Lois Maxwell (Miss Moneypenny), Tetsuro Tanba (Tiger Tanaka), Akiko Waka bayashi (Aki), Mie Hama (Kissy), Teru Shimada (Mr. Osato), Karin Dor (Helga Brandt). Directed by Lewis Gilbert.

**Synopsis:** An unidentified spacecraft has stolen US and Russian satellites, resulting in the two superpowers blaming each other and ready to start a nuclear war. Britain believes that the spacecraft belongs to another party and traces it to the Sea of Japan, and wishing desperately to avert World War III, Britain has James Bond (007), their best secret agent, fake his own death in order to throw possible spies off of his trail. Traveling to Tokyo, Bond meets up with Tiger Tanaka. , the head of the Japanese secret service, and his beautiful assistant Aki. Following a lead to a chemical warehouse, Bond and Tiger conclude that the stolen satellites may have been taken to a secluded volcanic island and that the evil organization S.P.E.C.T.R.E. may be involved. But in order to gain access to the island, Bond's face is changed to look like a Japanese, trains in the art of the ninja, and then takes a wife as cover. Once on the island, Bond sneaks inside the volcano that actually conceals a secret liar where the spacecraft are being kept. Trying to pass himself off as an astronaut, Bond is caught and comes face to face with the leader of S.P.E.C.T.R.E.—Ernst Stavro Blofeld (Donald Pleasence) who tells Bond that he has stolen the satellites to prompt America and Russia to go to war, thus eliminating his competition for world domination. Using a high-tech gadget from Q, Bond is able to escape from being killed and lets in Tiger's army of ninjas who proceed to destroy the secret lair. Realizing that he is defeated, Blofeld sets off a series of huge explosion inside the volcano that allows him to escape while Bond, Tiger, and the ninjas swim to safety with their mission completed.

**Commentary:** *You Only Live Twice was the last of the James Bond novels to be published during Ian Fleming's lifetime, and with a screenplay by* Roald Dahl, strays somewhat from the source material. *You Only Live Twice* is typical of the exciting James Bond films of the Connery era, filled with exotic locales, beautiful women, high-tech inventions, double-crossing agents, an evil villain, and in this case an elaborate volcanic hideaway for Blofeld and his henchmen. Plot-wise, *You Only Live Twice* utilizes the theme of America and Russia ready to go to war via the Cold War which was at its peak in the late 1960s with the US heavily involved in Vietnam to prevent the spread of communism. In addition, the "Space Race" was also in full swing some three years before the United States put a man on the moon. This was to have been Sean Connery's last turn as 007; however, after George Lazenby's single film in the series, Connery was brought back for *Diamonds are Forever* in 1971 and again in the non-Eon Films production of *Never Say Never Again* in 1983. As usual, Connery is in fine form for *You Only Live Twice*, arguably the best actor to have portrayed James Bond in the cinema.

It is easy to sum up Pleasence's Blofeld as an iconic figure, so much so that when comedian/actor Mike Myers decided to spoof the spy genre in *Austin Powers: International Man of Mystery* (1997), he chose Pleasence's Blofeld as the model for the villainous Dr. Evil in both looks and mannerisms. It is unfortunate that Pleasence did not live long enough to witness Myers' Blofeld spoof which demonstrates how ingrained in the public consciousness Pleasence's portrayal of Blofeld has become. In essence, it is Pleasence's interpretation of the villainous S.P.E.C.T.R.E. leader that immediately comes to mind, an evil, disfigured genius that wishes to rule the world. Newspaper reviews pointed Pleasence out for his contribution to the film, one example being, "Donald Pleasence is grandly grotesque as the evil genius who would rule the world." [96]

An interesting similarity between the fictional Blofeld and Pleasence is that they shared a great love of art. For example, when Bond does battle with the henchman Hans, a number of paintings can be seen adorning the walls of Blofeld's retreat. Another interesting note is Blofeld's white Persian cat that he often is seen stroking while issuing orders. Apparently, the cat was spooked by the explosions on the set and at one point clawed Pleasence; it did manage to escape but was tracked down later on. An example of this can clearly be seen when Blofeld's bunker is blown open during the ninja invasion—the Persian goes wide-eyed with Pleasence trying to hold it tightly against him as it starts clawing to escape.

# *Matchless* (1967)

**Cast:** Patrick O'Neal (Perry "Matchless" Liston), Ira von Furstenberg (Arabella), Donald Pleasence (Gregori Andreanu), Henry Silva (Hank Norris), Nicoletta Machiavelli (Tipsy), Howard St. John (General Shapiro), Sorrell Brooke (Colonel Coolpepper), Tiziano Cortini (Hogdon). Directed by Alberto Lattuada.

**Synopsis:** Perry Liston, a *New York Tribune* reporter who earned the nickname "matchless" while serving as a soldier in the Korean War, also writes a column under that name and is investigating a story in China. But he is picked up by the authorities and tortured by the Chinese military, believing that he is a spy. After frustrating the Chinese general, Perry is thrown in a jail cell to await execution along with an American spy named Hank Norris and an old Chinese man. Taking pity on the old man, Perry assists him for which he receives a mysterious ring with supposed powers before the old man dies. Upon being dragged out of his jail cell for the firing quad, Perry squeezes the ring, making him invisible and able to escape. Perry makes it to the home of a woman named O-Lan who helps him to hide from the soldiers and places him on a plane back to the US. But she also drugs him and Perry wakes up being tortured once again but this time by the US government. After General Shapiro determines Perry to be legitimate, he sends him on a mission to infiltrate the inner circle of the notorious Gregori Andreanu (Donald Pleasence) who has hidden some secret vials wanted by the US. After traveling to England, Perry meets his beautiful contact Arabella who has already worked her way into Andreanu's organization. Using his ring to turn invisible, Perry rigs a boxing match and wins a bet against Andreanu who then invites Perry to his home to collect his winnings. Once there, Perry and Arabella work together to steal the key to Andreanu's bank vault. Complicating everything is Hank Norris who is now working for the Chinese government. However, Perry and Arabella successfully steal the briefcase with the vials and after a chase by Andreanu and his henchmen, make it out to sea. But upon seeing American, Chinese, and British ships heading for them, Perry makes a last minute decision to end the chase.

**Commentary:** *Matchless*, a.k.a. *Mission Top Secret*, was Pleasence's next film role after appearing in the classic Bond film *You Only Live Twice* and as a spy spoof, it cleverly pokes fun at the main ingredients of the James Bond series—agents and double-agents, bizarre villains, beautiful women, and cool gadgets. Patrick O'Neal makes for a more everyman instead of the sophisticated Bond, while Ira von Furstenberg is on hand to lend plenty of glamour as his partnered spy. This film actually does quite well on its own with some amazing action scenes, such as when Perry runs away from Hank Norris and hides underneath a moving train to avoid him, and later on when Perry jumps his car onto the top of a train with Andreanu's car in hot pursuit.

Following his iconic Bond villain Blofeld, Pleasence creates another unique villain in the form of Gregori Andreanu, an evil mastermind bent on world domination. Andreanu surrounds himself with robots to do his bidding, uses sunglasses as a pacifier when stressed, and has a habit of quoting himself; he is also impeccably dressed and sports a very neatly trimmed goatee, but his perfect exterior hides a fragile ego. When Perry wins the bet related to the rigged boxing match, Andreanu tries to win his money back during a card game, but when this fails, he offers Perry a job working for his organization. Andreanu's final scene is true to his character, for after realizing that he has failed to stop Perry, he quotes himself once more—"When the leader has failed, the waters will close over his head"—before walking fully dressed into the ocean to meet his demise.

# Creature of Comfort (1968)

**Cast:** Donald Pleasence (James Thorne), Arthur Adams, Marjorie Bennett, Virginia Crawley, Maida Severn, Jon Stone, Bill Williams. Director: Graham Driscoll.

**Synopsis:** A mysterious, carnivorous being that is able to disguise itself as a bedcover is sold by a shop owner to various customers. The customers that display evil or greed are absorbed into the being's body, while the innocent are left unharmed.[97]

**Commentary:** Because Donald Pleasence appeared in well over a hundred films during his career, one would expect that some of them might wind up being difficult to track down, or as in the case with *Creature of Comfort*, "lost" in the annals of film history. The production company for this "lost" film apparently went bankrupt and was unable to pay off its creditors, causing the prints to be seized by a Canadian bank just after production finished. Trying to uncover information on this film proved most difficult, as all the actors listed are either deceased or never made any other films. However, one never knows and a print may turn up someday. A similar situation occurred with the 1978 Peter Cushing comedy *Son of Hitler* that was locked in a vault due to money being owed; however, it eventually leaked out into collectors' markets. Interestingly, *Creature of Comfort* is described as a horror anthology, much like those made popular by the British-based Amicus Productions. In fact, the plot of mean-spirited people being punished by something purchased from a store is very similar to the plot of the 1974 Amicus horror anthology *From Beyond the Grave* with Pleasence as Jim Underwood in Segment Two "An Act of Kindness."

# *Will Penny* (1968)

**Cast:** Charlton Heston (Will Penny), Joan Hackett (Catherine Allen), Donald Pleasence (Preacher Quint), Lee Majors (Blue), Bruce Dern (Rafe Quint), Ben Johnson (Alex), Slim Pickens (Ike Walterstein), Clifton James (Catron), Anthony Zerbe (Dutchy), Roy Jenson (Boetius Sullivan), G.D. Spradlin (Anse Howard), Quentin Dean (Jennie), William Schallert (Dr. Fraker), Lydia Clarke (Mrs. Fraker), Matt Clark (Romulus Quint), Gene Rutherford (Rufus Quint). Directed by Tom Gries.

**Synopsis:** Will Penny is an aging cowboy who makes his living moving from job to job. At the end of a cattle run, Penny hitches a ride with fellow cowboys Blue and Dutchy in search of work as winter approaches. While camping during their journey, they encounter Preacher Quint (Donald Pleasence) and his three sons and daughter. Quint shoots at Blue and Dutchy after a dispute over an elk and Penny returns fire, killing one of Quint's sons. Enraged, Quint swears vengeance on Penny before retreating. After seeking help in a nearby town for Dutchy who mistakenly shot himself, Penny goes off and gets a job on a ranch riding the line of the property, keeping the cattle in line, and making sure there are no squatters. To Penny's surprise, Catherine, a husbandless mother, and her child are squatting in his cabin up in the mountains. Not wanting to kick them out, Penny agrees to let them stay until the spring. Isolated together with winter quickly approaching, Penny and Catherine begin to fall in love, but their new romance is broken up when Quint and his family track Penny down and hold him, Catherine, and her son hostage. Realizing the danger of their situation, Penny makes a break from the cabin and is pleasantly surprised to run into Blue and Dutchy who help him drive out and kill Quint and his sons. Now free from danger, Penny makes a hard choice and decides that he is too old to start a new life with Catherine and instead leaves with Blue and Dutchy in search of a new job.

**Commentary:** *Will Penny* is not your usual western, due to taking an accurate look at the hardships faced by cowboys in the "Old West." They are always on the move for the next job, eat whatever they can, and hardly bathe. There are no welcoming towns for these cowboys, only open expanses and sparse places to seek shelter from the cold. The film depicts an overall dreary life and shows the cowboys as workers, rather than as heroes. This depiction follows the film right to the end when the main character fails to get the girl and instead rides off with his buddies in search of the next job. Not exactly a typical glamorized Hollywood western.

Pleasence shines as Preacher Quint, the crazed patriarch whose family has a fateful encounter with Will Penny. When Quint is first seen, arriving at the river's edge after shooting an elk, it is not easy to distinguish his intentions as he talks kindly with Blue and Dutchy who also spotted the elk. But once Dutchy asks to share the elk, Quint's facade slips away and he quickly pulls out a rifle and starts shooting. After one of Quint's sons is shot dead by Penny, it seems like Pleasence's steel blue eyes are swearing revenge on Penny. He makes a powerful speech at the river's edge, crying and screaming about the Lord's revenge and good to his word, Quint and his family track down Penny when he is alone and brutally beat and torture him. You can just feel the impending danger as Quint tells Penny of a man he once saw bleeding to death after being impaled by a wagon wheel spoke, and then saying it will not be that easy for him just before shoving a burning branch into an open wound.

Pleasence does go a bit over the top in the scene where he celebrates the capture of Penny and Catherine by dancing wildly on tables in the cabin, but the character of Quint sort of calls for this type of performance. Also, *Will Penny* provides an interesting look at the opposing sides of Christianity with Catherine trying to care for and set a good example for her son, and Quint who distorts religion to suit his own needs, such as when he says a prayer over Penny after leaving him for dead. Pleasence's powerful performance was noted by a reviewer for *The New York Times* as a "dangerous religious fanatic… out to kill Will Penny, played with terrifying piety by Donald Pleasence." [98]

Like Robert Mitchum in *Night of the Hunter* (1955), Pleasence's Preacher Quint is a religious zealot who often quotes the Bible, but certainly does not follow its path. He is willing to commit murder at the blink of an eye which makes one wonder just how Quint became knowledgeable in religion; it does show that he has book smarts which Penny does not, being illiterate. But Quint doesn't seem to have passed on his religious knowledge to his brood, for they seem content to violently take whatever they wish. This also seems to give Quint more control over his family because he can send them out like a long arm of destruction but still rein them in if necessary, using the Lord's words as his own. Without more background, one tends to think that the desolate surroundings must have played a role in shaping Quint as a man trying to survive with his family in a hostile environment. But unlike Penny and the other cowboys, something has twisted Quint's mind (perhaps the death of an unexplained missing wife) into seeking vengeance on the Lord Himself by mocking his words while committing some very devilish actions.

Upon its release, *Will Penny* did not fare too well, probably because of the fact that it does not present a happy ending which disappointed theatre-goers. Screenwriter Tom Gries adapted the film from an episode called "Line Camp" in the television series *The Westerner* which he had also directed. Gries shopped the script around to a few studios before selling it to Paramount with the stipulation that he would get to direct the film, his very first. Besides Heston and Pleasence, the rest of the cast provides some fine performances, including Joan Hackett as the struggling mother, Ben Johnson as the prickly ranch boss, and Bruce Dern as a vicious member of the Quint clan. Also giving a solid performance is Lee Majors in his very first credited film. Heston's character of Will Penny was surely a highlight of his long career as the crafty veteran cowboy who knows that his best days are behind him. He accepts his fate and is content with surviving. The speech Penny gives Catherine about how ranching life is too difficult and not wanting to be responsible for the care of a woman and her child is very poignant. Heston himself was full of praise for the film and was happy with his role—"It turned out to be one of the best I've made, certainly among my best performances." [99] Yet despite this comment, Heston explains in his autobiography that *Will Penny* was more or less ignored by Paramount's new management which was more concerned with its roster of films already in production, and as a result, *Will Penny* languished in the theatres. Also, it probably did not help matters that *Will Penny* opened one week after another Heston film that was drawing huge audiences—*The Planet of the Apes*.

# *Sleep is Lovely* (1968)

**Cast:** Peter McEnery (Peter), John McEnery (John), Olga Georges-Picot (Elsa), Donald Pleasence (Clive), Bruce Robinson (Colin), George Coulouris (Police Inspector). Directed by David Hart.

**Synopsis:** Even though an entire year has gone by, Peter is having a hard time dealing with the breakup with the beautiful Elsa. Feeling down and out, Peter spends most of his time with his best friend John and his younger brother Colin on their barge. One morning, they notice a man who has fallen into the water from a motor cruiser and quickly rescue him. They then decide to improve their financial situation by holding the man hostage for a £1,000 ransom. What they do not realize is that the man, a wealthy middle-aged pornographer named Clive (Donald Pleasence), is actually Elsa's father. As their plan is carried out, Peter actually gets back with Elsa, although their second chance at love prematurely ends when Elsa begins an affair with Colin. Complications ensue when they pick up the ransom money that fails miserably with Peter, John, and Colin losing everything. On top of this, Elsa ends her relationship with Colin, thus placing him and Peter in competition for her affections.

**Commentary:** Unfortunately, *Sleep is Lovely* is considered as yet another of Pleasence's "lost films". It never seems to have received a proper release and soon after it somehow disappeared. [100] Adding to the confusion is that *Sleep is Lovely* went by other titles, including *The Other People* and *I Love You, I Hate You*. The plot is a dark drama with comedic overtones and in some ways is reminiscent of *Cul-de-sac*. The director is said to have made the film in order to capture the feel of late 1960s London and decide to use a stylized camera editing technique to give the film a unique look. An interesting note is that *Sleep in Lovely* was made by Oakhurst Productions, co-founded by actor Stanley Baker who had previously worked with Pleasence on *Hell is a City* and went on to work with him again in *Innocent Bystanders*.

# *Mr. Freedom* (1969)

**Cast:** Delphine Seyrig (Marie-Madeleine), John Abbey (Mr. Freedom), Donald Pleasence (Dr. Freedom), Jean-Claude Drouot (Dick Sensass), Serge Gainsbourg (M. Drugstore), Yves Lefebvre (Jacques Occident), Rufus (Freddie Fric). Directed by William Klein.

**Synopsis:** Mr. Freedom is a superhero dedicated to eradicating the evil influence of the Reds, or Communists. He is sent by Dr. Freedom (Donald Pleasence) on a mission to France where their superhero Captain Formidable has been killed. While in France, Mr. Freedom teams up with freedom fighter Marie-Madeleine and the rest of the French freedom organization. Apparently, Red Chinaman, a former friend of Mr. Freedom, is behind the Red assault on France which turns Mr. Freedom's mission into a search and destroy to prevent France from becoming a communist nation. However, a meeting with Super Frenchman does not go well and after discovering that he has been spied on, Mr. Freedom and his freedom fighters are attacked by the Reds, led by Marie-Madeleine who has defected to the other side. Following this sneak attack, the working class turns against Mr. Freedom and his violent ways. Feeling that he has been backed into a corner, Mr. Freedom sets off a huge bomb, severely injuring himself. Dr. Freedom gets in touch with him and explains that they lost a small skirmish but not the war. Mr. Freedom is ordered back to America where he is promoted but he falls amid the rubble from the blast and dies.

**Commentary:** *Mr. Freedom* was written and directed by William Klein, a photographer and filmmaker who has long been openly critical of America's foreign policy which clearly shows in the film. As a satirical look at America, its patriotism, and dealings with other countries, *Mr. Freedom* stands as a bitter commentary by Klein which often seems very dark, especially because Mr. Freedom is a racist, a sexist, and boasts a huge ego. The look of this film is quite unique with Mr. Freedom donning hockey gear and other superheroes appearing in abstract form, such as Super Frenchman and Red Chinaman represented by balloon bodies. At times, the dialogue is difficult to follow but does not serve as a distraction.

Donald Pleasence portrays Dr. Freedom, a pseudo-evangelist who spouts messages of pro-freedom and anti-communism to his agent Mr. Freedom. Dr. Freedom only appears on television monitors and Mr. Freedom's wristwatch but calls all of the shots in the war to save France. His patriotism is so strong that it actually blinds him from what is really going on. Overall, Dr. Freedom is a brief but interesting role for Pleasence who is allowed to shout out patriotic songs with Mr. Freedom throughout the film. One odd note is that Pleasence is credited as "Don" Pleasence, a first in his acting career.

# *The Madwoman of Chaillot* (1969)

**Cast:** Katharine Hepburn (Countess Aurelia), Paul Henreid (The General), Oskar Homolka (The Commissar), Yul Brynner (The Chairman), Richard Chamberlain (Roderick), Edith Evans (Josephine), Donald Pleasence (The Prospector), Joellina Smadja (Prospector's girlfriend), Henri Virlojeux (The Peddler), John Gavin (The Reverend), Gordon Heath (The Folk Singer), Nanette Newman (Irma), Danny Kaye (The rag picker). Directed by Bryan Forbes.

**Synopsis:** In Paris, the announcement that France now has a nuclear bomb results in massive youth riots in the streets. Meanwhile, a group of powerful elite men—the Chairman, the General, the Commissar, and the Reverend, meet at a local cafe to create a new organization to further their greed and military ambitions. The Chairman is convinced a stranger will advise them and sure enough, seated at a nearby table is a prospector (Donald Pleasence) who only too willing to "assist" them in their quest and share his plan for untold wealth. After searching all over France, the prospector has discovered through drinking tap water that there is a major oil reserve right in the heart of Paris. However, a city planner has put a crimp in his plans by not approving his request to drill. But now, with the help of political influence of the organization, the prospector decides to take action by sending his idealistic nephew Roderick to unwittingly blow up the city planner's office in order to get a more agreeable replacement. However, the prospector's plans go awry when Roderick changes his mind at the last minute and is accosted and knocked out by a cop who thinks Roderick wants to commit suicide. Coming to Roderick's aid is Countess Aurelia, also known as the "Madwoman of Chaillot." Together with the beautiful waitress Irma, and the fellow commoners of Paris, the Countess devises a plan to stop the organization's efforts to destroy her beloved city. With the rag picker standing in for them, the Countess puts the organization on trial in absentia and finds them guilty. Shortly after, the organization arrives at the Countess's house under the ruse that they will get an exclusive contract for the oil. But the Countess sends them down into the deep cellar and locks them up. As the Countess goes to return to the streets of Paris where she strolls with the pleasure of life, Roderick and Irma fall in love.

**Commentary:** *The Madwoman of Chaillot* is an interesting vehicle and features some powerful performances by Katharine Hepburn, Yul Brynner, Donald Pleasence, and Danny Kaye. The plot is a political satire that looks at the socio-economic differences and values of the French classes, and although it does get bogged down at times through lengthy debates, the performances are nothing less than spectacular. Brynner works wonders as the egotistical chairman with the idea that a stranger will give him the answers he wants. One great scene defines his character when the rag picker finds money on the floor next to the chairman's seat. The rag picker asks the chairman if he dropped the money to which the chairman replies "I never drop anything," and then snatches it anyway, declaring "All money is mine!" Hepburn plays the leader of the people with conviction and a determination to save the values of the past which the modern world has seemingly forgotten. Danny Kaye, in his last film role, also does well, particularly during the trial when he defends the interests of the wealthy with some thoughtful logic.

Pleasence portrays the rich, cunning, and devious prospector who thinks of nothing else but how to further increase his wealth which is showcased by his apartment with its walls decorated with collected examples of restroom artifacts, such as a bathroom door from Johannesburg, Africa which he proudly tells the stunned movers was purchased for one million franks. There is a great scene with Pleasence and Richard Chamberlain as Roderick, trading barbs over their clashing ideologies. Upon realizing his nephew's trusting nature, the prospector uses him as a pawn in his plan to gain access to the oil.

But later, when the chairman declares that the prospector has the face that he can tell his innermost secrets to, the ball is in the prospector's court and his collecting secrets from the organization, followed by his explanation on how he discovered the oil, truly highlights Pleasence's acting abilities.

# *Arthur! Arthur!* (1969)

**Cast:** Shelley Winters (Hester Green), Donald Pleasence (Arthur Brownjohn / Sir Easonby "E" Mellon), Terry-Thomas (Clennery Tubbs), Tammy Grimes (Lady Joan Mellon), Margaret Courtenay (Clare Brownjohn), Oliver Tobias (Peter "Bobo" Jackson). Directed by Samuel Gallu.

**Synopsis:** Arthur Brownjohn (Donald Pleasence) is a timid and unsuccessful man at work and gets bossed around constantly at home by his obnoxious wife. Upon visiting a psychiatrist to discuss his problems, Arthur is told to get out into society and find some way to escape his stress-filled life. After deciding to take the psychiatrist's advice to heart, Arthur creates a new persona—the suave and womanizing Sir Easonby "E" Mellon that gives him the freedom he has always wanted. But as he continues to live two separate lives, problems begin to arise that force him to make a major decision to end his charade as Mellon and return to his original life; however, he must first end his relationship with Lady Joan Mellon—through murder. While thinking about how to commit the perfect crime, Arthur suddenly realizes that he can pin the murder on Mellon and then make him disappear, but all does not go according to Arthur's plan and he ends up having to pay for his indiscretions.

**Commentary:** As an unusual psychological film, *Arthur! Arthur!* did not receive a proper theatrical release and was rarely shown on television. The plotline concerning a timid man pinning his murderous actions on his alter-ego is somewhat unique and Pleasence tackles the complexity of Arthur Brownjohn with great style. Much like his television performance in *The Man with the Power*, Pleasence's take on Arthur is that of a beaten man but also someone who is capable of at least trying to break free of his self-imposed ordeal. Rounding out the cast are Shelley Winters, Terry- Thomas and Oliver Tobias in his film debut.

# Soldier Blue (1970)

**Cast:** Candice Bergen (Kathy Maribel "Cresta" Lee), Peter Strauss (Honus Gent), Donald Pleasence (Isaac Q. Cumber), John Anderson (Colonel Iverson), Jorge Rivero (Spotted Wolf), Dana Elcar (Captain Battles), Bob Carraway (Lieutenant McNair), Martin West (Lieutenant Spingarn). Directed by Ralph Nelson.

**Synopsis:** The Colorado 11th Cavalry is accompanying a pay wagon while also transporting Kathy Maribel "Cresta" Lee, a young bride-to-be whose fiancée awaits her at Fort Reunion. While in route, the cavalry is ambushed by rifle-wielding Cheyenne Indians. The entire cavalry is killed with the exception of Private Honus Gent who was ahead scouting and away from the battle. Cresta, who also survived the attack, spots Gent and the two decide to travel onward to Fort Reunion. On their journey, Gent is disgusted to learn that Cresta who spent time living with the Cheyenne, is very much anti-U.S. and pro-Indian and does not really care about what happened to the cavalry because they were on Indian land. Even though their views put them at odds, Gent and Cresta slowly build an attraction to one another. During their travels, they encounter trader Isaac Q. Cumber (Donald Pleasence) and although he appears friendly at first, Gent becomes suspicious of Cumber and after searching his wagon while he is gone discovers that Cumber is really a gun runner providing rifles to the Cheyenne. Cresta then admits that she met Cumber before and that the guns are necessary for Spotted Wolf and the Cheyenne to survive. Cumber returns and takes Gent and Cresta prisoner, but they escape after Gent destroys the rifles. Cumber pursues them and shoots Gent in the leg, forcing him to stay hidden in a cave while Cresta continues on. She is then found by soldiers from Fort Reunion and is taken back to her fiancée, but she is upset to find out that the troops are planning an attack on the Cheyenne village the next morning. Escaping to the Cheyenne village, Cresta alerts Spotted Wolf, but he refuses to move the Cheyenne, believing the peace treaty will protect them. Gent is also picked up by the Fort Reunion troops and is brought along as the soldiers fire upon and invade the Cheyenne camp, brutally torturing, raping, and murdering mostly innocent women and children. Gent tries to stop the savagery and is arrested for his efforts while Cresta is left behind with the remaining survivors of the massacre.

**Commentary:** Although its shocking, violent, and downbeat ending is what most viewers will remember after viewing *Soldier Blue*, there is also the excellent chemistry between Candice Bergen as the Indian sympathizer and Peter Strauss as the naive soldier whose values clash at first but then slowly merge together. With her powerful performance, Bergen was singled out in reviews as a "Foul-mouthed, belching, natural aristocrat (who) embodies not so much women's lib as a liberated woman, and therefore (is) a better anachronism than most you will find at home on the range." [101] Due to its release date of 1970, *Soldier Blue* is often compared to another American atrocity, the My Lai Massacre of the Vietnam War; however, it should really stand alone for its depiction of the mistreatment of Native American Indians. Certainly standing out from the great number of westerns that depict Indians as bloodthirsty savages, *Soldier Blue* rectifies this with its reenactment of the Sand Creek Massacre, one of the most heinous acts in U.S. history.

Despite his comical name, Pleasence's Isaac Q. Cumber is an unsavory character. He works hard to keep up the façade, wearing a too-tall top hat and capped teeth while trying to appear jolly, but Gent quickly sees right through him. Cumber knows full well that the rifles he sells to the Cheyenne will be used to kill U.S. soldiers, but this apparently does not bother him as long as he makes a tidy profit. Interestingly, Cresta sees Cumber as a necessary evil, for without his rifles, the Cheyenne stand no chance against marauding U.S. soldiers. Pleasence plays Cumber as a man trying to pass for a good, honest trader but brimming just below the surface is a greedy, calculating devil. Even when he takes Gent and Cresta prisoner, he still makes the point of acting like their tour guide on an unwilling journey.

# *THX 1138* (1971)

**Cast:** Robert Duvall (THX), Donald Pleasence (SEN), Don Pedro Colley (SRT), Maggie McOmie (LUH). Directed by George Lucas.

**Synopsis:** As a factory worker, THX lives in a futuristic society where the government controls everything, sex is outlawed, and all citizens are controlled by a mandatory drug intake that assists them in the ability to work at dangerous jobs for long periods of time. But THX is beginning to feel differently than his coworkers and makes a confession in his unichapel to the all powerful being OMM. What THX does not realize is that his female roommate LUH who has made a conscious effort to stop taking her pills has also been slowly substituting a placebo for THX's drugs and when his mind clears up from not taking the real drugs, his sexual desire returns and he makes love to LUH, but their illegal act is captured on video. THX and LUH then make plans to escape from the city but when THX's boss SEN (Donald Pleasence) discovers what is going on, he transfers LUH out of the apartment to try and get THX to help him escape instead. THX is later arrested for drug evasion, convicted, and placed in a limbo section of the city, where he meets LUH once again as well as SEN whom THX had turned in. LUH is taken away by the police and THX, SEN, and SRT who formally appeared as a hologram in the city attempts to escape. Only THX makes it out successfully, due to the police going over their budget of 14,000 credits for his capture. Finally free, THX climbs to the surface and stands for the first time on solid ground.

**Commentary:** Based on his 1967 student film *Electric Labyrinth: THX 1138 4EB*, George Lucas' *THX 1138* was a groundbreaking science-fiction drama for its style and use of computer technology. The story itself is not unique, due to relating the tale of a powerful futuristic, dystopian society, much in line with George Orwell's novel *Nineteen Eighty Four*. But the visual look of the film that makes use of an all white background with futuristic technology, provides a unique and unnerving portrayal that paved the way for future sci-fi films. For this reason alone, *THX 1138* is a masterpiece of cinema, especially related to the escape element that provides much suspense and visual appeal via THX's escape in a speeding jet car. *THX 1138* also serves as commentary on corrupt governments, organized religion, and the basic needs and desires of the people.

Pleasence's performance as SEN is yet another of his well-known film roles, and the fact that the inhabitants of the city have shaven heads works to Pleasence's advantage. As a higher echelon worker in the city, Pleasence's SEN is a sympathetic figure who also desires his freedom but lacks THX's intestinal fortitude. By attempting to get THX to take him along on the escape, SEN inadvertently sets into motion the delay of the plan, the arrests, and the eventual termination of LUH. In one poignant scene, SEN turns away from the sewer system and from freedom in order to return to the city where he chats with some children while waiting for the police to arrest him. In a review of the film, Pleasence's performance is singled out—"*THX 1138* is aided by lovely performances, including Donald Pleasence who with typical appeal plays a pathetically enterprising wheeler-dealer in a world that makes no deals."[102] An interesting note is that some of Pleasence's dialog as SEN actually came from speeches by former US President Richard Nixon.

## *Wake in Fright* (1971)

**Cast:** Donald Pleasence ('Doc' Tydon), Gary Bond (John Grant), Chips Rafferty (Jock Crawford), Sylvia Kay (Janette Hynes), Jack Thompson (Dick), Peter Whittle (Joe), Al Thomas (Tim Hynes), John Meillon (Charlie), John Armstrong (Atkins). Directed by Ted Kotcheff.

**Synopsis:** John Grant is a school teacher stuck in a barren Australian outback posting due to a policy whereby he must pay back his educational grant before moving on somewhere else. Christmas vacation arrives and with six weeks off, Grant makes plans to travel to Sydney to visit his girlfriend. During a stop-over in the mining town of Bundamyabba, known as Yabba by the locals, Grant decides to take a flight out to Sydney the next day, and after checking into his hotel, he heads for the local bar which is packed with men doing some heavy drinking and flipping coins in a gambling game. Here, Grant meets the local lawman Jock Crawford who tells Grant about the town while buying him numerous beers. Thinking that the locals are quite beneath him, Grant is shocked by their aggressive hospitality, although after getting drunk, he finds the atmosphere very intoxicating. After initially winning a large pot of money flipping coins at the bar, Grant decides to let it all ride hoping to win enough to pay off his bond, but instead, he loses everything. Now stuck in Yabba with no money, Grant relies on the generosity of Tim Hynes, a local who takes Grant back to his house where the drinks flow freely. A couple of Hynes's friends soon arrive including Dick, Joe, and the enigmatic "Doc" Tydon (Donald Pleasence) who proceeds to lead everyone in a wild drinking spree. Grant continues drinking until he passes out and wakes up the next day in Tydon's cabin. Picking up where they left off, the drinking begins anew and when Dick and Joe arrive, the four men go on an out of control bender, hunting kangaroos and trashing a stranger's house. That night, Grant passes out only to awaken and find that Tydon has taken advantage of him. Desperate to get away from Yabba, Grant hitches a ride only to be taken right back to town. Mentally and physically broken, Grant returns to Tydon's house where he unsuccessfully tries to commit suicide. Awakening in a hospital, Grant finds that Tydon has taken care of his medical bills and sees him off on the train back to his job in the outback.

**Commentary:** Also known as *Outback* in some markets, *Wake in Fright* is a truly harrowing look at the underside of Australian culture, and the fact that it was directed by a Canadian director and shows a very unglamorous side of Australia, pretty much doomed its domestic life in the theatres. In fact, *Wake in Fright* was almost lost forever when the negatives went missing, only to be rediscovered in 2004 in a Pittsburgh, Pennsylvania warehouse inside a film container marked "For destruction." Since this time, the film has been restored and has won much acclaim in its native Australia as well as at the International Cannes Film Festival. From the opening panoramic shot of a barren landscape, reminiscent of a Sergio Leone spaghetti western, *Wake in Fright* reveals the true desolation of certain parts of Australia. Gary Bond's John Grant is a sympathetic character, held hostage to the education system, the town of Yabba, and to his new 'friends' who succeed in bringing him down to their barbaric level. As Grant begins drinking, his situation quickly deteriorates from a dead-end job to a literal dead-end situation. In his last film role, Chips Rafferty gives a somewhat chilling portrayal of the lawman that looks the other way as his town drinks its way into oblivion. One of the most shocking things about *Wake in Fright* is the scene involving the kangaroo hunt, taken from actual footage of the killing of the native Australian marsupials. Thus, after viewing this film, one can easily understand why Australia was not so keen on initially embracing it.

As "Doc" Tydon, Pleasence provides the moral and social corruption that causes Grant's breakdown. A self-confessed alcoholic, Tydon was banished to Yabba due to his excessive drinking, but instead of this being a demotion, Tydon revels in it because he has free reign in the town to continue his chosen lifestyle. This he does with an over-the-top embrace of his disease, from drinking while standing on his head, living in an abandoned cabin, and spending his nights drinking until he passes out. Tydon walks a fine line between his former refinements and new lifestyle as he describes the medical effects of drinking while getting sloshed, or listening to operatic music while cooking kangaroo meat and hunting flies in his cabin. Grant makes the mistake of trusting Tydon because they both have educated backgrounds and ends up paying for it with his sanity. After mentally chipping away at Grant with his lifestyle, Tydon takes it to a whole other level when one night, he sexually assaults Grant while he is passed out. This is the moment when Grant goes over the edge in reference to the film's title as he awakens from an alcohol-induced stupor to find Tydon lying next to him in a woman's nightgown. For his fans, Pleasence's performance in *Wake in Fright* is a must see example on how commanding he could be in a film role.

# *Kidnapped* (1971)

**Cast:** Michael Caine (Alan Breck), Lawrence Douglas (David Balfour), Vivien Heilbron (Catriona Stewart), Trevor Howard (Lord Advocate), Donald Pleasence (Ebenezer Balfour), Jack Hawkins (Captain Hoseason), Gordon Jackson (Charles Stewart), Freddie Jones (Cluny), Jack Watson (James Stewart), Peter Jeffrey (Riach). Directed by Delbert Mann.

**Synopsis:** David Balfour, recently orphaned, goes to the home of his uncle Ebenezer (Donald Pleasence) to hopefully gain an apprenticeship; however his uncle is anything but hospitable and after almost sending David to his death on the night of their first meeting, sells him the next day to Captain Hoseason who promptly knocks him out and takes him aboard his ship where David is forced to be a cabin boy and learns he will be sold as an indentured servant in the Carolinas. During the sea voyage, Hoseason picks up Alan Breck, a Scotsman adrift in a small boat. At first agreeing to take Alan to France for a price, Hoseason decides to rob him with the help of his scurvy crew. After Hoseason orders his crew to arm themselves, David decides to alert Alan and they end up fighting off the Hoseason and his crew until the ship crashes upon the rocks of Scotland, sending everyone overboard. Upon rescuing David from the frigid waters, Alan explains that he is wanted by the British government for attempting to reinstate the Stuart royal family in Scotland. Together, they make their way to the home of Alan's kinsman James Stuart where David meets James' daughter Catriona to whom David is highly attracted. The next day, British soldiers arrive at the house and before anyone can escape, British captain Mungo Campbell is shot dead and James Stuart is severely injured. Alan, David, and Catriona then run for their lives and upon regrouping they learn that James was taken prisoner by the British and is being charged with the death of Campbell even though he never fired a shot. David wants to testify on James' behalf to the Lord Advocate but Alan advises him against it because it is a British court and it would never be a fair trial. Instead, Alan makes plans to hitch a boat ride back to France, but being short on money, he decides to help David seek revenge on his uncle Ebenezer by blackmailing him. David then discovers that he is the true and legal owner of the Balfour family estate. As a result, Catriona wishes to settle down with David but he continues to insist on testifying in court that causes Alan to strike a deal with the Lord Advocate by turning himself in for James' freedom and David's safety.

**Commentary:** *Kidnapped* is actually based on two novels by Robert Louis Stevenson—*Kidnapped* and its sequel, *Catriona*. Stevenson's classic tale of intrigue and betrayal has been filmed many times with the most popular being the 1960 Disney version, but unlike this upbeat swashbuckler, Delbert Mann's *Kidnapped* is rooted in the political turmoil of Great Britain and features a more downbeat angle. Filmed within the beautiful lush landscapes of Scotland, the bitter struggle between the British soldiers and Scottish rebels is carried out, and while

Lawrence Douglas as David Balfour provides a rather naive perspective on all that is occurring around him, it is Michael Caine's portrayal as Alan Breck that gives this version some backbone. Breck's deep commitment to restoring the Stuart royal family in Scotland creates tunnel vision in his character which causes him to lose sight of the individuals who were once so important to him, but Breck's turnaround truly serves as the impetus for most of the emotion in this film.

Pleasence plays Ebenezer Balfour, a man who truly lives up to his name by living in a large estate, dressing in rags, and being so cheap that he saves the leftover food from the plates of his guests. With wispy hair and a Scottish accent, Ebenezer first appears to be a dotty but harmless uncle to David, at least until he gives him the keys to a nonexistent room in the tower and prays while his nephew climbs the stairs. His betrayal of David comes on the following day when he sells him off to become a slave. It is only later when Alan Breck blackmails Ebenezer that his true motives are revealed—David's father stole the woman that Ebenezer loved which broke his heart. Ebenezer's heart does eventually give out but not before telling David not to let the visiting doctor charge him too much.

## *The Jerusalem File* (1972)

**Cast:** Bruce Davison (David Armstrong), Nicol Williamson (Professor Lang), Daria Halprin (Nurit), Donald Pleasence (Major Samuels), Ian Hendry (General Mayer), Yair Rubin (Barak), Ze'ev Revach (Rashid), David Semadar (Herzen), Jack Cohen (Altouli), Yitzhak Ne'eman (Yussof), Ori Levy (Captain Ori). Directed by John Flynn.

**Synopsis:** David Armstrong is an American student studying archaeology in Jerusalem, and while visiting Rashid Rifaat, his friend and fellow student from Yale, David becomes the victim of a drive-by shooting but survives. Major Samuels (Donald Pleasence) then becomes very interested in David because he knows Rashid is a terrorist who is rumored to be taking over in his organization. Refusing to turn in his friend, David leaves the hospital after Professor Lang pulls strings to get him released. In return, Samuels takes away David's passport and decides to follow him, hoping to locate Rashid. Once back at the dig site, David meets up with Nurit, a student he has a crush on, and her friend Barak. David gets to know Barak who expresses an interest in meeting Rashid with a few fellow students. In the meantime, Samuels is following a trail of dead bodies, courtesy of one of the terrorist groups out to eliminate their competition. David decides to help Barak and sets up the meeting, but Lang becomes upset, knowing that it could end badly and wants it called off. When David does not comply with his wishes, Lang contacts Samuels for his help, and together, they eventually get to David, but Barak has already left for the meeting, along with Nurit and some other fellow students. The Israeli army then sends word to Samuels regarding where the meeting took place, and when they arrive, they find Barak, Nurit, and Rashid among the dead, courtesy of a sniper by a rival terrorist group.

**Commentary:** Much like *The Ambassador*, *The Jerusalem File* revolves around the Israeli/Arab conflict, and even though it does not feature big name stars like the former, it is still superior and unfortunately less known. As a political thriller set shortly after the Six-Day War between Israel and its Arab neighbors, *The Jerusalem File* adheres more to suspense and intrigue, rather than the actual events of the war, thus making it a fast moving thrill ride that demands the attention of the viewer. Bruce Davison as the young and naive student David Armstrong does a good job by eliciting sympathy when he finally realizes how he has been used and the violent outcome that occurs as a result of his help. Not surprisingly, the fact that things have not changed much in this region of the world has resulted in numerous copycat productions up until the present day.

As Major Samuels, Pleasence is in fine form as a man on a mission fighting against a deadline to track down a possible terrorist leader. At first almost appearing villainous because of his unscrupulous methods of trying to get results and answers, it slowly becomes evident that Samuels is the real hero of this film, due to his efforts to protect his country and avoid the inevitable violent showdown. There are many great scenes with Pleasence, such as when Samuels and his men raid and ransack a local house looking for photos. He asks his captain, "Did they know that they were sheltering terrorists?" and when told that the owners said they had no choice in the matter, Samuels coolly replies, "Then neither had we." In a contemporary film review, Pleasence was singled out for his gritty performance—"Donald Pleasence emerges as a convincingly human, if implacable, sleuth." [103]

# *The Pied Piper* (1972)

**Cast:** Jack Wild (Gavin), Donald Pleasence (The Baron), John Hurt (Franz), Donovan (The Pied Piper), Michael Hordern (Melius), Roy Kinnear (Burgermeister Poppendick), Peter Vaughan (Bishop), Diana Dors (Frau Poppendick), Cathryn Harrison (Lisa), Keith Buckley (Mattio), Peter Eyre (Pilgrim), John Welsh (Chancellor), Hamilton Dyce (Papal Nuncio), Arthur Hewlett (Otto). Directed by Jacques Demy.

**Synopsis:** In 1349 in Northern Germany, the Black Death is ravaging the population. A group of traveling entertainers, along with a Christian pilgrim and a piper travel to Hamelin where a big wedding between the Baron's son and the burgermeister's daughter is being held. But upon arriving, they are locked out of the city, due to a quarantine to keep the town safe from the plague. But within Hamelin all is not well as Lisa, the burgermeister's daughter, has taken extremely ill and is feared to be infected with the plague. Melius, the town alchemist, is called in by the burgermeister and deduces that Lisa only has a bad fever and will recover with rest, but the church priests condemn him for being a Jew and prepare to give Lisa her last rites when a musical flute stirs her from her illness. Desperate for a possible cure, the burgermeister orders his guards to find the source of the healing music. Outside the town gates, they find the piper playing his flute and bring him in along with the entertainers. The piper plays for Lisa who makes a miraculous recovery much to the burgermeister's delight. Lisa's fiancé, Franz, is only happy that she will make it to the altar so he can receive her dowry to support his army. But his father the Baron (Donald Pleasence) has other plans for the dowry because he needs the funds to complete the building of a cathedral so he can save his soul. A wrench is thrown into all of their plans when rats begin to invade Hamelin. Melius tries to work on a cure but is stopped and arrested by Franz for not making him fool's gold to help raise an army. The piper answers the burgermeister's plea for help and uses his flute to lure the rats to a lake to drown. But upon not being paid for his services, the piper plays a song that lures all the children out of town, never to be heard from again. Melius is placed on trial by the Inquisition and is soon put to death. Gavin, his assistant, sees no hope left in the town because the plague has already taken hold and leaves with the entertainers.

**Commentary:** *The Pied Piper* is a well-made film that closely follows the German fairy tale "The Pied Piper of Hamelin" and one that utilizes remarkable set and costume designs, giving it a rich and realistic look. Much like the fairy tale, *The Pied Piper* is a bit depressing with the plague, greedy officials and church members, child marriages, abused villagers, and the piper enacting his vengeance by taking the town's children away. The most heroic figure is the educated and innovative alchemist Melius, for unlike the medieval church, Melius does not rely on superstition but on science which not surprisingly draws the ire of the church. The fact that Melius is a Jew living in a Christian town incites more anger in church officials who are eager to dispose of him and seize the opportunity when he is arrested by Frantz. This sort of conflict provides an interesting look at anti-semitism which many Jews faced in medieval Europe. As such, *The Pied Piper* is an excellent social commentary on life during the Middle Ages. The roles are all well-acted with two stand-out performances by John Hurt as the sadistic and greedy Frantz and Roy Kinnear as the inept burgermeister Poppendick. The only slightly weak point in this film is the Piper himself, played by 1960s folk singer Donovan. Although his musical numbers are well-done, his acting is marginal and possibly because the producers knew this, the Piper's role is kept to a minimum despite the film's title.     As the Baron, Pleasence is a most colorful character who provides some comic relief in a mostly dreary story. Dressed in a ridiculous-looking, two-foot tall headpiece, the Baron is always trying to come up with schemes to wring more money from the townspeople so he can build his new cathedral. Pleasence has some great interactions with a young John Hurt as his son and wearing equally bizarre headgear. When the church officials tell the Baron that the cathedral will guarantee his entrance into Heaven, Frantz quips that his father never behaved like he believed in God, thus making the church's guarantee redundant. But right on cue, the Baron replies, "But Hell? I can buy my way out of that!" Yet Frantz will not back down on his need to keep the dowry for himself which makes the Baron even more desperate, such as when he refuses to drink at his son's wedding, fearing that it would only be a waste of precious money.

# *Henry VIII and His Six Wives* (1972)

**Cast:** Keith Michell (Henry VIII), Donald Pleasence (Thomas Cromwell), Charlotte Rampling (Anne Boleyn), Jane Asher (Jane Seymour), Frances Cuka (Katherine of Aragon), Lynne Frederick (Catherine Howard), Jenny Bos (Anne of Cleves), Barbara Leigh-Hunt (Catherine Parr), Michael Gough (Duke of Norfolk), Brian Blessed (Duke of Suffolk), Michael Goodliffe (Thomas More), Bernard Hepton (Archbishop Thomas Cranmer). Directed by Waris Hussein.

**Synopsis:** As England's King Henry VIII lies on his deathbed, he thinks back on his life, monarchy, and his six wives. In Henry's first marriage to Catherine of Aragon who had previously been married to his now deceased brother, problems quickly arise when Catherine suffers a number of miscarriages with her only surviving child being a daughter named Mary. Desperate for a male heir to inherit his throne, Henry falls in love with Anne Boleyn and petitions the Pope for an annulment, but the legal battle gets stuck in the courts, due to Catherine's brother being the former Holy Roman Emperor. But when Anne becomes pregnant, Henry decides to break away from the Catholic Church and the Pope's rule by having his archbishop grant him the annulment. However, like Catherine, Anne gives birth to a daughter named Elizabeth that leads to Henry seeking out the affections of Jane Seymour. Thomas Cromwell (Donald Pleasence), Henry's Chief Minister, uses his power to persuade Henry to put Anne on trial for treason for alleged past liaisons. After Anne is beheaded, Henry marries Jane who gives birth to a son named Edward; however, Jane later dies as a result of childbirth complications. After another short-lived marriage to Anne of Cleves, Henry marries the much younger Catherine Howard who then carries on an affair and as a result is executed. With his health beginning to deteriorate, Henry marries for the last time Catherine Parr who outlives him. In the end, Henry is at least content that he has a male heir to the throne of England.

**Commentary:** *Henry VIII and His Six Wives*, adapted from a six-part 1970 BBC television mini-series *The Six Wives of Henry VIII*, are both very well-made historical dramas based on the exploits of one of the most controversial monarchs in British history. Keith Michell as King Henry VIII in both versions, gives the performance of his life in tracing the beginnings of the young, carefree king and upwards through political shenanigans, health issues, and six loves and losses. Michell sets the personality of the king in motion during an exchange with his first wife Catherine—"Princes don't marry for love, my lady, but to beget children." For the viewer, King Henry is presented as not only the monarch who split from the Catholic Church to create his own religion (Anglicanism) and who goes through wives like discarded clothing, but also as a sort of pawn pulled and pushed by his own counsel and their personal desires for advancement.

Pleasence portrays Chief Minister Thomas Cromwell, a character full of conflict who uses the king's trust to help fatten his pockets and courtly influence. With a pageboy haircut to more closely resemble the historical Cromwell, Pleasence does a good job at displaying his dual nature as unassuming and acting like Henry's good friend while at the same time making behind-the-scenes deals and holding power over other members of the king's court. In effect, Pleasence presents Cromwell as a man who proudly wears his medals from the king and feels that he is superior, at times even over Henry himself. But when Henry's marriage to Anne of Cleves goes sour, Cromwell bears the brunt of the king's wrath and in a powerful scene is stripped of all his medals and rings by the counsel and left with a bloody nose in return as the guards arrest him for treason. An interesting note is that in the original BBC mini-series, Pleasence's daughter Angela played King Henry's fifth wife Catherine Howard.

# Innocent Bystanders (1972)

**Cast:** Stanley Baker (John Craig), Geraldine Chaplin (Miriam Loman), Donald Pleasence (Loomis), Dana Andrews (Blake), Sue Lloyd (Joanna Benson), Derren Nesbitt (Andrew Royce), Vladek Sheybal (Aaron Kaplan), Warren Mitchell (Omar), Ferdy Mayne (Marcus Kaplan). Directed by Peter Collinson.

**Synopsis:** Aaron Kaplan, a Russian agronomist who has made a breakthrough in creating arable land in the desert, escapes from a work camp in Siberia and goes into hiding. The U.S. intelligence agency Group Three wants Kaplan but is afraid of an internal leak so their leader Blake meets with his British counterpart Loomis (Donald Pleasence), the operator of Department K to obtain his assistance. But when Blake refuses to meet Loomis's demand for intelligence on some Hong Kong strike plans, Loomis decides to take on the case anyway. John Craig, a past his prime agent stuck in limbo at Department K, is sent by Loomis to find Kaplan's brother in New York; however, two new agents, Andrew Royce and Joanna Benson, have been sent as well and if Craig fails, his career is over. But when Craig arrives in New York, he discovers that Loomis set him up to fail; no gun is provided and Royce and Benson turn out to be competing with him instead of acting as decoys. More trouble comes for Craig when he finds out that the KGB is also after Kaplan and is picked up and interrogated by Group Three. Fed up with everyone, Craig decides to go solo and kidnaps Miriam Loman, a friend of Kaplan's brother, who knows the location of Kaplan in Turkey. Along the way, Loman finds herself falling in love with the hard disciplined Craig, and although captured and tortured by Royce and Benson in Turkey, Craig and Loman still beat the competition to find Kaplan, now hiding as a local goat herder. Craig then makes a deal with Loomis who agrees to pay 100,000 pounds for Kaplan as long as Royce and Benson accompany them to get their man. But more trouble arrives when two of Kaplan's former prison mates sent by the KGB follow and engage Craig, Royce, and Benson in a firefight at a secluded villa. Craig outwits the assassins and gets Kaplan to Loomis to claim his money. Loman, who is really an agent for Group Three, is sent on her way by Craig who then disappears with his money as Loomis fails to try and capture his former agent.

**Commentary:** In the 1950s, Welsh actor Stanley Baker was one of Britain's top stars and *Innocent Bystanders* was one his last films before dying from lung cancer a few years afterwards. In this film, Baker's character of John Craig fits in very well with his canon of tough guy-type roles. Looked down on by his boss and new recruits who all call him "old man," Craig knows that his career as a government agent is at a standstill, but Loomis explains that no one who signed on to Department K can ever leave which equals a virtual death sentence. *Innocent Bystanders* is often considered as a James Bond imitation but is quite different in practically every respect. The idea of an agent psychologically scarred and on his way to being replaced by new recruits is quite fascinating and was executed by director Collinson with great style. One scene illustrates this when Craig is picked up by Group Three to be interrogated on his involvement in the Kaplan case. Blake is told about Craig's former torture at the hands of the KGB, so he tells Craig that he is sending high voltage currents through his body which makes Craig scream in pain, even though the machine is not plugged in. Along with Miriam, other characters in *Innocent Bystanders* turn out to be not so innocent, especially toward the conclusion of the film.

Although Pleasence's character is named Loomis (a name that he would become associated with six years later in the original *Halloween*), this is mere coincidence, as John Carpenter had actually named the heroic psychiatrist in the original *Halloween* after the Sam Loomis character in Alfred Hitchcock's 1960 thriller *Psycho*. But as the icily cool leader of Department K, Loomis has no qualms about sending an agent to his death just to get what he wants. In an exchange with Craig about Royce complaining of being beaten by him when not looking, Loomis sums up his philosophy perfectly when he replies, "Cheated? You mean he still believes there are rules?" Loomis backs up this revelation of utter indifference throughout the film as he double-crosses Craig and sets him up to fail at every turn; however, as a highly experienced agent, Craig still has a few tricks up his sleeve for his boss.

# *Wedding in White* (1972)

**Cast:** Carol Kane (Jeannie Dougall), Donald Pleasence (Jim Dougall, Sr.), Doris Petrie (Mary Dougall), Leo Phillips (Sandy), Christine Thomas (Sarah McCarver), Paul Bradley (Jimmie Dougall), Doug McGrath (Billy), Bonnie Carol Case (Dolly). Directed by William Fruet.

**Synopsis:** Jeannie Dougall is a shy, awkward teenager living in a small Canadian town during World War II. She constantly dreams of a romantic future, finding her dream husband like in the movies. One day, her brother Jimmie returns home on leave with his friend and fellow soldier Billy and start drinking heavily along with Jeannie's dad Jim Dougall, Sr. (Donald Pleasence); of course, mischief follows wherever they go. Upon returning home late at night after hanging out with her friend Dolly, Jeannie finds Billy still drinking downstairs, while her brother and father have passed out upstairs. When Jeannie tries to go to sleep on the couch, Billy takes advantage of her and rapes her. Embarrassed, Jeannie says nothing about the encounter until months later when her mother finds some baby mittens stolen by Jeannie and confronts her about them. Jeannie confesses about what happened with Billy and then reveals that she is pregnant. Her mother starts crying in shame while her father slaps and knocks her around out of rage for dishonoring the family. Because Jeannie has no husband, Mr. Dougall wants her out of the house but her mother pleads to let her stay. A compromise is reached when Sandy, Mr. Dougall's best friend and fellow guard at work, declares his interest in Jeannie, even though he is old enough to be her father. A wedding takes place in the house and Jeannie is forced to marry Sandy, thus breaking her heart and her hopes for a loving marriage.

**Commentary:** *Wedding in White* provides a harrowing look at the familial stigma that was created when a baby was born out of wedlock during the era of World War II. While not producing the same effect on the families of today, women, even innocent ones like Jeannie, became social outcasts if they gave birth sans a husband. In her debut film role, Carol Kane excels as the shy Jeannie Dougall whose bedroom is plastered with images of romantic scenes from various films that she idolizes. But Jeannie is much too innocent in matters of love and has learned most of what she knows from Dolly, her more adventurous friend. The terror that Jeannie feels when her own family treats her like an outcast and their horrible solution to the "problem" remains potent and heartbreaking. In essence, all of the performances in this film are quite spectacular and are helped along by accurate period clothing, music, and dialogue.

As the somewhat simple-minded, chauvinistic, and hard drinking Jim Dougall, Pleasence gives a very powerful performance as the source of a number of disastrous consequences for his own family. When his son Jimmie and his friend Billy return home on leave, it is Mr. Dougall who encourages their frat boy behavior, drinking so much that they pass out and unknowingly leave Jeannie in the clutches of the sadistic Billy. With a spot on Canadian accent, Pleasence portrays the traditional paternalistic figure that is more concerned with what his buddies think of him than the welfare of his own wife and daughter, a basic recipe for disaster, especially when combined with the typical macho drinking culture. Although a somewhat scary premise, this sort of behavior was a way of life for many families during the 1940s. In a contemporary film review, Pleasence's performance in *Wedding in White* was singled out and the reviewer notes that "Donald Pleasence is Jeannie's dad, "a top-notch bowler and a triple-threat man at darts" who also manages to suggest the existence of evil in the most commonplace of personalities." [104]

# *The Rainbow Boys* (1973)

**Cast:** Donald Pleasence (Ralph Logan), Don Calfa (Mazella), Kate Reid (Gladys). Directed by Gerald Potterton.

**Synopsis:** Ralph Logan (Donald Pleasence) is an eccentric gold miner living in a cabin he built by the river in British Columbia. One day, he runs into Mazella, a New Yorker who arrives in town on his custom three-wheeler motorcycle. Mazella accidentally crashes into a car and Logan takes him to his friend Gladys' house to get his injured arm treated. After sitting down to rest, the conversion of gold comes up and Logan reveals that his father had left him a gold mine called The Little Lemon far up in the hills. As a result, an unlikely bond is formed between Logan, Gladys, and Mazella and as a team, they decide to take a ride up to try and locate the mine and the riches it may hold. Along their journey, they learn more about each other's background and recognize that they are kindred souls. Traveling on Mazella's motorcycle, they stop by Logan's cabin to get the map, are thrown off Indian land, and later due to Logan's mistake, they watch their ride roll over a cliff and smash into the river below. Just when they are about to call it quits, Logan spots the Little Lemon mine. Elated, they reach the mine entrance only to have their hopes crushed when they see the mine shaft is blocked by a cave-in. Logan then recalls that his father stashed some gold under the floor of a nearby shack during one of his travels. After ripping up the floor of the shack, they discover what they have come for—a chest full of gold nuggets. Taking some lumber from the shack, they build a makeshift raft to get home, but an accident during the raft's launch sends the chest of gold floating down the river by itself while Logan, Mazella and Gladys watch in disbelief from the shore line.

**Commentary:** *The Rainbow Boys* (released on video with the more appropriate title *The Rainbow Gang* considering Kate Reid's involvement), is a quirky little gem of a film. Essentially a buddy road picture, the plot is not as important as the interaction and dialogue between the three main stars. Each character is an outsider, a soul cast off from society, from the forgetful and sometimes childlike Logan, to Mazella the dreamer, and to the grumpy but level-headed widow Gladys, and the fact that they are traveling through Indian land further highlights their roles as outcasts. *The Rainbow Boys* was written and directed by Gerald Potterton for his own production company. Potterton had mostly done shorts and besides *The Rainbow Boys*, his other well-known film is the 1981 animated fantasy *Heavy Metal*. As Mazella, Don Calfa is an excellent character actor with a great understanding on how to make a character appear as natural and real. Kate Reid, who plays Gladys as the voice of reason in the trio, was a well-known Canadian actress. What makes this film really work is the dialogue between these three friends during their journey. There is a great scene between Mazella and Logan in his cabin where they begin to arbitrarily discuss their interests which makes the bond between them even stronger. *The Rainbow Boys* is also not without some amusing scenes, such as when Logan remembers that he hid his map in the barrel of a rifle and when Mazella becomes enraged over Gladys calling his now wrecked motorcycle a piece of junk and uses a pickaxe to open a can of beans which explodes all over Logan's face.

As Ralph Logan, Pleasence demonstrates his acting range by choosing to portray a character totally off the beaten path. Although not explained, it seems as if Logan has a short attention span and is prone to fits of frustration which is when he usually screams "Bastards!" or "Put your dukes up!" Logan is not successful by any means but seems to be perfectly content living the life of a gold panner down by the river's edge and visiting his friend Gladys. It is the arrival of Mazella who opens up Logan's world to attempt an adventure that he most probably would never have taken on his own. Logan often discusses his father in a heroic light as the man who helped England during the war and who later panned for gold in the Northwest. Gladys' attempts to knock him down are ignored by Logan who clearly misses his family, thus making him all the more likable. There are so many little nuances to Pleasence's character in this film that it takes more than one viewing to really catch them all, a true sign of a well-acted part. An interesting side note is that Pleasence would work with Gerald Potterton once again in a totally different media for Pleasence's 1977 book *Scouse the Mouse*, illustrated by Potterton.

## *Death Line* (1973)

**Cast:** Donald Pleasence (Inspector Calhoun), Norman Rossington (Detective Sergeant Rogers), David Ladd (Alex Campbell), Sharon Gurney (Patricia Wilson), Hugh Armstrong (The 'Man'), June Turner (The 'Woman'), Christopher Lee (Stratton-Villiers, MI5), Clive Swift (Inspector Richardson), James Cossins (James Manfred, OBE), Hugh Dickson (Dr. Bacon). Directed by Gary Sherman.

**Synopsis:** A young couple, Alex and Patricia, after leaving the Russell Square tube station, spot a man slumped over on the staircase. They are not sure if the man is drunk or injured, so after looking at his wallet for identification, Alex and Patricia go and get a constable, but when the constable returns to the scene with them, the man has disappeared. Later, the constable's report ends up at the local police station, where it attracts the interest of Inspector Calhoun (Donald Pleasence) upon learning that the man on the staircase was James Manfred, a high-level government official. Adding to the mystery is that a number of people have gone missing in the same subway over the years. Together with Detective Sergeant Rogers, Calhoun begins to piece together the puzzle; however, after bringing in Alex for questioning, Rogers wonders if they should turn the case over to MI5, but Calhoun is determined to solve the case without bringing in the government. Detective Richardson, who is also working the case with Calhoun, turns up information on the location of the missing persons and their disappearances—there had been an attempt to extend the tunnel back in 1892 before a roof collapse buried a number of workers, and because the company involved went bankrupt, the people and the line they were working on were abandoned. Meanwhile, deep in the labyrinth of underground tunnels, Manfred has been killed and dragged into the abode of the last surviving descendant from the 1892 incident who has managed to survive like all the others before him by practicing cannibalism. His pregnant companion unexpectedly dies much to his horror, and acting out in frustration and anger, the cannibal returns to the station, where he attacks and kills three subway workers. Calhoun receives information on the deaths and after sending out a blood sample from the crime scene learns that the killer suffers from vitamin deficiencies and is also a carrier of the plague. While returning to their apartment, Alex and Patricia become separated in the subway, resulting in Patricia being taken hostage by the cannibal. Desperate to find her, Alex contacts Calhoun and then goes searching on his own. Patricia has been chosen by the cannibal to be his new mate, but she manages to escape and is caught once again. While searching nearby, Alex hears her screams and ends up fighting the cannibal and mortally wounding him. Calhoun and his men arrive and bring Alex and Patricia back to safety, and upon searching the lair, they find the remains of Manfred's body.

**Commentary:** *Death Line*, a.k.a. *Raw Meat*, is one of the most underrated horror films of the 1970s; in fact, although lacking the significance of *Halloween*, one could argue that *Death Line* is probably Pleasence's best overall horror film. The film just oozes with style, wit, and the right amount of horror from writer and director Gary Sherman, making his film debut. Unlike other horror films that often show only quick cut away shots of the monster in question, *Death Line* pulls no punches with a seven minute-long scene that takes the viewer through the visceral lair of the cannibal, stocked with half-decayed corpses amid maggots, rats, dripping water, and complete darkness, a truly unnerving experience which counterbalances the sarcastic humor of Inspector Calhoun. Likewise, another interesting aspect of *Death Line* is the humanization of the cannibal, for he is not presented as a stereotypical blood-thirsty monster but as a tragic survivor, abandoned by society and trying to eke out an existence the only way he knows how. The scene involving the cannibal and his dead companion is as touching as could be considering the unusual circumstances. Also, the underground subway setting lends a natural horror that completes the effect; viewers might look around cautiously the next time they hear the phrase "Mind the doors!"

Pleasence as Inspector Calhoun practically 'owns' *Death Line* via his non-stop tour de force and looks like he is clearly enjoying chewing up all the scenery in sight. Wearing a crumpled hat and using an East End accent, his Calhoun is a very sarcastic, working-class policeman who loves to intimidate those higher up in the chain of command. The interaction between Pleasence's Calhoun and Norman Rossington's Detective Sergeant Rogers is pure delight, especially during the pub scene, and will keep viewers smiling long after the film ends. Watching Calhoun getting upset because his tea was made from tea bags, a cheap alternative, and fishing them out with a throwing dart or using a fake upper-crust accent when calling Manfred's office is quite amusing. Horror legend Christopher Lee shares a cameo with Pleasence as an MI5 agent, but even he cannot steal the thunder from Pleasence's performance. In character as Calhoun, Pleasence is determined against all odds to get his man and solve the case and manages to steal the film in the process. It all comes down to *Death Line* being a definite must-see for all Donald Pleasence fans.

# Tales That Witness Madness (1973)

**Cast:** Donald Pleasence (Professor R.C. Tremayne), Kim Novak (Auriol), Georgia Brown (Fay Patterson), Joan Collins (Bella Thompson), Jack Hawkins (Dr. Nicholas), Donald Houston (Sam Patterson), Michael Jayston (Brian), Suzy Kendall (Ann/Beatrice), Peter McEnery (Timothy Patrick), Michael Petrovitch (Kimo), Russell Lewis (Paul Patterson), Leslie Nunnerley (Vera), Leon Lissek (Keoki), Mary Tamm (Ginny). Directed by Freddie Francis.

**Synopsis:** Dr. Nicholas pays a visit to the Department of Psychiatric Medicine run by Professor R.C. Tremayne (Donald Pleasence). Of interest to Nicholas is Tremayne's claim to have made a major breakthrough in his field which he proceeds to explain through the stories of four of his patients. The first patient is a young boy named Paul whose parents fight constantly and being an only child, feels the need to create an imaginary friend, Mr. Tiger. Embarrassed by their son's behavior, Paul's parents simply look the other way until Paul starts stealing meat to feed Mr. Tiger and they find scratch marks on the doors. Their eventual confrontation with Paul in his bedroom about Mr. Tiger ends in a bad way. The second patient is Timothy who runs an antique store and has just acquired the belongings from an aunt who passed away. Among the curios are a penny farthing and a portrait of the mysterious Uncle Albert. These two items are eerily connected because Uncle Albert has the power to force Timothy via the penny farthing to propel him back in time as himself to meet a lost love. Timothy's girlfriend sees the danger of the situation and tries to help him break Uncle Albert's hold, resulting in her death and a massive fire. The third patient is Brian and while jogging near his house, he discovers an odd-shaped tree stump that he drags home to the disappointment of his fiery wife Bella. An unusual relationship develops between Brian and 'Mel,' the newly named tree stump. Bella tries to intervene which leads to a deadly showdown. The fourth patient is Auriol, a literary agent who invites her most well-known and mysterious client Kimo to come for a special Hawaiian themed party she is throwing for him. But all does not go according to Auriol's plans, as Kimo has sinister plans of his own involving the seduction, murder, and eating of Auriol's daughter Ginny. At the wrap-up of all of the stories, Dr. Nicholas is very confused about the stories and Tremayne's explanation of their realities fails to convince him until it is too late.

**Commentary:** As a typical horror story anthology, *Tales That Witness Madness* possesses more misses than hits. Often mistaken as an Amicus production that specialized in these types of features, *Tales That Witness Madness* was instead produced by World Film Services which had previously released the excellent horror thriller *The Creeping Flesh* (1973). The company's attempt to cash in on the success of Amicus is fairly obvious and in fact seems to borrow heavily from the Amicus horror anthology *Asylum*, made in 1971. The stories here are all subpar; there is not much suspense and some of the stories like "Uncle Albert" are not fully explained, thus creating a lot of unanswered questions. However, this film does seem to have a grittier edge than the average Amicus film through additional gore and some nudity, but it still pales in comparison to its rival.

Donald Pleasence plays the eccentric Professor R.C. Tremayne, the head of a futuristic-looking asylum who delves into the minds of his hand picked patients. His role in this film is not really substantial, for he only appears in the linking of the stories; his character also is quite vague on the nature of his "breakthrough" discovery that serves as the impetus for the film's plot. His final revelation at the conclusion that proves his theory is also vague, leaving one to wonder whether Tremayne really does know what is going on or if he should be locked up along with his special patients. Pleasence would be much better off in his role for the Amicus horror anthology *From Beyond the Grave*.

# *From Beyond the Grave* (1974)

**Cast:** Ian Bannen (Christopher Lowe), Ian Carmichael (Reginald Warren), Peter Cushing (The Proprietor), Donald Pleasence (Jim Underwood), Diana Dors (Mabel Lowe), Margaret Leighton (Madame Orloff), Nyree Dawn Porter (Susan Warren), David Warner (Edward Charlton), Angela Pleasence (Emily Underwood), Ian Ogilvy (William Seaton), Lesley-Anne Down (Rosemary Seaton), Jack Watson (Sir Michael Sinclair). Directed by Kevin Connor.

**Synopsis:** Tucked away on an isolated side street is an antique store called Temptations Ltd., a very unusual place where the Proprietor sells special items to his customers that all walk away with an unusual tale related to the item. The first customer, Edward Charlton, convinces the Proprietor that an antique mirror is a reproduction to cheat him on the price, and when he takes the mirror back to his apartment, his friends conduct a séance for fun, not realizing they have just awakened an evil spirit in the mirror who will make Edward do his bidding for his need for blood. Then Christopher Lowe, an unhappily married office manager, strikes up a conversation with Jim Underwood (Donald Pleasence), an ex-service man selling laces and matches by the train station. Wanting to impress Jim, Christopher steals a medal of honor from the Proprietor's shop that allows him access to Jim's house where he meets his daughter Emily who will deliver his every wish and more. Then Reginald Warren comes into the Proprietor's shop and switches the tags on a snuff box to get a cheaper price. On the train ride home, a psychic named Madame Orloff tells him that he has a murderous elemental on his back. Reginald ignores Orloff's warning until he gets home and the elemental proceeds to try and kill his wife. Madame Orloff is called in to do an exorcism, but the elemental is not an easy creature to get rid of. Lastly, William Seaton purchases an unusual door for his home from the Proprietor, but what William does not know is that at midnight, the door opens to an alternate world inhabited by a stranger with dangerous intent.

**Commentary:** As the main competitor to Hammer Films in the horror genre, Amicus Productions, although a British company like Hammer, was actually formed by two Americans, Milton Subotsky and Max J. Rosenberg. Their first horror film, 1964's *Dr. Terror's House of Horrors*, was a big hit and helped paved the way for their success by using the anthology format that allowed for many big name stars to appear in small roles. By the 1970s, Amicus had truly hit their stride via the anthology format with *From Beyond the Grave*, one of their best-produced films. The stories are clever and frightening with horror star Peter Cushing linking the segments together as the bushy-eyed Proprietor with a Northern accent and something special for every customer depending on how they treat him. A plot very similar to *From Beyond the Grave* can be found in the film adaptation of Stephen King's *Needful Things*.

As with his sole connection to Hammer Films, Pleasence made only one film for Amicus, but his role as Jim Underwood turned out to be a big part of the film's effectiveness and success. For the very first time, Pleasence got to share the screen with his daughter Angela and in a bit of casting genius, they even play father and daughter in the segment *An Act of Kindness* with Pleasence as an ex-service man who relies on selling his wares by the train station to make a living. Once again, showing how well he could act with his eyes, Pleasence looks on nonchalantly until Ian Bannen's Christopher Lowe puts enough change in his box that causes Jim's eyes to come to life and initiates a conversation between the two of them. The real joy of this segment is seeing Pleasence and his daughter interact and slowly set up a neat twist ending. One great scene features Christopher paying a visit to the Underwood's apartment for the first time and Jim proudly proclaiming that his daughter Emily reads books with jaw-cracking words and then has her quote from one. Like her father, Angela Pleasence also makes good use of her eyes and the scene where they show up at Christopher's house for an impromptu wedding ceremony is quite powerful. An interesting note is that like his character Jim Underwood, Pleasence's background had ties to the railroad; another interesting aspect is that Angela Pleasence would later appear in the segment *Scream Satan Scream*, part of Steve Coogan's 2001 spoof of Amicus called *Dr. Terrible's House of Horrible.*

## *Watch Out, We're Mad!* (1974)

**Cast:** Terence Hill (Kid), Bud Spencer (Ben), Patty Shepard (Liza), Deogratias Huerta (Attila), John Sharp (The Boss), Donald Pleasence (The Doctor), Manuel de Blas (Paganini), Luis Barbero (Jeremias), Rafael Albaicin (Himself). Directed by Marcello Fondato.

**Synopsis:** Race car drivers Ben and the Kid enter into a road rally race in which the winner will receive a brand new dune buggy. After eliminating all of their competition, they wind up in a tie. With only one dune buggy as the prize, Ben and the Kid come up with a way to decide who gets to ride away with the buggy—a beer and hot dog eating contest at the local amusement park. But their contest ends early when a group of mobsters show up, wreck the bar and scare away the visitors at the park. As Ben and the Kid try to leave the park in their new buggy, the mobsters stop them and their prize ends up destroyed when they get rear-ended. The Mob Boss and his personal doctor (Donald Pleasence) have plans to raze the amusement park to make way for a skyscraper that will demonstrate their wealth and power. When Ben and the Kid show up to confront the Boss at his restaurant about replacing their destroyed buggy, he responds by having Attila, his main henchman, try and take them out. But Ben and the Kid have other plans and make quick work of Attila and a gym full of thugs. The Kid then outsmarts the Boss's hired assassin who tries to kill them at a chorus tryout Ben attends. When the Boss has Ben's assistant mechanic Jeremias beat up, Ben and the Kid can no longer contain their anger. They drive right through the Boss's restaurant and destroy it and everyone inside. The next day, the Boss, his Doctor, and his henchmen show up and deliver two brand new dune buggies to Ben and the Kid. Everyone celebrates as the amusement park is now saved. Ben and the Kid happily race their new dune buggies until the Kid accidentally rear-ends Ben's dune buggy, causing it to explode. Down to one dune buggy again, Ben and the Kid decide to have another beer and hot dog eating contest.

**Commentary:** Bud Spencer and Terence Hill were a most formidable box office team that specialized in Italian spaghetti westerns during the 1960s and 1970s. Spencer's large six foot, four-inch frame was perfectly suited for playing imposing characters which was complimented by Hill's easy and comedic demeanor. *Watch Out, We're Mad!* is not a western but a most enjoyable comedy which ranks as one of the pair's best films. Spencer and Hill share some great comedic scenes, such as the chorus scene when they outwit an assassin and when they continually upstage the Boss's lead henchman. *Watch Out, We're Mad!* also boasts some amazing stunts, from the opening road rally race to a battle with a motorcycle gang and to the finale in which Spencer and Hill drive a car into the Boss's restaurant and use it as their personal battering ram. One would think they might pass on the prized dune buggy though as they seems to easily burst into a fireball from any rear end collision! Every confrontation Spencer and Hill get into in this film is accompanied by the song "Dune Buggy" by the Italian duo Oliver Onions, a rather delightful melody which one will be humming after the film ends.

Donald Pleasence is allowed to play a good comedic role. His self-professed Freudian doctor is a real hoot; with a German accent, he bullies the babyish Mob Boss and feeds him his bizarre psychology about projecting the image of an evil leader. In one very funny scene, the Doctor and the Mob Boss practice tripping a waiter to show the power of evil. The waiter turns on the Doctor who then cowers behind the Boss, pleading it was only an accident. Amusingly, it is the Doctor's idea to destroy the amusement park to build the skyscraper. As he puts it, "The Boss is filthy rich and the Doctor is 10% filthy rich." The intrusion of Ben and the Kid into the Doctor's plans infuriates him, and he refers to them as little children whom the Boss must make obedient so as to further both their goals. The Doctor also has an amusing habit of going berserk, yelling "Nien! Nien!" when the Boss does not immediately conform to his somewhat well thought out plans.

Signed Donald Pleasence agency photo, circa 1950s.
From the Christopher Gullo collection

Donald Pleasence opposite Donald Sinden in his first film role from *The Beachcomber*, 1954. From the Christopher Gullo collection

Donald Pleasence with his parents in New York, 1961.
From the Christopher Gullo collection

Donald Pleasence 1958 agency photo.
From the Christopher Gullo collection

Signed Donald Pleasence publicity photo from the Hammer film *Hell is a City*, 1960.
From the Christopher Gullo collection

Donald Pleasence in and out of makeup for *The Twilight Zone* episode "The Changing of the Guard," 1962. From the Christopher Gullo collection

Robert Shaw and Donald Pleasence from *The Caretaker*, 1963. From the Christopher Gullo collection

Director Alberto Lattuada and Donald Pleasence kidding around at the London airport before filming *Matchless*, 1966. From the Christopher Gullo collection

Patricia Neil, Donald Pleasence, and Yul Brynner, at a party in London, 1967. From the Christopher Gullo collection

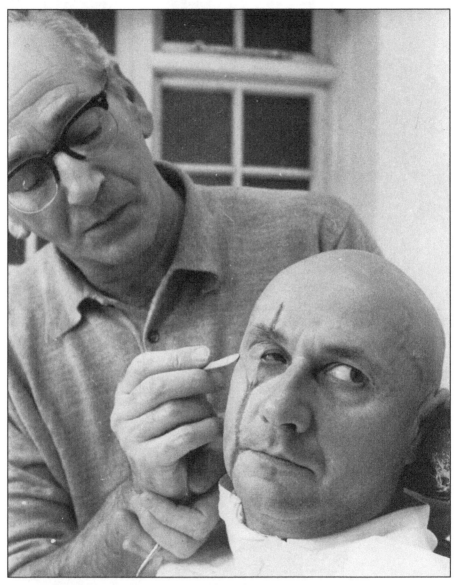

Donald Pleasence getting his 'scar' applied by makeup artist Paul Rabinger for the film *You Only Live Twice*, 1967. From the David Vaskas collection

Donald Pleasence having a tea break on the California set of *Will Penny*, 1968.
From the Christopher Gullo collection

Donald Pleasence and Lawrence Douglas filming *Kidnapped*, 1971.
From the Lawrence Douglas collection

Donald Pleasence and Keith Michell meet Princess Ann at a film gala night in
London, 1972. From the Christopher Gullo collection

The two Logans – the real life Logan and the person who played him – Donald Pleasence, 1973. From the Gerald Potterton collection

Donald Pleasence being filmed during *From Beyond the Grave*, 1974. From the Kevin Connor collection

Donald Pleasence holding his young daughter Miriam at a Pro-Israel rally in Trafalgar Square, London, 1973. From the Christopher Gullo collection

Donald Pleasence at home and relaxing in his favorite chair, circa 1970s.
From the Christopher Gullo collection

British cinematographer Ossi Rawi, director Martyn Burke, David Hemmings, and Donald Pleasence having a lunch break during the filming of *Power Play* at Canadian Armed Force Base Borden, 1977. From the Martyn Burke collection

Donald Pleasence and Leif Garrett at the *Sgt. Pepper and His Lonely Hearts Club Band* wrap party in Los Angeles, 1978. From the Christopher Gullo collection

Donald Pleasence cleaning the town with MP Peter Walker on a London Street, 1979. From the Christopher Gullo collection

Donald Pleasence and Dorothy Tutin during rehearsals from the Haymarket Theatre production of *Reflections*, 1980. From the Christopher Gullo collection.

Donald Pleasence with daughter Angela in a publicity photo for *The Barchester Chronicles*, 1982. From the Tony Earnshaw collection

Donald Pleasence with his wife Linda outside Buckingham Palace where he displays his O.B.E. award, 1994. From the Tony Earnshaw collection

Donald Pleasence discussing a scene with director Joe Chappelle as Paul Rudd looks on from *Halloween: The Curse of Michael Myers*, 1996.
©1996 Kent Miles / www.kentmiles.com

# *The Black Windmill* (1974)

**Cast:** Michael Caine (Major John Tarrant), Donald Pleasence (Cedric Harper), Delphine Seyrig (Ceil Burrows), Clive Revill (Alf Chestermann), John Vernon (McKee), Joss Ackland (Chief Superintend Wray), Janet Suzman (Alex Tarrant), Catherine Schell (Lady Melissa Julyan), Joseph O'Conor (Sir Edward Julyan), Denis Quilley (Bateson). Directed by Don Siegel.

**Synopsis:** Major John Tarrant is a spy working for the British government to infiltrate a sabotage ring. At a meeting with his boss Cedric Harper (Donald Pleasence) and higher ups including Sir Edward Julyan, Tarrant receives a call from his wife explaining that their son David has been kidnapped. Tarrant returns home and takes the call from the kidnapper known as Drabble who demands to be put in touch with Harper. After reluctantly agreeing to talk to the kidnapper, Harper is shocked to hear the demand of the exact amount of uncut diamonds recently purchased by the department. Believing it is an inside job and that Tarrant may have kidnapped his own son to get the money, Harper has Tarrant tailed by Scotland Yard. But McKee, the real kidnapper, has his partner Ceil Burrows set up Tarrant by leaving photos in his apartment for Scotland Yard to discover. Meanwhile, Harper tells Tarrant the department will not pay the ransom for his son because it would open the floodgates for terrorists. Desperate, Tarrant steals the diamonds himself and brings them to McKee in France, but this backfires when the diamonds are stolen and Tarrant is knocked unconscious and left next to the murdered Ceil Burrows. Soon after, Harper and Scotland Yard show up and arrest Tarrant and drive him back to England. But McKee's thugs knock over the van and free Tarrant. Now on the run, Tarrant is aided by his wife Alex in figuring out that someone on the inside wants him dead so no more questions will be asked. Posing as Drabble, Tarrant draws out the inside man behind the kidnapping, Sir Edward Julyan, and forces him to reveal where his son is being held. Holed up in a windmill, McKee attempts a last ditch effort to save himself, but Tarrant kills him and rescues David.

**Commentary:** *The Black Windmill* was the third and last film for Pleasence acting alongside the great Michael Caine, and while basically a standard spy thriller, *The Black Windmill* did rise above, thanks to some crisp direction and wonderful performances by Caine, Pleasence, and John Vernon. As one of the most respected British actors of his generation, Michael Caine had a number of spy films under his belt prior to this film, starting in 1965 as Harry Palmer in *The Ipcress File*. There is some genuine tension as Tarrant attempts to hold everything together in order to save his son David. Separated from his wife because of constraints related to his job and suspected by his own boss of staging the kidnapping, Tarrant is desperate but still manages to keep his cool and turn the table on the kidnappers. This film also is unique in featuring the only imitation of Donald Pleasence in one of his films, done by Caine as he poses as his boss on the phone to steal the diamonds.

Pleasence has a particularly juicy role in *The Black Windmill* as the by the books, unsympathetic head of MI6. His character of Cedric Harper seems out of touch with his feelings, due to his inability to console his agent whose going through a horrible ordeal. Otherwise, he acts like a kid in a candy store at the shooting range and in showing off his new 007 style gadgets. Pleasence also gives Harper some nervous ticks like twirling his moustache, picking his nails, and uncontrollable swallowing when he witnesses his boss's wife acting very affectionate. There is also a great scene in which Harper finishes blowing his nose with a tissue and then fitting for his demeanor, proceeds to put the tissue through a shredder. A *New York Times* reviewer actually pointed out Pleasence as the person who steals the show—"Still, the flatness of the Caine persona is balanced by Donald Pleasence in his best form as the phobic but stony head of the Department of Subversive Warfare." [105] *The Black Windmill* also showcases Pleasence speaking French which he does quite fluently while trying to track down Tarrant. Pleasence also has one of the best lines in the film when he flubs a suspect's name and as a result pokes fun at 007—"And whom I believe to be a soviet agent, Sean Connery. Er… Kelly, Sean Kelly."

# *The Wolf and the Dove* (1974)

**Cast:** Donald Pleasence (Martin Zayas), Carmen Sevilla (Sandra), Michael Dunn (Bodo), Muriel Catala (Maria), Aldo Sambrell (Atrilio), Jose Jaspe (Acebo). Directed by Gonzalo Suarez.

**Synopsis:** After years of searching, Martin Zayas (Donald Pleasence) and his friend Acebo discover a rare diamond-encrusted gold statue in a cave that will make them very wealthy. But Zayas gets injured trying to leave the cave and when he finally makes it back to Acebo's house, the statue has apparently disappeared. Thinking that his friend is trying to cheat him, Zayas goes mad and in a struggle stabs Acebo to death with a knife. As Zayas staggers back, he notices that Acebo's daughter Maria saw the whole event and is holding the statue in her hands as a toy. Years later, Zayas is released from prison for murder and immediately makes his way back to Acebo's old house where he finds Sandra, Acebo's niece, along with her husband Atrilio and her brother Bodo. Upon learning that Maria went into a comatose state after the murder and was placed in a mental institution, Zayas makes a deal with Sandra because she is Maria's legal guardian. The four devise a plot to free Maria and bring her back to the house so she can reveal the whereabouts of the statue so they can share in the profits. But this proves to be more difficult than they had imagined because Maria is now a mute and cannot speak. Eventually, distrust and greed turns everyone against each other, resulting in their deaths.

**Commentary:** *La Loba y la Paloma*, translated as *The Wolf and the Dove*, a.k.a. *House of the Damned* (the American video title), is a low budget Spanish thriller with a small cast and some good tension. Everything revolves around a golden statue with a large diamond embedded in it that ultimately becomes the source of greed, jealousy, violence, and murder. The premise of the young girl who witnesses the brutal murder of her father over an item she was playing with and is then placed in a mental institution only to be taken out by her greedy relatives and abused, is truly horrific. The entire dialog is dubbed into English with the exception of Pleasence and Michael Dunn in one of his last film roles. Dunn, a dwarf who first made a name for himself after being nominated for a 1964 Tony Award for Best Supporting Actor in *The Ballad of the Sad Café*, had by the 1970s appeared in a number of genre films. Following *House of the Damned*, Dunn teamed up with Pleasence again in their next film *The Mutations*.

Pleasence portrays Martin Zayas, a role that seems to draw some parallels with his Ralph Logan character from *The Rainbow Boys*. Both men are obsessed with finding gold, although Zayas is much more forceful and dangerous. After understandably being upset at his friend leaving him bloodied and with a broken foot in the cave, Zayas goes over the edge and kills Acebo when he cannot locate the statue. Acebo's relatives fear Zayas for good reason when he returns from his stint in prison and openly threatens their lives. But then Zayas seems to do an about face toward the latter half of the story when he saves Maria from a brutal beating by Atrilio. Zayas then manages to get Maria to talk but as she is about to hand over the well-hidden statue, Zayas once again goes mad (understandably because Brodo shot him) and kills once more. However, Zayas does make an attempt to spare Maria from further abuse when he begs her to speak to the authorities in order to stay out of the institution.

## *The Mutations* (1974)

**Cast:** Donald Pleasence (Professor Nolter), Tom Baker (Lynch), Brad Harris (Brian Redford), Julie Ege (Hedi), Michael Dunn (Burns), Scott Antony (Tony), Jill Haworth (Lauren), Olga Anthony (Bridget). Directed by Jack Cardiff.

**Synopsis:** Professor Nolter (Donald Pleasence) is a biology expert whose main goal is to create a hybrid plant/animal which he believes will be a new evolutionary species. His experiments involve mutations that are created artificially in the laboratory in his house, but in order to continue his work, Nolter needs subjects which turns out to be his own biology students, acquired through underhanded means by his deformed henchman Lynch who runs a circus freak show where Nolter's failed experiments end up. When their friend Bridget disappears, her fellow students Hedi, Tony, and Lauren, all wonder and worry about what has happened to her. When Tony's curiosity gets him too close to the truth of what happened to Bridget, he is grabbed by Lynch who brings him to Nolter to use as another subject. Succeeding with Tony, Nolter creates his first successful plant/human hybrid, but the transformed Tony manages to escape into the night. Making his way back to his girlfriend Lauren, Tony is forced to run away when she screams upon seeing what he looks like. Meanwhile, Lynch is pressured by Nolter who promises to fix his glandular disorder if he will get him another test subject. This causes tension between the rest of the freaks, terrified that Lynch will abuse them. Lynch eventually kidnaps Hedi and brings her to Nolter for his latest experiment, but her boyfriend Brian manages to track her to Nolter's home where he is attacked by Lynch, knocking him out before being killed by his fellow freaks. Meanwhile, Tony breaks through a skylight in Nolter's lab and kills him, setting off a huge fire. Brian comes to the rescue and saves Hedi, although she may not have escaped unchanged.

**Commentary:** Although unconventional, *The Mutations*, a.k.a. *The Freakmaker*, succeeds quite well, due to its star and the use of real freaks along with good special effects. Jack Cardiff who had previous directed Pleasence in *Sons and Lovers*, is widely hailed as one of the great cinematographers with classic films like *The African Queen* and *Ghost Story* as part of his repertoire. Cardiff's mastery behind the camera is also evident in *The Mutations*, especially with the film's exterior shots. *The Mutations* also features some neat time-lapse photography of various plants growing which compliments the storyline. Besides its star, *The Mutations* also features Tom Baker (pre-Doctor Who) as Nolter's henchman who manages to elicit some sympathy through his desperation to be normal and his servitude to Nolter and his promises. Another stand out is Norwegian actress Julie Ege, mostly recognized for her appearances in Hammer films. Rounding out the cast is an entourage of real freaks that are used to great effect and remind one of Tod Browning's 1932 classic *Freaks*. Although these freaks are displayed in a circus (the show is mind boggling, especially the literally eye-popping Popeye), Cardiff does not exploit them and in fact portrays them as sympathetic human beings who just want to feel that they have a safe place to live as normal a life as possible.

As Professor Nolter, Pleasence portrays a typical mad scientist that in many ways is on par with Baron Frankenstein. As he gleefully lectures to his students about the benefits that his scientific work can produce, Nolter does not express any kind of guilt when he recognizes one of his students while lying on his experimental table. This scene highlights Nolter's complete separation from reality and mankind via his quest to create mutations as a new species of human beings. He also manipulates Lynch with his promises to cure him, all the while luring him from one job to another. One great scene shows Nolter calmly taking a rabbit from its cage, petting it gently, and then feeding it to his giant carnivorous hybrid plant. Pleasence's calm demeanor as Professor Nolter highlights these and other scenes which masks his true intentions even from those close to him.

# *Malachi's Cove* (1974)

**Cast:** Donald Pleasence (Malachi), Veronica Quilligan (Mally), David Bradley (Barty Gunliffe), John Barrett (Vicar Polwarth), Peter Vaughan (Mr. Gunliffe), Lillias Walker (Mrs. Gunliffe), Arthur English (Jack Combes). Directed by Henry Herbert.

**Synopsis:** In North Cornwall in the 1880s, an orphaned teenage girl named Mally lives with her grandfather Malachi (Donald Pleasence) down by a cove. In order to make money, Mally collects seaweed and sells it to help buy necessities and care for Malachi who is wheelchair bound. Upon making the occasional trip into town, Mally is scorned by many of the villagers who see her as a dirty tramp. In return, Mally blames the town for her mother's death because no one came to help her when her mother was drowning. When Mally finds out that Barty, a local boy her age, is taking seaweed from the cove, she becomes enraged but the town lawyer quickly explains that the cove is public property and that anyone can take whatever they like. One day, Mally spots Braty on the rocks and watches as he falls and hits his head before the tide begins to take him away. Thinking fast, Mally grabs Braty with her seaweed hook and runs to get his parents. Braty is saved and thanks to Mally, they decide to work together collecting seaweed and a new friendship is formed.

**Commentary:** *Malachi's Cove* is a bittersweet film about Mally, an outcast through no fault of her own and because of her anger toward the townspeople who did nothing to help save her mother from drowning, Mally has carved out a new life with her grandfather Malachi and prefers to remain isolated by the ocean. Veronica Quilligan does a great job as the spiteful and headstrong Mally who deep beneath longs to be like other kids her age. The only real issues with this film are two unexplained occurrences—first, why Mally's father was out at sea and the other as to why Barty's mother has so much hatred for Mally. Also in the cast are a number of well-known British actors like Arthur English and Peter Vaughan, Pleasence's best friend in real life.

Receiving top billing, Pleasence plays Malachi, the father of Mally's deceased mother. As a character, Malachi is an old man with old vices and prefers to drink and smoke his pipe which is causing him chest problems. In addition, Malachi is confined to a wheelchair that requires assistance on the part of Mally when he needs to get up. Pleasence portrayed a similar old miser in *Kidnapped*, but in *Malachi's Cove*, his character is truly a good soul. The relationship between Malachi and Mally is beautifully portrayed with her caring for him and he singing to her and in a demonstration of his true self, Malachi manages to drag himself over the rocks by the ocean to stand vigil with the injured Barty while Mally runs to town for help.

# *Barry McKenzie Holds His Own* (1974)

**Cast:** Barry Crocker (Barry McKenzie/Reverend Kevin McKenzie), Barry Humphries (Aunt Edna Everage/Dr. Meyer Delamphrey/Senator Douglas Manton), Donald Pleasence (Count Erich von Plasma), Dick Bentley (Colin "The Frog" Lucas), Louis Negin (Hugo Cretin), Paul Humpoletz (Modeste Imbecile). Directed by Bruce Beresford.

**Synopsis:** Barry McKenzie and his aunt Edna Everage are on a flight back to Australia when two henchmen of Count Plasma (Donald Pleasence), a vampire and the communist ruler of Transylvania, mistakes aunt Edna for the Queen of England. Desperate to revive his country's tourism industry, Count Plasma orders his henchmen to kidnap Edna and bring her back to his castle to attract tourists. In response, McKenzie seeks out the Australian Embassy and leads up a team to rescue aunt Edna, his twin brother Reverend Kevin McKenzie, a close friend of Colin "The Frog" Lucas, and a group of fellow Australians. After parachuting into Transylvania, they meld into a group of tourists visiting the castle where they wage war against Count Plasma and his henchmen to save aunt Edna and return to Australia as heroes.

**Commentary:** *Barry McKenzie Holds His Own* is the zany comedy sequel to the smash hit *The Adventures of Barry McKenzie* (1972), the first Australian film to earn a million dollars. The character of Barry McKenzie was the creation of comedian/actor Barry Humphries who became famous for his own Aunt Edna Everage (later Dame Edna Everage). Humphries and singer Barry Crocker co-wrote the film that features some funny musical numbers like *Rat Bag*. The film is way over the top and pokes fun at many stereotypes, especially the Australian drinking culture, exemplified by the non-stop consumption of Fosters Lager that serves as a multi-purpose tool, such as bringing down a mad Bruce-Lee like chef and as a cross made from beer cans to dispose of Count Plasma.

In a brilliant stroke of casting, Pleasence portrays Count Erich von Plasma, decked out in a Bela Lugosi style outfit complete with widows peak, pancake white skin, and a gold tooth between his fangs, a send-up of his on-screen horror image with lots of laughs. Ranting and raving when upset, Count Plasma hisses through his teeth which sounds much like Daffy Duck. One great scene shows Count Plasma ordering his waiter to give him his "special" drink; the waiter simply opens a tap on his neck and pours out a glass of blood. In effect, *Barry McKenzie Holds His Own* highlights Pleasence's great ability to play comedic roles that were few and far between during his career.

# *The Devil Within Her* (1975)

**Cast:** Joan Collins (Lucy Carlesi), Eileen Atkins (Sister Albana), Ralph Bates (Gino Carlesi), Donald Pleasence (Dr. Finch), Caroline Munro (Mandy Gregory), Hilary Mason (Mrs. Hyde), John Steiner (Tommy Morris), Janet Key (Jill Fletcher), George Claydon (Hercules). Directed by Peter Sasdy.

**Synopsis:** In a London hospital, Lucy Carlesi experiences a difficult birth but produces a rather large and strong baby boy. Her attempts to bond with the baby are unsuccessful as he immediately scratches up her face and sucks her blood from his fingers. Lucy's husband Gino discusses this with Dr. Finch (Donald Pleasence) and is told that it is nothing more than the baby's survival instinct. Back at home, Lucy continues to have trouble with the baby and relates her concerns to her friend Mandy who works as a stripper at a club, where Lucy also used to work as a stripper. Lucy believes that the problems with her baby are related to a curse that a dwarf named Hercules placed on her when she spurned his advances. Gino's sister Albana, who just happens to be a nun, comes to London to visit and when she see the new baby, she becomes suspicious when the baby screams in agony while blessing him. When the baby struggles with the priest during his baptism, Lucy and Gino realize that something is very wrong and begin searching for answers. Albana then convinces Dr. Finch to take the baby in for observation at the hospital which will give Lucy and Gino a much-needed break. But the baby has other plans and begins a violent and deadly string of attacks on everyone who comes into contact with him. No one is spared from the horrific attacks until Albana resorts to performing an exorcism on the baby that breaks the curse.

**Commentary:** Known by a slew of different titles like *I Don't Want to be Born* and *Sharon's Baby*, the plot for *The Devil Within Her* was obviously inspired by two of the biggest blockbusters of all time—*Rosemary's Baby* (1968) and *The Exorcist* (1973), both of which opened a floodgate of similar films in the 1970s concerning the Devil and his influence on infants, children, and adults. A number of articles reported on this phenomenon with one example declaring, "If you care about the welfare of films, of women and little boys, these movies, to say nothing of the dozens of sequels already planned, represents a long step sideways onto the soft shoulders of puerility." [106] As a result, the low budget Gothic horror films of the previous generation faded away in favor of Hollywood big budget adaptations, although some low budget adaptations like *I Don't Want to be Born* still made the rounds. While somewhat campy, *The Devil Within Her* does have its creepy moments, such as when Lucy realizes that her own baby may be out to do her in. The cast does their job well and the attempt by Ralph Bates to mimic an Italian accent is quite amusing. The plot involving the Devil, strippers (including nude scenes for Joan Collins), and a dwarf is certainly exploitative and failed to impress the critics—"The film is a smear to dwarfs everywhere." [107]

Acting as the good doctor who brings the demonic baby into the unsuspecting world, Pleasence portrays a man of medicine who will not accept supernatural explanations for the bizarre events occurring in the Carlesi household. When Lucy continues to complain of the baby's violent behavior, Dr. Finch responds by telling her that she should seek out psychiatric help. It takes a meeting of the minds when Sister Albana comes to plead the Carlesi's case to convince Dr. Finch to take the baby in for a series of tests at the hospital. This is the film's best scene with Sister Albana's spiritualism coming into direct opposition with Dr. Finch's modern medicine. They argue back and forth about the possibility of an inherent evil but end with a compromise via Finch telling Albana that she would make a great doctor and Albana telling Finch that he would make a horrible nun.

# Escape to Witch Mountain (1975)

**Cast:** Eddie Albert (Jason O'Day), Ray Milland (Aristotle Bolt), Donald Pleasence (Lucas Deranian), Kim Richards (Tia Malone), Ike Eisenmann (Tony Malone), Walter Barnes (Sheriff Purdy), Reta Shaw (Mrs. Grindley), Denver Pyle (Uncle Bene). Directed by John Hough.

**Synopsis:** Siblings Tony and Tia Malone become orphans when their foster parents pass away and because they do not know about their real parents or any relatives, the only clue to their past is Tia's strange star box which she has always had. Along with a mysterious past, Tony and Tia also possess the mysterious powers of telepathy and telekinesis and the ability to see into the future which Tia uses while on an orphanage trip to the movies to warn a certain Lucas Deranian (Donald Pleasence) not to stay in his parked car or something bad will happen to him. Deranian decides to heed Tia's warning and sure enough only moments later, an out-of-control tow truck plows into his car. But unbeknownst to Tia and Tony, Deranian works for megalomaniac Aristotle Bolt who is always looking out for the next big thing to help increase his vast fortune. When Deranian tells Bolt of Tia's powers, they hatch a plot whereby Deranian poses as the sibling's long-lost uncle so he can adopt them. While at first amazed at how much Bolt provides for them, Tony and Tia quickly realize that they are in danger and that Bolt will never allow them to leave his mansion. Tia then discovers that her star box has a secret compartment with a map that helps the siblings to plan their escape and try to unravel their mysterious past.

Using their powers, Tony and Tia sneak away but not before the security alarms ring out, prompting Deranian and his guards to begin a search to hunt them down. After making their way into town, Tony and Tia hide in the back of a camper owned by a crusty local named Jason O'Day. At first, O'Day puts up an angry front after finding Tony and Tia, but soon decides to help them after they describe their flight from Bolt and Deranian and the search for their past. Upon reading the map on the star box, Jason drives Tony and Tia toward his brother's cabin, but on the way, he drops them off and drives on so as to throw Deranian off their track. The local sheriff, paid off by Bolt, grabs Tony and Tia and locks them up, but they use their powers to break out of the jail and escape again. Racing against time as the sheriff rounds up hunters, thinking that Tony and Tia are witches, and with Deranian closing in, Tia finally recalls that Uncle Bene saved them from drowning when they were very young and that they are actually from another planet in another solar system. O'Day then meets up with Tony and Tia and gets them safely to Uncle Bene who thanks O'Day for his help before taking the kids back to their interstellar home.

**Commentary:** *Escape to Witch Mountain* was Disney's first take on the Alexander Key's classic novel of the same name, and after hiring director John Hough to helm the picture, he went on to direct the film's sequel and a few other productions for Disney during the 1980s. The film itself is a welcomed change of pace from Disney's usual cartoon fare, yet it still caters to children. The two young leads, Ike Eisenmann and Kim Richards, make believable siblings and are well-balanced by veteran actors Donald Pleasence, Ray Milland, and Eddie Albert. The special effects in *Escape to Witch Mountain* which are the hooks of the storyline are handled fairly well, even despite one scene with a "floating" gun which turns laughable because of the clearly visible supporting wires. Nonetheless, *Escape to Witch Mountain* was successful enough to warrant a sequel, *Return to Witch Mountain*, in 1978 which follows the same formula, and a more modern remake in *Race to Witch Mountain* in 2009.

Pleasence's role as Lucas Deranian is basically that of a henchman for Milland's Aristotle Bolt. Although portrayed as one of the main villains in the story, Deranian exhibits some personal restraint, such as when he is forced to nab Tony and Tia in order to keep his job and tries unsuccessfully to object to Bolt's harsh demands on the children early on. Though these are only two small blips, most of *Escape to Witch Mountain* has Deranian doggedly pursuing Tony and Tia at all costs. In one enjoyable scene, a bear sneaks into Deranian's car and Pleasence's face lights up and his eyes twitch like he cannot believe his misfortune upon seeing the animal—perhaps a bad memory from his fate in *Circus of Horrors*—only this time with a real bear. *Escape to Witch Mountain* was not the first time Pleasence had worked for Disney, which was in the 1961 television series *Walt Disney's Wonderful World of Color* in which he starred in *The Horsemasters*. Pleasence would also go on to star in an additional Disney production, coincidentally also directed by John Hough—the 1985 television production of *The Black Arrow*.

## *Journey into Fear* (1975)

**Cast:** Sam Waterston (Howard Graham), Zero Mostel (Kopelkin), Donald Pleasence (Kuyetli), Vincent Price (Dervos), Yvette Mimieux (Josette), Shelley Winters (Mrs. Mathews), Stanley Holloway (Mr. Mathews), Joseph Wiseman (Colonel Haki), Ian McShane (Banat), Meira Shore (Maria), Scott Marlowe (Jose), Jackie Cooper (Eric Hurst). Directed by Daniel Mann.

**Synopsis:** Howard Graham is a geologist for an American oil company doing work in Turkey, and while conducting surveys for research, Graham uncovers vital information that will greatly affect foreign treaties and the price of oil. As a result, a concerned group tries numerous times to kill Graham before he can deliver his research to the company. After a third attempt on his life at an airport, Colonel Haki puts Graham on a boat to keep him safe on his journey. Graham is pleased that the beautiful singer Josette is on board and strikes up a relationship. But as the ship travels to its destination, Graham finds out that someone on board was sent to kill him. After befriending a cigarette dealer named Kuyetli (Donald Pleasence) and Dervos, an Arab archaeologist, Graham learns that the two men have secret agendas—Kuyetli turns out to be a Turkish agent sent to watch over him, while Dervos is actually a mercenary named Muller who forcefully insists that Graham comes with him when the ship docks. But when Graham finds Kuyetli murdered in his cabin, he has no choice but to go with Muller. But Graham is not about to walk away quietly and outwits Muller's men, escaping and turning the tables on his captors to bring about their end and his freedom.

**Commentary:** Based on the novel by Eric Ambler, *Journey into Fear* was earlier adapted into a 1943 film version of the same name with Joseph Cotton and Orson Welles, but this 1975 version, the first major Hollywood film made in Vancouver, Canada, turned out to be an inferior attempt at bringing the novel to the screen. This was not however because of a lack of talent, due to the presence of Daniel Mann who had directed several actors in Oscar winning performances and a number of big name actors, such as Pleasence, Vincent Price, Shelley Winters and Zero Mostel. But unfortunately, the talents of these standout performers are mostly wasted and the film's star, a young Sam Waterston years before he found success in the television series *Law and Order*, does not bring much to his role as Howard Graham.

Pleasence was cast as Kuyetli, a passenger on the ship who presents himself as a tobacco seller before later revealing his true identity—a Turkish agent in charge of keeping an eye on Graham. Most of Pleasence's performance basically serves as a red herring as to the actual identity of the killer, and an excursion to Athens in which Kuyetli accompanies Graham almost results in the geologist's murder when they become conveniently separated. Also, Kuyetli ineffectively attempts to act as Graham's savior before being bumped off. But the real reason for Pleasence fans to see *Journey into Fear* is to spot then-wife Meira Shore in her only film role in a bit part as Maria.

# *Hearts of the West* (1975)

**Cast:** Jeff Bridges (Lewis Tater), Andy Griffith (Howard Pike), Donald Pleasence (A.J. Neitz), Blythe Danner (Miss Trout), Alan Arkin (Bert Kessler), Richard B. Shull (Stout Crook), Herb Edelman (Polo), Alex Rocco (Earl), Frank Cady (Pa Tater), Anthony James (Lean Crook), Burton Gilliam (Lester). Directed by Howard Zieff

**Synopsis:** While living in Iowa during the 1930s, Lewis Tater dreams of becoming a famous writer of western prose like his hero Zane Grey. He believes he has finally gotten a break when he receives a letter notifying him of his acceptance to a writing program at a university in Nevada. After quickly deciding to throw caution to the wind and head for the scenic West to begin his writing career, Tater's dreams are crushed when he arrives and finds out there is only a post office box and no actual university. A woman checking on the university's mail takes pity on Tater and drives him to a local hotel which she runs. Besides Tater, also staying at the hotel are the two 'owners' of the university scam who plan to rob him. Tater fights off one of the crooks and manages to escape in their car, but when it runs out of gas, Tater looks in the trunk and finds the university money and a gun which he takes as he runs off into the desert. Tater seems to luck out again, for after passing out in the harsh desert, he is rescued by a group of B-film western extras shooting on location. After making friends with the secretary for the director Miss Trout, Tater gets hired as an extra and works his way up the ranks. He then becomes friends with Howard Pike, one of the veteran extras whose advice to Tater on asking for a high raise promptly gets him fired. Now in love with Tater, Miss Trout gets him a meeting with a friend in touch with famed producer and director A.J. Neitz (Donald Pleasence). At the meeting, Tater shows Neitz a western novel he wrote only to find out that Pike passed off a copy he was lent as his own and is now considered as the author. Broken-hearted and disillusioned by the whole film industry, Tater goes back to his apartment to talk to Miss Trout but is surprised by the two university crooks that assault and shoot him. But Pike comes to the rescue in the nick of time, foiling the crooks and saving Tater. While being led out on a stretcher, Tater realizes that he has lived his dream of being a real cowboy in a shootout and sells his first novel on his experiences.

**Commentary:** In the mid 1970s, a slew of films delved into Hollywood's early days of the 1930s, such as *The Day of the Locust* (1975), *W.C. Fields and Me* (1976), and *Gable and Lombard* (1976). *Hearts of the West* fits well within this category and is easily among the best, not so much for its story, but for the wonderful drawn-out characters that frequent this delightful comedy from director Howard Zieff. Most of the film rests on the shoulders of a young Jeff Bridges who demonstrates his charisma and physical comedic style throughout. Viewers find themselves immediately rooting for the naive Lewis Tater as he chases his dreams in a town looking to knock him down time and time again. In one of his best film roles, Andy Griffith as Howard Pike is a crafty survivor of Hollywood and most likely was like Tater when he was younger but learned the tricks of the trade and uses them for his own benefit. The scenes between Bridges and Griffith are certainly the best parts of this film; the rest of the cast, made up of veterans and new faces alike, creates fascinating characters that revolve around the story. A review of this film highlights this novel approach—"*Hearts of the West*, with an original screenplay by a new writer named Rob Thompson, dawdles. It gives its actors time to embroider their roles at the expense of narrative drive."[108]

Pleasence's role as A.J. Neitz is small yet very amusing as the western writer and director whom Tater hopes will make his future. Unlike other characters in this film, Pleasence's role was based on the real A.J. Neitz who started in Hollywood in the 1910s and wrote and directed dozens of poverty row westerns from the silent to the talkie era. In 1932, he began working under the pseudonym of Alan James until his retirement from the film industry in the early 1940s. Pleasence paints Neitz as a somewhat eccentric character that obsesses over hats in a meeting and later shows up for brunch with Tater in a red and white striped robe. Neitz represents a turning point in the film, as after Tater learns through him that Pike duped him, Tater goes into a downward spiral.

## Trial by Combat (1976)

**Cast:** John Mills (Colonel Bertie Cook), Donald Pleasence (Sir Giles Marley), Barbara Hershey (Marion Evans), David Birney (Sir John Gifford), Margaret Leighton (Ma Gore), Peter Cushing (Sir Edward Gifford), Brian Glover (Sidney Gore), John Savident (Commissioner Oliver Griggs), John Hallam (Sir Roger Moncton), Keith Buckley (Herald), Neil McCarthy (Ben Willoughby). Directed by Kevin Connor.

**Synopsis:** In modern-day England, a group of men still live as medieval knights at a castle founded by Sir Edward Gifford. Sir Giles Marley (Donald Pleasence), the grandmaster of the Order of the Knights of

Avalon, has taken it upon himself to have the knights pursue a new challenge—capturing criminals that have evaded the law and punishing them according to the laws of chivalry. When Gifford unexpectedly comes across Marley and his knights dispatching a criminal, he protests and is killed for his efforts. Along with his father's ally Colonel Bertie Cook, Gifford's son Sir John arrives from America for the reading of the will and to investigate his father's murder. At the reading of the will, John learns that he is the sole beneficiary but only as long as he works and resides at the estate; otherwise, everything goes to the Knights of Avalon. John decides to try and make the best of it and befriends Marion Evans, Marley's assistant. Meanwhile, as the former Commissioner of Police at Scotland Yard, Bertie pursues Sir Gifford's murder and the Red Banner butcher killings which he believes are related. In time, Bertie discovers the connection when a gangster named Sidney Gore is kidnapped by the knights. Bertie is also captured while patrolling the grounds of the castle, and Marion soon joins him after helping Gore to escape. Before Marley and his knights can do them harm, John arrives after learning of their involvement in his father's death from the gamekeeper and challenges Marley to a trial by combat. Trained by his father in medieval combat as a boy, John dispatches the knights and pursues Marley who meets his end courtesy of the castle gates.

**Commentary:** *Trial by Combat*, a.k.a. *A Choice of Weapons* and *A Dirty Knight's Work*, is a fun *Avengers* style film that incorporates several different genres. Part mystery/thriller, adventure, and comedy, *Trial by Combat* manages to blend them all seamlessly, mostly due to stars Donald Pleasence and John Mills who portrays Colonel Bertie Cook, friend of the murdered Sir Edward Gifford and who advises Gifford's son John on medieval etiquette while trying to solve Sir Edward's murder. Mills' character is interesting and humorous, practically a Dr. Doolittle at times as he interacts with a guard dog, a horse, pigeons, a parrot, a monkey, and a goat. Also in the cast is American actor David Birney who interacts well with his fellow cast members, and Brian Glover as the colorful Cockney gangster Sidney Gore.

Pleasence plays Sir Giles Marley, a man whose views on society turns him and his knights into a dangerous vigilante group. As the leader of the Knights of Avalon, Pleasence is in medieval armor for a good portion of the film and it is interesting to see him in battle, wielding a lance or an axe. Pleasence also interacts with John Mills and watching these two film veterans together is quite a delight. Although quite a villainous character, Pleasence provides one of the best lines during the climax when Sir John Gifford does battle with him in the dungeon area and Colonel Bertie Cook lends a helping hand by throwing bottles of wine from a rack. When Cook grabs one particular bottle of wine to hurl at Marley, Pleasence's eyes go wide and he deadpans "Not the Chateau de Temniac!"

# *The Devil's Men* (1976)

**Cast:** Donald Pleasence (Father Roche), Peter Cushing (Baron Corofax), Luan Peters (Laurie Gordon), Costa Skouras (Milo Kaye), Fernando Bislani (Sergeant Vendris), Anna Mantzourani (Mrs. Mikaelis), Nikos Verlel Verlekis (Ian), Vanna Reville (Beth), Bob Behling (Tom Gifford). Directed by Kostas Karagiannis

**Synopsis:** In a small Greek village, the locals have come under the influence of Baron Corofax and have taken to worshipping the spirit of the legendary minotaur that demands human sacrifices. On the outskirts of the village, Father Roche (Donald Pleasence) runs a small Christian ministry, and one day, Beth and Tom, an American couple, and their friend Ian, due to their shared interest in archaeology, pay Roche a visit on their way to the ruins. Ian shows Roche a golden miniature minotaur head that he had found when previously digging. Roche, an authority on ancient religions, recognizes the statuette as belonging to the minotaur cult and warns the trio not to go near the ruins. They leave anyway in the middle of the night, and before long disappear without a trace. Soon after, Ian's girlfriend Laurie arrives at Roche's ministry in search of Ian. Roche, fearing the worst, contacts his former student Milo, now a private investigator living in New York. Milo agrees to come to Greece and along with Roche and Laurie, they start searching for the missing trio. In the village, they discover that the locals are very reluctant to help and soon after Laurie is kidnapped by Corofax who orders the villagers to drive out Roche and Milo. However, they manage to sneak back to the village, only to find that Beth and Ian have been sacrificed. Knowing that Corofax plans on sacrificing Ian and Laurie next, Roche leads Milo to the entrance of the underground secret temple. After entering, Milo fends out the cultists while Roche uses his own religion to combat and destroy the cult of the minotaur.

**Commentary:** After working together in a few productions, *The Devil's Men* marks the last time that Donald Pleasence and Peter Cushing appeared side by side in this sub-par chiller set among the fabulous ruins of ancient Greece. The script is at times ludicrous which explains the confused direction of the plot. In the U.S. version of this film (*Land of the Minotaur*), all of the nude scenes were deleted which unfortunately butchered almost the entire scene explaining Milo's connection to Father Roche. Most of the budget obviously went to paying Pleasence and Cushing to appear in the film, as the minotaur is simply a statue that shoots fire through its nose as it commands that all intruders of its labyrinth must die. The majority of the cast were recruited locals and it unfortunately shows; however, the various locations in the film are very scenic, highlighted by mountains and temple ruins. Another plus is the chilling synthesizer score by Brian Eno who later gained fame for his involvement in the British band Roxy Music, along with a very successful career doing film scores.

As Father Roche, Pleasence really does get to star in this film and appears throughout the entire production—for good or bad. His character is a Van Helsing-like figure that recognizes the supernatural but faces resistance by the more modern fact-based reasoning of private investigator Milo. Pleasence does offer some comedic bits during the film, such as his concerns over Milo's driving—"I'm not afraid to meet my maker. I just don't want to meet him today." The best part of *The Devil's Men* are the scenes that Pleasence shares with Cushing, for both were experienced acting veterans in the horror genre and it clearly shows. At the end of the film, Father Roche tells Milo he may need to call on him again in the future to root out other evils, obviously a set-up for a sequel that never happened.

# *Goldenrod* (1976)

**Cast:** Tony Lo Bianco (Jesse Gifford), Gloria Carlin (Shirley Ashbee Gifford), Will McMillan (Ethan Gifford), Andrew Ian McMillan

(George Gifford), Donald Pleasence (John Tyler Jones), Patricia Hamilton (Mrs. Gunderson), Ed McNamara (Johnson), Donnelly Rhodes
(Keno McLaughlin). Directed by Harvey Hart.

**Synopsis:** Jessie Gifford is the Canadian rodeo champion of 1952 and
lives for the competition of the rodeo despite the fact that his wife Shirley longs for a ranch to settle down from life on the road. At a small-time
local rodeo, Jessie is severely injured after he falls off his horse that crashes down on his leg, breaking it. As a result, Shirley wants Jessie to take
the opportunity to finally quit the rodeo circuit and buy a farm but he
refuses because his doctor gives him clearance to compete. When Keno
McLaughlin, his main competitor, becomes the new rodeo champion in
his absence, Jessie becomes determined to regain his title, but Shirley,
seeing no hope in changing Jessie's mind, leaves him with Keno who is
also a rancher while their two sons Ethan and George remain with their
father. Months later and not fully recovered from his injuries, Jessie ends
up reduced to a farmhand working for other ranchers. Then one night
he meets John Tyler Jones (Donald Pleasence) in a bar and after a lot of
talking, Jones offers Jessie a lucrative job caring for his large ranch. Convinced that his luck has finally changed, Jessie quits his job as a farmhand and takes his two sons with him to Jones' ranch. However, Jones
does not even remember Jessie because he was too drunk the night they
met, not tot mention that his ranch is a rundown operation with some
sheep and one horse. Taking pity on the desperate Jessie, Jones agrees
to let him work for him and allows him and his sons to live in a cabin
on the property. When Jones eventually learns that Jessie was a former
rodeo champion, he offers to be his manager for a share of the winnings.
At first, Jessie declines but the attraction proves too great when his son
Ethan enters the junior rodeo division and wins. Unfortunately, Jessie's
attempt at a comeback is short-lived as he is quickly thrown from his
horse into the dirt. Feeling worthless, Jessie attempts suicide but fails
and Ethan who helps save his father, hatches a plan to save the family.
Faking a run away, Ethan gets Jessie to care once more about the family
and even rekindles his desire to compete in the rodeo with the goal to
raise money to buy a ranch. A wrench is thrown into Ethan and Jessie's
plans when the former owner of the ranch breaks his leg, but Shirley
does return to care for her sons and in time her husband.

**Commentary:** *Goldenrod*, a.k.a. *Glory Days*, refers to the flowers that Jessie presents to Shirley during their first meeting and is essentially a love story set in 1950s Calgary, Canada, a very male dominated society that was also explored in a previous Pleasence film *Wedding in White*. The story of a rodeo rider who rises to the top of his profession only to fall and hit rock bottom before making the slow climb back up, is so well done that viewers may think it is a Greek tragedy. In the lead role is Tony Lo Bianco in one of his early film roles. Bianco carries the pride of Jesse Gifford very well and makes the character quite believable. His belief in living the life of a rodeo champion is also very convincing but at the same time turns out to be the undoing of his family. Another standout actor is young Will McMillan in his film debut as the elder son Ethan who is always dreaming up schemes to bring his mother back into the family while at the same time wishing to follow in his father's footsteps, a fine line that McMillan achieves with ease.

Pleasence has the choice role of John Tyler Jones, better known as J.T., a washed up rancher past his prime who spends his time with the bottle when not driving his Cadillac like a madman. When drinking, J.T. boasts about how well connected he is and his expansive ranch, but he just likes to talk which deflates Jessie's dreams very quickly. However, J.T. is good hearted and cannot turn Jessie away and so stands by his offer even though he cannot remember saying it. J.T. also plays a pivotal role in helping Ethan get his father back into the rodeo circuit, knowing all along that he stands to make a profit from doing so; even as a failed rancher, J.T. knows how to make a buck. In the end, J.T. sells his ranch and becomes a very successful indoor rodeo promoter back East but he is always amazed at his success and continues to wish Jessie well.

# *The Passover Plot* (1976)

**Cast:** Harry Andrews (Yohanan the Baptist), Hugh Griffith (Caiaphas), Zalman King (Yeshua), Donald Pleasence (Pontius Pilate), Scott Wilson (Judah). Directed by Michael Campus.

**Synopsis:** Yeshua, the Aramaic name for Jesus, believes that he is the Messiah of his people and is helped along by his brother James and Judas Iscariot. A religious underground group known as the Zealots are fed up with the corrupt policies of King Herod and Pontius Pilate (Donald Pleasence) and decide to support Yeshua in an attempt to overthrow the Roman government. However, the attempt fails and the Zealots then decide to increase their influence by having Yeshua sacrificed to fulfill his prophesy. Yeshua then tells Judas to report him to the Roman authorities while James concocts a drug to simulate Yeshua's death on the cross. The Zealots are then instructed to secretly remove Yeshua's body from the tomb, thus creating the idea that he has risen from the grave and is indeed the real Messiah who has come to rally the people for Jewish liberation.

**Commentary:** Based on Hugh J. Schonfield 's best-selling book, *The Passover Plot* generated some controversy upon its release because of its biblical conspiracy scenario, something that would be done to a much greater effect in Dan Brown's 2006 bestseller *The Da Vinci Code*. The story proposes that Jesus faked his own death in order to perform the ultimate miracle of resurrection that understandably drew ire from the Christian church. In addition, the film was poorly reviewed and eventually languished and has rarely been shown.

Having previously played Satan in *The Greatest Story Ever Told*, Pleasence was chosen to play another of Jesus' opponents, Pontius Pilate. However, unlike Telly Savalas' portrayal of the Roman Prefect, Pleasence portrays him as more of a villain who actively conspired with the Jewish high priests to control the people. In this respect, Pleasence does a good job as an authoritarian figure that demands strict discipline and dishes out harsh punishment in order to maintain law and order, thus making Pontius Pilate an excellent unknowing helper in *The Passover Plot*.

# *The Last Tycoon* (1976)

**Cast:** Robert De Niro (Monroe Stahr), Tony Curtis (Rodriguez), Robert Mitchum (Pat Brady), Jeanne Moreau (Didi), Jack Nicholson (Brimmer), Donald Pleasence (Boxley), Ray Milland (Fleishacker), Dana Andrews (Red Ridingwood), Ingrid Boulting (Kathleen Moore), Peter Strauss (Wylie), Theresa Russell (Cecilia Brady), Tige Andrews (Popolos). John Carradine (Tour guide). Directed by Elia Kazan.

**Synopsis:** Monroe Stahr is a movie producer and is regarded as a genius by the heads of the studio that employs him. Because his true value lies in being able to perceive what the public wants to see, Stahr oversees all film-related cuts and edits, and is responsible for firing incompetent directors, mentoring his actors, and dealing with writers. Although everyone looks to him for guidance, the corporate head Pat Brady, and lawyer Fleishacker constantly look for ways to try and keep Stahr from driving up film budgets. However, one of their biggest concerns comes from a movement out of New York City to unionize writers. Stahr is not that concerned, and the issue slips his mind when he spots a woman named Kathleen Moore on a film set who happens to be a dead ringer for his late wife. He becomes obsessed with Kathleen to the point where Brady takes notice and his daughter Cecilia turns jealous. Kathleen is mysterious, meeting with Stahr only to keep telling him that they cannot meet again. While neglecting some of his duties, Stahr continues to pursue Kathleen and wants her to be with him. At the studio, Stahr's actions have attracted the attention of the board, and his call to reshoot a costly scene by the writer Boxley (Donald Pleasence) has everyone up in arms. Although a rendezvous at his unfinished beach house gives him hope, Stahr's dreams are crushed when Kathleen reveals in a letter that she is now married and will no longer be able to see him. Despondent, Stahr's meeting with Brimmer, the writers' representative from New York, turns disastrous and ends with him trying to unsuccessfully attack Brimmer. News quickly reaches the board who seizes the opportunity to fire Stahr. Now all alone, Stahr is left to ponder about his lost love.

**Commentary:** Producer Sam Spiegel's interpretation of F. Scott Fitzgerald's unfinished novel is a very hit and miss affair. *The Last Tycoon* features some wonderful performances though it gets bogged down in a love story with a rather wooden female lead. Originally set to be directed by Mike Nichols who was still editing *The Fortune*, Spiegel decided to go instead with veteran director Elia Kazan, a proponent of the method approach to acting which probably helped to draw Robert De Niro and Jack Nicholson to the project. De Niro's character study of Irving Thalberg, the young producer that gained fame at M-G-M, is quite moving. His need to control the entire studio, contrasted with his infatuation with Kathleen and his eventual downfall, is fascinating to watch. Unfortunately, Kazan's decision to bring in newcomer Ingrid Boulting, a.k.a. Ingrid Brett, proved to be unsuccessful as she simply could not bring to the screen the allure of the mysterious woman whom Stahr desires. The rest of the cast does turn in some great performances including Robert Mitchum, Jack Nicolson, Ray Milland, and of course, Donald Pleasence.

In a 1976 interview, Sam Spiegel admitted "I don't know a director (i.e., Kazan) who is as skillful at releasing an actor of his inhibitions." [109] This skill certainly benefited Donald Pleasence as he shines in *The Last Tycoon* as the British writer who cannot get the hang of American pictures. In his first scene, Boxley shows his impatience with everyone including Stahr about the boring material he has to work with. But instead of firing him on the spot, Stahr gives Boxley a moving pep talk in how to create a suspenseful and watchable scene with the classic line "You've been fighting duels all day." This same pep talk is used again at the end of the film with Stahr delivering it to the audience, presumably now concerning his thoughts about Kathleen. Viewers should watch the reaction in Pleasence's eyes as his character is won over with wonder by Stahr, but unfortunately for Boxley, his creative spark is still not engaged and he winds up holed up in a hotel room, drunk and angry. Pleasence's best bit is when he snaps at Stahr and then ingeniously uses a fan to blow the page he wrote across the room into Stahr's hands. It is interesting to note that Pleasence the writer and the film's screenwriter Harold Pinter both gained fame for the play *The Caretaker* in 1960.

## *The Eagle Has Landed* (1976)

**Cast:** Michael Caine (Colonel Steiner), Donald Sutherland (Liam Devlin), Robert Duvall (Colonel Radl), Jenny Agutter (Molly), Donald Pleasence (Himmler), Anthony Quayle (Admiral Canaris), Jean Marsh (Joanna Grey), Sven-Bertil Taube (Captain von Neustadt), John Standing (Father Verecker), Judy Geeson (Pamela), Treat Williams (Captain Clark), Larry Hagman (Colonel Pitts), Alexei Jawdokimov (Corporal Kuniski), Michael Byrne (Karl), Joachim Hansen (SS-Obergruppenfuhrer), Jeff Conaway (Frazier), Maurice Roeves (Major Corcoran). Directed by John Sturges.

**Synopsis:** In late 1943, Adolf Hitler orders the seemingly impossible task to capture his main opponent, British Prime Minister Winston Churchill. Admiral Canaris who was consulted by Hitler about the feasibility of this operation, orders Colonel Radl to conduct a study and report back to him. After hearing back from German intelligence, Radl is surprised to learn that the plan is indeed possible because Churchill is scheduled to spend a weekend at a Norfolk country manor in a town seven miles away from a deserted coastline. Canaris, however, does not want to carry out Hitler's orders, due to seeing them as ludicrous, and tells Radl to scrap his research. But fate intervenes when Himmler (Donald Pleasence) gets wind of the plan and gives Radl free reign to undertake the mission. Making up the team to capture Churchill are Liam Devlin, a university professor and supporter of the Irish Republican Army, Colonel Steiner, a military hero who was court martialed for protecting a Jewish woman, and Steiner's soldiers who were also drawn up on charges. Under the guise of the new marsh warden, Devlin helps Steiner and his men to sneak into the town and set up their cover as Polish soldiers on maneuvers. Things go well until one of Steiner's men dies rescuing a local girl and his German uniform is spotted by the town priest. With their cover blown, Steiner orders his men to hold the townspeople hostage inside of a church while continuing their mission. However, one of the villagers manages to escape from the church and alerts the nearby-stationed U.S. National Guard under the command of Colonel Pitts who foolishly confronts Grey on his own and ends up killed for his efforts. The second in command, Captain Clark, orders his men to surround the church following a brutal firefight with Steiner and his soldiers. Devlin then points out an escape tunnel in the church and leads Steiner through it so he can try to complete his mission while his men fight to the death against the U.S. forces. After slipping into a British soldier's uniform, Steiner tracks down Churchill and shoots him dead as he stands on a patio. In return, Steiner is shot dead by British soldiers, and as they look on, their commander reveals that the man thought to be Churchill was a look-alike decoy to fool the Germans and draw in their forces while the real Churchill was elsewhere planning the final strike against Hitler and his Third Reich.

**Commentary:** In filming Jack Higgins' bestseller as his last film, director John Sturges achieved something quite unique by making viewers feel some sympathy for the German soldiers. Normally cast as villains in films concerning World War II, this approach by Sturges is very rarely seen. Sturges carefully makes the case for the Germans portrayed in *The Eagle Has Landed*, beginning with Michael Caine's first scene as Colonel Steiner in which he views German Jews as being forced to board the trains bound for Nazi concentration camps. After declaring that he is highly opposed to brutally hauling away innocent people who did not put up any fight, Steiner tries to protect a young Jewish woman, but she ends up being killed by one of the Nazi soldiers. As a penalty for their disobedience, Steiner and his men are court marshaled and are essentially given a death sentence in a German penal colony. Thus, the audience quickly sides with Steiner because he is obviously proud of his native Germany and openly condemns the actions of the Nazi Party. Also, the viewing audience supports Steiner as a good-natured and honorable German officer and actually hopes for the success of Steiner and his men, as impossible as we know it is. The fact that the whole mission is exposed when one of Steiner's men instinctively saves a drowning village girl only to die himself and expose his German uniform speaks volumes about his character. Likewise, Robert Duvall's stand-out performance as Colonel Radl elicits much sympathy, due to expressing to the viewer that he has no control over the events occurring in Nazi Germany and can only hope that this impossible mission will somehow redeem his unfortunate fate.

*The Eagle Has Landed* features a big name cast which for Sturges worked out very well. Instead of standing out from the story and slowing it down, each actor provides great depth of character which helps moves the plot along at a steady pace. In a *New York Times* review of the film, it is noted that *The Eagle Has Landed* is a "good old-fashioned adventure movie that is so stuffed with robust incidents and characters that you can relax and enjoy it without worrying whether it actually happened or even whether it's plausible." [110] Some of the other stand-out performances includes Donald Sutherland as the jovial IRA man who incidentally took over this role when Richard Harris dropped out after garnering negative publicity for attending an IRA fund raiser in the U.S.; Treat Williams as an intelligent military man; and of course Donald Pleasence as Himmler, the ruthless Reichsfuhrer of the dreaded S.S. The only weak characters are Larry Hagman's Colonel Pitts who plays a stereotypical southern "Good old boy" for laughs, and Jenny Agutter's Molly who was simply thrown into the cast as a love interest for Devlin.

Although only appearing in three main scenes, Pleasence makes the most of his role as Heinrich Himmler by providing a truly chilling performance. In fact, his character is one of the only real "villains" in the film, and with a striking physical similarity to the real Himmler, Pleasence's calculating demeanor is truly unnerving as he manipulates the lives of people within his iron grip. Radl, initially drawn in by Himmler with the understanding that he would have free reign in the mission, thanks to a letter from Hitler, is played like a puppet. Himmler jokes in order to put Radl at ease, but the wheels in his head are turning all of the time because he plans to take credit for any possible successes and lay the blame on others for any failures. Along these lines, Pleasence's strongest scene occurs when Himmler takes the letter from Radl and rips it up which foreshadows Radl's death sentence later on when he is charged with exceeding his orders. Although certainly not a horror film by any definition, Pleasence's turn as Heinrich Himmler in *The Eagle Has Landed* is one of his most terrifying performances and truly reflects the real-life human monster known as Heinrich Himmler.

# *The Uncanny* (1977)

**Cast:** Peter Cushing (Wilbur Gray), Ray Milland (Frank Richards), Donald Pleasence (Valentine De'ath), Samantha Eggar (Edina Hamilton), Susan Penhaligon (Janet), Alexandra Stewart (Mrs. Joan Blake), John Vernon (Pomeroy), Joan Greenwood (Miss Malkin), Catherine Begin (Madeleine), Roland Culver (Wallace), Chloe Franks (Angela Blake), Renee Girard (Mrs. Nora Maitland), Katrina Holden Bronson (Lucy), Jean LeClerc (Bruce Barrington), Sean McCann (Inspector). Directed by Denis Heroux.

**Synopsis:** Author Wilbur Gray visits the home of his publisher Frank Richards with his latest manuscript that details cases involving the evil nature of cats. Although skeptical, Richards agrees to hear about the cases. The first takes place in London in 1912 with Janet, a maid who works for a wealthy ailing woman and conspires with her boyfriend (the ailing woman's nephew) to get her inheritance. Because the woman has left her entire estate to her numerous cats, her nephew asks

Janet to steal the will so they can change it which proves to be deadly difficult, due to the feline heirs of the estate. The second case takes place in Canada in 1975 when Lucy, recently orphaned following her parent's death in a plane crash, comes to live with her aunt's family. Lucy's cousin Angela is extremely cruel to her and proceeds to torment her, but with the help of her black cat Wellington and a special book on magic, Lucy has her revenge. The final case takes place in Hollywood in 1936. Valentine De'ath (Donald Pleasence), the noted horror actor, has just killed his wife via an "accident" with a set prop while making his latest film. To fill in for his wife, Valentine recommends her stand-in Edina Hamilton who also happens to be his mistress. Later on, Valentine brings Edina back to his home where they find that his wife's cat has given birth to kittens. Not wanting to have anything to do with his wife's pet, Valentine drowns the kittens, but the mother cat escapes, only to give Valentine exactly what he deserves.

**Commentary:** Originally planned to be another anthology horror film by Amicus Productions, *The Uncanny* was instead taken up by producer Milton Subotsky after a falling out with his partner Max Rosenberg. Unfortunately, the film does not hold up to Amicus' previous forays into the genre, such as the excellent *From Beyond the Grave* that also features Pleasence. While *The Uncanny* does offer up horror star Peter Cushing and a couple of well-known character actors like Pleasence and Ray Milland, the end result is far from anything special. The biggest issue are the evil felines that often fail to produce the intended dreaded effects, and combined with some predictable stories, *The Uncanny* falls short as a horror film. Amazingly, Subotsky co-produced another anthology about cats in 1985's *Cat's Eye*, written by horror master Stephen King which did make it worthwhile.

As the preposterously named Valentine De'ath, Pleasence seems to be the only actor in the film who obtains some enjoyment out of the resulting chaos and is therefore the highlight of *The Uncanny*. Pleasence's segment is the best of the three as a hammy horror actor, kind of a cross between Vincent Price and William Shatner. Pleasence clearly has a ball throughout the segment and provides many tongue-in-cheek intentional laughs. Valentine's attempt to do away with his dead wife's cat allows for slapstick style humor and the scenes in which the cat strikes back on the film set almost resembles a *Tom and Jerry* cartoon. Valentine's much-deserved fate also gives new meaning to the old adage "cat got your tongue." Sharp-eyed viewers will notice that when Peter Cushing takes out his case file for the Donald Pleasence segment, he produces a photograph of Pleasence as Blofeld holding a cat from *You Only Live Twice*.

# *Oh, God!* (1977)

**Cast:** John Denver (Jerry Landers), George Burns (God), Teri Garr (Bobbie Landers), Donald Pleasence (Doctor Harmon), Paul Sorvino (Reverend Willie Williams). Directed by Carl Reiner.

**Synopsis:** One day, Jerry Landers, living a very ordinary life as an assistant manager at a supermarket, receives a letter for an interview. Out of curiosity, he goes to the interview and finds himself on a non-existent floor of a building and confronted by a voice claiming to be God. The voice then tells him that he was chosen to spread God's message, but Jerry doubts the voice until God appears to him in person in his bathroom to help him believe. God then performs a miracle in Jerry's car as a way of proving His divinity. Thoroughly convinced, Jerry starts to spread God's word, much to the embarrassment and disbelief of his wife Bobbi. The media eventually catches on to the story and soon Jerry is in the spotlight and comes to the attention of a theology group that wants to know if Jerry is telling the truth. God answers a questionnaire given to Jerry and tells him that a certain Reverend Williams is a phony. When Jerry delivers the message, he is hauled into court by the reverend for slander. With no one else to turn to, Jerry calls God as his witness who proves to the court that He does indeed exist and that they must listen to His message of faith.

**Commentary:** *Oh God!* is a charming and heartwarming family comedy about divine intervention. In the lead role is American folk singer John Denver in his first feature film and as a newcomer, Denver does a very credible job of playing store manager Jerry Landers, an honest and good father and at first a reluctant messenger of God. Opposite Denver is comedian George Burns, perfectly cast as a wisecracking God. Denver and Burns share some good chemistry and the scenes in which Landers attempts to convince everyone of God's presence are downright funny. Cast as priest Harmon, Pleasence has a small role and only appears in two scenes, such as when he hands over the questionnaire for Jerry to give to God, along with some instructions. In order to give his character a bit of depth, Pleasence portrays Harmon as a prim and proper religious man with his pencils all neatly laid out. There is also Paul Sorvino as the funny yet crooked televangelist. *Oh God!* turned out to be quite popular and resulted in the 1984 sequel *Oh God! You Devil* (1984); it was also the inspiration for *Bruce Almighty* in 2003 and its sequel.

## *Telefon* (1977)

**Cast:** Charles Bronson (Major Grigori Borzov), Lee Remick (Barbara), Donald Pleasence (Nicolai Dalchimsky), Tyne Daly (Dorothy Putterman), Alan Badel (Colonel Malchenko), Patrick Magee (General Stresky), Sheree North (Marie Wills), Helen Page Camp (Emma Stark), Roy Jenson (Doug Stark). Directed by Don Siegel.

**Synopsis:** Nicolai Dalchimsky (Donald Pleasence), a hard-line Stalinist Russian clerk for the KGB decides he wants to start World War III and proceeds to steal one of two code books to activate a Russian Cold War plan involving deep cover agents acting as human time bombs. When the KGB is not able to get to Dalchimsky due to escaping to America, General Stresky decides to call in Major Grigori Borzov to hunt down and kill Dalchimsky. Borzov is debriefed on the old secret mission and is then sent overseas, where he meets up with Barbara, his American counterpart. In order to operate this old Soviet secret mission, Dalchimsky places phone calls to the deep undercover Soviet agents in the US listed in the code book, then recites lines from the poem "Stopping by Woods on a Snowy Evening" by Robert Frost which activates the agent to do his/her dirty work, such as blowing up old military installations. Dalchimsky then stands back and watches the progress of the missions that always end with the Soviet agent committing suicide. After following behind from one victim to another, Borzov finally figures out Dalchimsky's code and tries to beat him to his next target. Barbara, who is actually an American double agent, receives instructions from both the Russians and the CIA to kill Borzov as soon as he completes his mission. Things come to a head in Texas when Borzov and Barbara are actually able to beat Dalchimsky to a target and activate and kill him ahead of time. Borzov then attempts to pass himself off as the target at a tavern, and when Dalchimsky arrives, the local police expose him for not being the person in question. In the tavern, Dalchimsky panics and starts calling the rest of the names in the code book. Borzov then instructs Barbara to cause a diversion and in the chaos, Borzov strangles and forces Dalchimsky to swallow cyanide, thus completing his mission. Already having fallen for Borzov, Barbara chooses to disobey her orders and not kill Borzov; instead, she informs her KGB and CIA superiors that they are leaving together and are no longer involved with either organization.

**Commentary:** *Telefon*, a reference to the Russian code name for the mission, is a well-crafted thriller by director Don Siegel, and due to its big budget features huge pyrotechnic effects, not to mention tense and fast-paced action. Although the plot of *Telefon* is a bit far-fetched, it does feature a novel idea involving a portion of Robert Frost's "Stopping by Woods on a Snowy Evening" which will certainly stick in the minds of viewers long after the film ends. The late Hollywood action star and tough guy Charles Bronson provides a variation on his usual film persona to a slightly above average effect, and Lee Remick gives an equal performance as the Soviet/US double agent in love with Borzov. However, the performer that really "steals the show" is Tyne Daly as Dorothy Putterman, the ever enthusiastic CIA whiz kid with a mind like a computer.

Although Pleasence appears as the main villain Dalchimsky, the need to keep him secretive in the plot as Bronson's Borzov tries to track him down equates to not much dialogue for him. Besides reciting the lines from the Frost poem over and over again to activate the deep cover agents, Pleasence does not really get to say much more, other than asking for directions on his way to Texas to set off one of his deep cover agents. His background is not fleshed out either which might leave some viewers assuming that Dalchimsky is simply unhappy with the current state of détente between Russia and the United States during the late 1970's when the Cold War was winding down. Amusingly, Pleasence is allowed to sport a Floridian disguise, complete with a blonde wig and Hawaiian shirt, and as a plot point, it would have been far more interesting to have Dalchimsky keep changing his appearance so as to avoid Borzov. Noteworthy is that *Telefon* reunites Pleasence with Charles Bronson, for both had appeared some fifteen years earlier in the classic film *The Great Escape*.

## Blood Relatives (1978)

**Cast:** Donald Sutherland (Steve Carella), Aude Landry (Patricia Lowery), Lisa Langlois (Muriel Stark), Laurent Malet (Andrew Lowrey), Donald Pleasence (James Doniac), David Hemmings (Armstrong). Directed by Claude Chabrol.

**Synopsis:** After a late night party, teenager Patricia Lowery, slashed and covered in blood, runs into a police station while her cousin Muriel Stark, lies dead in an alleyway. Detective Steve Carella takes the case and based on Patricia's description of the killer begins searching for a tall, dark-haired, blue-eyed man. Carella questions sex offenders that match the description and puts together a line up so that Patricia can point out the killer. However, after Muriel's burial, things take a different turn when Carella learns that Muriel was having a sexual relationship with Patricia's brother Andrew. Then Patricia changes her story and blames Andrew for the murder, but the more Carella digs into the case, the more he becomes convinced that the real killer is someone no one would ever suspect.

**Commentary:** As an effective crime drama, *Blood Relatives* is rarely shown which is a shame because Donald Sutherland was a big box office draw in the 1970s and plays the shrewd detective Carella quite well. In fact, his performance ranks up with some of his best screen portrayals. *Blood relatives* also benefits from a fine performance by David Hemmings as Muriel's boss who is carrying on a secret relationship with her. The reason for the film's neglect is mostly due to its uncomfortable topics—two cousins in a relationship, a pedophile, a married cheat, and a quite violent death. But director Claude Chabrol brings all the ugly factors together through a well-balanced storyline with lots of suspense that keeps the viewer interested in the characters and the outcome.

The Films • 201

Pleasence has basically a cameo in *Blood Relatives* as a pedophile named James Doniac. Brought in for questioning by Detective Carella, Doniac's eyes shift quickly and he squirms around in his seat. In his French accent, Doniac at first provides a vague alibi to Carella but under some intense questioning, he caves in and admits that he was with a thirteen year-old girl on the night of the murder. Credit Pleasence with creating such a loathsome character, perhaps one of the most foul and despicable in his long acting career.

# *Tomorrow Never Comes* (1978)

**Cast:** Oliver Reed (Jim Wilson), Susan George (Janie), Raymond Burr (Burke), John Ireland (Captain), Stephen McHattie (Frank), Donald Pleasence (Dr. Todd), Paul Koslo (Willy), Cec Linder (Milton), Richard Donat (Ray). Directed by Peter Collinson.

**Synopsis:** Jim Wilson is a retiring police officer who feels bitter concerning police corruption and his trigger happy colleagues in the department. Meanwhile, Frank, a local returning home after a three month long trip for work, finds that his girlfriend Janie is singing at a fancy hotel on the beach, due to dating the owner Robert L. Leer. After flying into a rage at Janie's betrayal, a police officer is called in to investigate, and when the officer questions Frank, a fight ensues in which the officer is shot with his own gun. Leer wants the situation immediately put to an end and calls in a favor to police chief Burke who sends officer Willy and some backup to storm the cabana where Frank is holed up with Janie. When Jim gets word of what is going on, he quickly rushes to the scene and takes command, trying to coax Frank into giving himself up without the use of deadly force. However, the tense negotiations between Jim and Frank are aggravated by Willy who wants to shoot first and ask questions later. Jim calls in Dr. Todd (Donald Pleasence) when he discovers that Frank has suffered a head injury that may cause his death or set him off like a ticking time bomb. Convinced that he can still end the situation without someone being killed, Jim convinces Leer to come to the cabana so Frank can meet him face to face, but when Frank come out of the cabana after seeing Leer and is about to hand his gun over to Jim, Willy shoots him dead.

**Commentary:** *Tomorrow Never Comes* is a mostly failed crime thriller effort despite the cast being full of veteran actors like Oliver Reed, Raymond Burr, John Ireland, and of course Donald Pleasence. There is also Susan George on hand who became well known in the 1970s for her various films like *Dirty Mary and Crazy Larry*. But *Tomorrow Never Comes* is pretty much stagnant with Frank and Janie stuck in a hot cabana for most of the film and Reed looking like he is almost sleepwalking through his role as officer Jim Wilson. The dialogue is quite wooden as are some of the secondary actors, but what truly makes no sense is why Jim would take this case anyway because he is a day away from retirement and knows that the department is crooked and willing to shoot on sight. One plus is a funny scene in which Jim has a table, an umbrella, and a beer stand set up on the beach to tempt Frank to come out of hiding.

Pleasence portrays Dr. Todd, a man who does not take himself too seriously. Called in by Jim, Todd explains in his French accent that the cop Frank shot will survive his wound. Then, Jim asks what effect the large gash on Frank's forehead will have on him. Todd's assessment lends more stress to the standoff—that Frank may have brain damage, could die within minutes or days, and that his injury may set him off on a violent killing rampage. After this initial input, Todd just hangs around to see the results. The only real plus here is getting to see Oliver Reed and Pleasence share some scenes.

# *Night Creature* (1978)

**Cast:** Donald Pleasence (Axel MacGregor), Nancy Kwan (Leslie), Ross Hagen (Ross), Jennifer Rhodes (Georgia), Lesly Fine (Peggy), Prackit Yaungsri (Tom), Rachan Kanghanamat (Nippon). Produced and directed by Lee Madden.

**Synopsis:** Axel MacGregor (Donald Pleasence) is a Pulitzer Prize winning novelist who makes his home on an island in the River Kwai of Thailand. He puts his restoration work of Buddhist temples on hold when a man-eating black leopard begins terrorizing the locals. As an experienced hunter, MacGregor successfully tracks the beast but is unprepared for its cunning and power and is almost killed in a close encounter. Frightened for the first time in his life, MacGregor is desperate to repair his ego, so he offers a $10,000 bounty on the leopard. When a group of Thai hunters capture the leopard, they deliver it to MacGregor's secluded island per his instructions. There, he releases the leopard after sending all his workers away with a plan to hunt the beast himself with only nine bullets in his rifle. But unbeknown to MacGregor is that his two daughters Georgia and Leslie, their friend Ross, and his granddaughter Peggy have all arrived at the island to surprise him with a visit. What follows is a deadly game of cat and mouse with MacGregor and his loved ones' lives at stake.

**Commentary:** Although this film features an interesting animal attack plot popular in the 1970s, *Night Creature* fails miserably, due to a low budget and very shoddy direction by Lee Madden who also served as the film's producer and writer. Madden only made a handful of films and if they are of the same quality as *Night Creature*, then it explains his short career. While the film provides a good jungle background (marking the first time Pleasence would appear in this type of setting) and ominous ruins of Buddhist temples, the script is wooden and attempts to make the leopard appear as a bloodthirsty beast. The point of view of the leopard while it stalks and attacks is exciting, as are some slow motion shots of the beast chasing its prey. But the attacks are not shown, only cutaways with close-ups of the leopard growling back at a bloodied victim. This simply does not do justice for a film that promotes an allegedly savage beast. Besides Pleasence, the only other name actor is Nancy Kwan as MacGregor's daughter Leslie. Kwan initially rose to fame with *The World of Suzie Wong* in 1960, but by the time of her appearance in *Night Creature*, her career had begun to fade.

Although Pleasence is the star of this film that is usually quite enjoyable, he had to contend with a shoddy script and does not even have a lot of dialogue. His portrayal of Axel MacGregor as an Ernest Hemingway type works well, but the viewer may question MacGregor's hunting prowess because he goes out on his first hunt wearing a bright yellow shirt and blue-striped hat more suited for a disco. His desire to hunt the leopard on his private island rings true of *The Most Dangerous Game* vibe that does add some suspenseful scenes. No one quite does 'crazy' quite like Pleasence and his wild eyes and ranting when he discovers that the leopard has killed his daughter is a sight to behold. One bizarre aspect of this film is Madden's decision to feature close-ups of Pleasence staring superimposed with the face of the leopard. Perhaps Madden's intention was to illustrate their shared animal instincts; if so, this is never explained.

# *Sgt. Pepper's Lonely Hearts Club Band* (1978)

**Cast:** Peter Frampton (Billy Shears), Barry Gibb (Mark Henderson), Robin Gibb (Dave Henderson), Maurice Gibb (Bob Henderson), Frankie Howerd (Mr. Mustard), Paul Nicholas (Dougie Shears), Donald Pleasence (B.D. Hoffler), Sandy Farina (Strawberry Fields), Dianne Steinberg (Lucy), Steve Martin (Dr. Maxwell Edison), Aerosmith (Future Villain Band), Alice Cooper (The Sun King), George Burns (Mr. Kite), Billy Preston (Sergeant Pepper golden weather vane). Directed by Michael Schultz.

**Synopsis:** Sgt. Pepper's Lonely Hearts Club Band was known in the town of Heartland for the peaceful and joyous effects their music had on listeners. His services were rendered during times of need including two World Wars before he eventually retired, but when Sgt. Pepper passed on in 1958, he left his musical instruments to the town for a museum dedicated in his honor and for a new Sgt. Pepper's band, comprised of Billy Shears and three brothers—Mark, Dave, and Bob Henderson. Slowly by word of mouth, their popular music was heard by B.D. Hoffler (Donald Pleasence), head of the world's most successful record label. Amazed by the group's sound, B.D. invites the band out to Los Angeles where he signs them as his new act. But as they experience the glamour of wealth and popularity, a villain named Mr. Mustard is sent by the Future Villain Band to steal Sgt. Pepper's instruments from the town to destroy it. Billy's girlfriend Strawberry Fields gets word to him about the plot and he organizes the band to reclaim all of the instruments that were given to various nefarious individuals. During the final battle with the Future Villain Band, Strawberry Fields dies, but all is put right once again for Billy and the two of Heartland when Sgt. Pepper works one more miracle.

**Commentary:** As a Beatles-inspired musical, *Sgt. Pepper's Lonely Hearts Club Band* borrowed its plot from a 1974 off-Broadway production. Although the Beatles do not appear in the film and were not involved in the production, their songs from the *Sgt. Pepper* and *Abbey Road* albums are covered by various musicians and groups like Peter Frampton, the Bee Gees, Steve Martin, Alice Cooper, Aerosmith, and Earth, Wind, and Fire. The plot itself is really not much more than a device to feature the songs of the Beatles with the lyrics acting as dialog. George Burns plays Mr. Kite, the mayor of Heartland, who also provides the film's narration. Produced by Robert Stigwood, best known for the smash hit *Saturday Night Fever*, *Sgt. Pepper* was expected to be a huge success, due to the music of the Beatles and the involvement of popular musicians. However, this would not be the case because after being released, critics trashed it, but for Beatles fans and admirers of the groups and singers, *St. Pepper* is definitely worth seeing.

As the ultra wealthy and somewhat devious record company owner B.D. Hoffler (though for some unknown reason the character is referred to as B.D. Brockhurst in publicity manuals), Pleasence looks the part of a late 1970s record producer, complete with a gold tooth, earrings, flashy clothes, and a golden blonde toupee that seems to fly off when he gets agitated. Pleasence does not have many lines but when he first meets the group, he gets to sing the first few verses of the Beatles' *I Want You* from the *Abbey Road* album. Despite this, Pleasence uses his physical acting abilities to convey the greed and underhanded tactics that Hoffler unleashes on the band, including drugging Billy Shears in order to get him to sign a contract.

## *Power Play* (1978)

**Cast:** David Hemmings (Colonel Anthony Narriman), Barry Morse (Dr. Jean Rousseau), Peter O'Toole (Colonel Zeller), Donald Pleasence (Blair), Jon Granik (Colonel Raymond Kasai), Gary Reineke (Aramco), Harvey Atkin (Anwar), George Touliatos (Barrientos), Chuck Shamata (Hillsman), Eugene Amodeo (Photographer), Dick Cavett (Himself), Eli Rill (Dominique). Directed by Martyn Burke.

**Synopsis:** The good people in a foreign nation are at the mercy of a corrupt government and its controlling police force. In response to this situation, a group of homegrown terrorists kidnap and execute the Minister of Economics. The President then calls a press meeting and declares that he has the military's support and that force will be met with force. However, Colonel Narriman is annoyed by the President playing politics with the military but he lets it go because his retirement is coming up in a few weeks. His good friend Dr. Rousseau pleads with him to assist in a coup d'état to bring down the government and bring democracy to the people, but Narriman wants no part of it, fearing the ensuing violence. His mind is changed however upon seeing the government at work when Blair (Donald Pleasence), the chief of the secret police, has a friend's daughter cruelly tortured and executed. Working with Rousseau to stage the coup, Narriman realizes the need for more support, so he brings in Colonels Kasai, Aramco and Zeller to leads the tank brigade. Trouble beings when Kasai goes to discuss the coup with another general who tries to inform the government, resulting in Kasai having to kill him. Part of the general's message gets to Blair who immediately attempts to identify those involved in the plot against the government. Narriman tries to keep one step ahead of Blair while finalizing the plans for the coup, but in turn, Blair uses every means at his disposal in his search including spies, blackmail, torture, and murder. After interrogating one of the colonels, Blair has the air force call in two battalions of soldiers to stop the coup, forcing Narriman to immediately enact the plan. Working together, Narriman, Rousseau, and the colonels manage to stop Blair and bring down the government, culminating with the arrest of the President. But all is not what it seems in the takeover, and surprises are in store for all involved.

**Commentary:** *Power Play*, a.k.a. *Coup d'état*, provides an interesting look at the complexities related to staging a government takeover and the possible disastrous consequences, no matter how good the intentions are at the beginning. This film does not shy away from the difficult questions that it raises, such as whose life is worth what and to what ends are the rebels willing to go. *Power Play* is also well plotted by director Martyn Burke and benefits greatly from an amazing cast. David Hemmings, serving double duty as a producer and starring as Colonel Narriman, is a truly noble character who faces ever-increasing difficult decisions as the planned coup moves ahead, and despite having the best intentions, things fail to work out as he would like. Barry Morse as Dr. Jean Rousseau, perfectly named after Jean-Jacques Rousseau who helped trigger the French Revolution, is an interesting character as the only non-military man in the coup which makes him the 'weak' link and the intellectual with the closest ties to the people. Also delivering a good performance is Peter O'Toole as the hotheaded Colonel Zeller, a necessary ingredient for achieving the goals of the coup. With similarly staged coups occurring in reality, *Power Play* is as relevant today as when it was released in 1978.

Pleasence channels a member of the dreaded Gestapo for his role as Blair, a character that certainly could have been featured in any film with World War II as the background. Blair is the watchdog of the government, responsible for rooting out all possible threats with the utmost authority. His calm overseeing of the torture of the girl is certainly one of the most brutal scenes of its kind ever committed to film. Cool and calculating, Blair promises Narriman that he will release the girl, but when he does, he has her shot, then later informs Narriman that the streets are no longer safe. Another example of Blair's ruthlessness is when he tries to blackmail Rousseau with photos of his wife cheating on him, all the while trying to play the concerned colleague but asking for information at the same time. His failure to ultimately stop the coup brings up more questions than answers when the information he was seeking is finally revealed. His pleading with a colonel that the new government will need "men like him" rings true in many newly-formed governments, particularly in Eastern Europe after World War II. In a twist ending, the viewer is left wondering who was right and wrong in the struggle that is *Power Play*.

# *Last In, First Out* (1978)

**Cast:** Bruno Cremer (Lucas Richter), Donald Pleasence (Rothko), Laure Dechasnel (Helene Lehman), Dennis Hopper (Medford), Joseph Cotton (Foster Johnson), Gabriele Ferzetti (Herzog), Michel Bouquet (Banquier Muller). Directed by Claude d'Anna.

**Synopsis:** Helene Lehman is traveling on a train to Zurich to end an affair. Seated in her cabin is Lucas Richter and during the train ride to Zurich, their passwords are somehow mixed up, but when Helene realizes what has happened, it is too late because Richter is long gone. The mix-up draws the interest of an agent named Medford who thinks she knows the location of Richter. Scared and frightened, Helene manages to elude Medford and jumps on a train to Paris where she locates Richter and learns that he is a former journalist who spent time in prison for writing about secret government contracts with foreign companies. He is now wanted for a file in his possession that would expose the illegal dealings of an American company involved in Africa. Medford turns out to be a hired killer for the company and is also on the Paris bound train, a situation that will put to the test the wills of Helene and Lucas as they attempt to outsmart and outmaneuver their opposition.

**Commentary:** *Last in, First Out*, a.k.a. *L'ordre et la Securite du Monde*, is a French made political thriller similar in style and scope to *Journey Into Fear*, due to focusing on an individual who by doing his job honestly exposes a corrupt system and as a result becomes a target. Both films are also not terribly exciting nor well directed which makes the proceedings plod along at a slow pace. The cast is mostly made up of French actors with a few name actors thrown in the mix, such as Dennis Hopper, Pleasence, and Joseph Cotton. As the character of Rothko, Pleasence has a very small role but is given a large billing, a sign that the producers were basically looking to cash in on his name.

# *Halloween* (1978)

**Cast:** Donald Pleasence (Dr. Sam Loomis), Jamie Lee Curtis (Laurie Strode), Nancy Kyes (Annie Brackett), P.J. Soles (Lynda van der Klok), Charles Cyphers (Sheriff Leigh Brackett), Kyle Richards (Lindsey Wallace), Brian Andrews (Tommy Doyle), John Michael Graham (Bob Simms), Nancy Stephens (Marion Chambers), Mickey Yablans (Richie), Brent Le Page (Lonnie Elamb), Adam Hollander (Keith), Robert Phalen (Dr. Terence Wynn), Sandy Johnson (Judith Margaret Myers), Peter Griffith (Morgan Strode), Nick Castle (The Shape). Directed by John Carpenter.

**Synopsis:** In 1963, on Halloween night in Haddonfield, Illinois, six year-old Michael Myers finds his sister making out with her boyfriend. For reasons that are unclear, Michael retrieves a butcher knife from the kitchen and stabs his sister to death. Fifteen years later, we find

Michael's psychiatrist Dr. Loomis (Donald Pleasence) driving with a nurse to take Michael before the state board for a hearing. As they approach the Illinois State Hospital, they see that the power has gone out and the patients are running loose on the lawn. Dr. Loomis goes to call for help but Michael steals his car and escapes into the night. Back in Haddonfield, high school student Laurie Strode places the key to the old and dilapidated Myers home under the front mat, as her father will be showing the house to prospective buyers. Unlike her friends Annie and Lynda, Laurie does not have a boyfriend and will be busy babysitting little Tommy Doyle on Halloween night. Unbeknownst to Laurie, Michael Myers has returned to his home and has taken a murderous interest in Laurie and her friends. One day, while Laurie is walking to school, she notices a slow moving car with a masked man behind the wheel who watches her intently and then disappears. On the trail of Michael is Dr. Loomis, intent on putting him back in isolation and keeping him away from society. He teams up with Brackett, the local sheriff, to scour the neighborhood for signs of Michael. As Annie and Lynda make plans for a romantic Halloween night with their boyfriends, Michael stalks and kills them one by one. Laurie, who is babysitting a few houses away from Annie, goes to see why no one is answering the phone and runs into Michael who proceeds to try and stab her with a knife. She runs back to the Doyle house with Michael in pursuit. He manages to get into the house and chases Laurie into a closet where she gets the upper hand by sticking a wire coat hanger in his face. When Michael drops his knife, Laurie picks it up and stabs him with it. However, Michael will not die and continues to try and kill Laurie. As Tommy and Lindsey run out of the house screaming, Dr. Loomis spots them and runs into the house, sees Michael attacking, and empties his pistol into him forcing him through the second floor window. When Dr. Loomis walks to the shattered window and looks down outside, he sees that Michael Myers has mysteriously vanished.

**Commentary:** Made on a small budget of $300,000, *Halloween* would go on to make more than $60 million and shock Hollywood to become one of the most successful independent films of all time. It also proved that filmmakers did not need to sink millions into a film to deliver a hit, and its success bred a whole new genre—the slasher film. Director John Carpenter was a horror film fan himself and understood what audiences wanted to see—"The reason these films have been popular is that audiences want to see something that's forbidden. They do touch some sort of awful nerve. And the more forbidden, the more alluring."[111]

Even before the opening credits, Carpenter pulls the audience in by placing them in the eyes of the killer as he stalks his prey and murders them. The Carpenter film score, now a classic horror riff, provides a chilling accent to Michael Myers and was reused in many of the sequels. The unnerving killer, a.k.a. "the Shape," never utters a single word, but his horrendous actions related to stalking and murdering innocent young girls speaks volumes. During the killing of Lynda's boyfriend, Michael actually pivots his head back and forth like a curious dog, truly a separation from humanity. Indeed, Carpenter created a new type of monster and draws a parallel in *Halloween* as Tommy watches a TV airing of the sci-fi classic *The Thing* (1951) which Carpenter would later remake according to his own vision in 1982. It should be mentioned that "the Shape" or the mask that Michael Myers wears throughout *Halloween* was actually a life mask of actor William Shatner as Captain Kirk from the sci-fi TV classic *Star Trek*.

For Donald Pleasence, lightning struck twice in his career, for as in the James Bond vehicle *You Only Live Twice*, Pleasence was not the first choice to play Dr. Loomis in *Halloween*; in fact, he was not even the second choice this time around. Director John Carpenter had originally invisioned horror star Peter Cushing in the role of Dr. Loomis, but Cushing's agent turned him down. Carpenter's second choice for Dr. Loomis was another horror star, Christopher Lee, who also turned him down. It was producer Irwin Yablan who suggested trying to get Pleasence for the role, but Pleasence was not sure of taking the role. But one of Carpenter's daughters was a fan of Pleasence's work, so he agreed to star in the film. So Pleasence could thank Carpenter's daughter for bringing him into the spotlight as never before, and although Pleasence had certainly done his share of horror films prior to 1978, *Halloween* made him a horror icon for a new and young audience, much like Peter Cushing and Christopher Lee. In effect, Carpenter's *Halloween* made Donald Pleasence a household name for a new American generation.

As the veteran actor in a film with many fresh faces like Jamie Lee Curtis, Pleasence as Dr. Loomis provides an air of respectability that helps highlight the bloodcurdling terror of the antagonist Michael Myers. Dr. Loomis is indeed a heroic figure who realizes the danger that awaits him but is willing to risk his life to stop Michael Myers from his reign of terror in Haddonfield. Pleasence has some great scenes in this film, such as when he discusses how Michael is the personification of evil in an attempt to convince the sheriff to heed his warnings. Just as Michael Myers is on a mission to kill, Dr. Loomis is on a mission to stop him. Loomis never seems to stop and relax except in one scene when he pulls a Halloween prank to scare some curious boys away from the old Myers house; only then does he crack a smile. In the final scene, Pleasence demonstrates his skill at acting only with his eyes, for they convey his disbelief and then wonderment as to where Michael Myers might show up next.

## *Jig-Saw* (1979)

**Cast:** Luno Ventura (Romain Dupre), Angie Dickinson (Karen), Laurent Malet (Julien Dupre), Hollis McLaren (Nancy), Donald Pleasence (Albert Pumpelmeyer), Lisa Pelikan (Anne), Chris Wiggins (MacKenzie), R.H. Thompson (Borke), Peter Hicks (Lentini). Directed by Claude Pinoteau.

**Synopsis:** Romain Dupre is called from his home in France to Canada where his son Julien has been reported killed, but when Romain arrives to identify the body, he discovers the body of another man with his son's passport. The police then realize the mix up and tell Romain his son is now wanted on a charge of murdering an officer. Romain's search for his son leads him to a crime syndicate whose boss turns him away and has him beaten up for his efforts. Dumped in a car that gets wrecked, Romain later contacts Karen, the car's owner, who lends him a sympathetic ear and a helping hand in trying to locate Julien. During their search, Romain meets Albert Pumpelmeyer (Donald Pleasence) who puts him in touch with Julien's girlfriend Anne. After questioning Anne, Romain learns that Julien began working for the syndicate soon after arriving illegally in Canada because he had no money. He was also part of a smuggling ring that went bad, resulting in the death of a police officer, and is now on the run. Romain eventually finds Julian, only to discover that he possesses a bag full of the syndicate's money and wants to use it to start a new life with Anne. But when Anne is brutally beaten and Romain takes a bullet during a clash between the police and the syndicate, Julien realizes the errors of his ways and comes forward to the police with the money.

**Commentary:** *Jig-Saw, a.k.a. L'homme en Colere, is a crime drama that mostly succeeds, due to the talents of longtime character actor* Luno Ventura as Romain Dupre, the dedicated father in search of his missing son. In this film, Romain portrays a man in a foreign land with little help and not much time to locate his son before other forces find and kill him. Adding to the drama is a backstory in which Romain's wife dies in a car accident that eventually creates a large rift between father and son to the point where they lose contact. What Romain goes through to save his son's life is a harrowing journey that almost takes his own life on numerous occasions. Also standing out among the cast is Angie Dickinson in a good supporting role as Karen, a kind-hearted woman with a questionable background who aids Romain when no one else will.

Pleasence has a small and somewhat deceiving role in *Jig-Saw*. His character of Albert Pumpelmeyer first appears in Romain's hotel lobby posing as a laundromat owner who hands over some clothes Julien left behind, along with a piece of information on Julien's girlfriend Anne. Later on, Pumpelmeyer picks up Romain in his car and questions him harshly about Julien's whereabouts, an indication that he apparently also worked for the syndicate. After receiving no answers, Pumpelmeyer drops Romain off and coldly lights a cigarette as a group of thugs chase down Romain. Career-wise, this is yet another villainous role for Pleasence.

# *Good Luck, Miss Wyckoff* (1979)

**Cast:** Anne Heywood (Evelyn Wyckoff), Donald Pleasence (Dr. Steiner), Robert Vaughn (Dr. Neal), Earl Holliman (Ed Eckles), Carolyn Jones (Beth), Ronee Blakley (Betsy), Dorothy Malone (Mildred), Doris Roberts (Marie), John Lafayette (Rafe Collins), Directed by Marvin J. Chomsky.

**Synopsis:** Evelyn Wyckoff, known to her friends as Eve, is a thirty-five year old, single schoolteacher living in the town of Freedom, Kansas in 1954. For unknown reasons, she begins to develop bouts of panic, illness, and anger, and after deciding to find the cause, she makes an appointment with Dr. Neal who after examining her asks if she has ever had relations with a man. Eve reveals that she has never been with a man that leads Dr. Neal to believe that this is the source of her ailments. In response, he refers her to a psychiatrist in Wichita, and after traveling by bus, Eve begins sessions with psychiatrist Dr. Steiner (Donald Pleasence) who manages to uncover Eve's uncomfortable and explosive childhood home life. He then encourages her to continue the sessions and try to make a connection with a man for her own experience. Eve takes an interest in a married bus driver, but he is gone before she gets over her hesitation. Feeling stronger for taking the first steps in her rehabilitation, Eve goes about her daily routine until one fateful day she is confronted by Rafe Collins, a young black football player that also works as a janitor in her school. Rafe first exposes himself to Eve and later brutally rapes her in her own classroom. Humiliated but not wanting to turn in her attacker for fear of ruining his academic future, Eve tells no one which only convinces Rafe to continue his 'visits' to her classroom after school. Eve, confusing her new sexual encounters with Rafe for a relationship, begins to willingly accept him in her life, but after their school trysts are discovered, Eve is forced to resign from her teaching position. She also finds herself unwanted in her own town, thus forcing her to leave to start anew somewhere else.

**Commentary:** *Good Luck, Miss Wyckoff,* a.k.a. *The Shaming,* is a well-acted film all around, though it does raise more questions than answers. Because the story takes place in the 1950s, issues like communism, McCarthyism, women's independence, and racism are all tackled. Anne Heywood is remarkable as the troubled Evelyn Wyckoff, and after watching this film, viewers will appreciate Heywood's role for its difficulty. Eve is a defender of the rights of others, even when her rights are being trampled into the ground. She actively stands up for a fellow colleague branded as a communist for teaching the theory of Communism in his history class. Eve's struggle to desegregate her school is also brought up which ironically would allow her attacker into the building. This is where the story gets a bit convoluted and may raise the ire of some viewers. The idea that a woman who is raped would give in and later defend her attacker is certainly not going to appeal to any women's rights advocates. In addition, the portrayal of Rafe is presented as the negative stereotypical image of a black man that might incense some viewers. For those wishing to view the film, they should seek out the longer, uncut print because it packs a more powerful emotional impact.

As Miss Wyckoff's psychiatrist, Pleasence is not given too much to do other than open up Eve's past a bit to try and explain why she has never been with a man. Dr. Steiner comes across naturally as quite Freudian, due to the subject matter, and Pleasence makes himself quite believable in the role. His explanation of Eve experiencing a "rebirth" and her need to make her own decisions and live with the consequences sounds very convincing. Steiner also tries to convince Eve to separate what she perceives about herself from watching movies in relation to her true identity. But once she is raped by Rafe, Eve is unable to get in touch with Dr. Steiner as he is ironically away on an emergency call, but by the time he calls the house to get in touch with her, Eve has decided to accept her new "relationship." If ever there was a film with a message not to quit one's therapy before issues are resolved, then *Good Luck, Miss Wyckoff* is it.

# *Dracula* (1979)

**Cast:** Frank Langella (Count Dracula), Laurence Olivier (Professor Abraham Van Helsing), Donald Pleasence (Dr. Jack Seward), Kate Nelligan (Lucy Seward), Trevor Eve (Jonathan Harker), Jan Francis (Mina Van Helsing), Janine Duvitski (Annie), Tony Haygarth (Milo Renfield), Sylvester McCoy (Walter). Directed by John Badham.

**Synopsis:** A Romanian ship caught in a severe storm crashes and breaks up among the rocks near an English asylum run by Dr. Jack Seward (Donald Pleasence). His daughter Lucy discovers the ship's lone survivor, Count Dracula, lying in a cave near the beach. The next morning, the ship is searched during which it is discovered that the crew was slaughtered by some unknown beast. Jonathan Harker, a solicitor that represents Dracula, arrives to bring him to his new home in

England. Seward invites Dracula to his home to welcome him, and his guest takes an immediate interest in Mina Van Helsing, a friend of the family. Later that night, Dracula comes to Mina through her bedroom window and drinks her blood. The next morning, Lucy finds Mina dead that leads Seward to call for her father Professor Abraham Van Helsing to come immediately. Van Helsing is suspicious of his daughter's sudden death and when he notices two bite marks on her neck, he begins to conduct research on vampirism. Meanwhile, Dracula has taken notice of Lucy and she of him and they spend time together even though she is Harker's girlfriend. Van Helsing's suspicions are confirmed when he tracks down Mina, now a vampire herself, and kills her with the assistance of Seward. They continue to follow the trail of the unexplained until Van Helsing concludes that Dracula is the source of the unexplained deaths. He then confronts Dracula who proves too powerful to stop and after escaping from Seward's home, he returns and takes Lucy with him. Van Helsing, Seward, and Harker soon embark on a desperate chase until they learn that Dracula and Lucy are on a ship bound for Romania. Van Helsing and Harker board the ship and do battle with Dracula who seems to have the upper hand until a mortally wounded Van Helsing brings about his demise by using a hook to hoist Dracula up into the sunlight.

**Commentary:** Frank Langella first donned the cape of the infamous Count on Broadway in 1977 with 925 performances at the Martin Beck Theatre and received rave reviews as well as a Tony Award nomination. Of course, because of Langella's outstanding performance and success as Dracula on Broadway, a film adaptation was not far behind and fortunately, director John Badham convinced Langella to reprise his role. The resulting film benefits greatly from the complex and sensual presence of Langella as the infamous Count and due to having a large budget, the sets are quite impressive, not to mention on location shooting that lends a true Gothic atmosphere to the film's storyline. Many actors have portrayed Count Dracula in film and Langella's performance occupies the higher end along with Christopher Lee and Louis Jordan. Another big plus is the beautiful score by composer John Williams.

Pleasence plays Dr. Jack Seward, the administrator of Billerbeck Hall asylum who brings in Abraham Van Helsing when his daughter Mina dies. Seward is portrayed as a man of science who refuses to accept the concept of vampirism until he comes face to face with the undead Mina. In Bram Stoker's 1897 novel, the character of Seward is more prominent and complex and he does his best to understand Renfield's psychological neurosis. In addition, Seward in Stoker's novel is but one of three suitors vying for the affections of the beautiful Lucy, but in most film adaptations including Badham's version, Seward is portrayed as her father. Basically, Pleasence's role in *Dracula* is to advance the story by bringing Van Helsing into the picture and as a result, Pleasence does share several pivotal scenes with Sir Laurence Oliver.

## *Jaguar Lives!* (1979)

**Cast:** Joe Lewis (Jonathan Cross/Jaguar), Christopher Lee (Adam Caine), Donald Pleasence (General Villanova), Barbara Bach (Anna Thompson), Capucine (Zina Vanacore), Joseph Wiseman (Ben Ashir), Woody Strode (Sensei), John Huston (Ralph Richards), Anthony De Longis (Bret Barrett). Directed by Ernest Pintoff.

**Synopsis:** Jonathan Cross, also known as Jaguar, is an international agent working for G6 and while on a mission to stop a bomb from exploding, Jaguar is shot and his partner Bret Barrett dies in the explosion. Years later and after recovering from his injuries, Jaguar is asked to re-enlist with G6 to track down and stop a new global drug cartel run by the mysterious Estoban. Traveling around the world chasing leads, Jaguar is double-crossed, avoids death, and does battle with the killers of various drug lords, including General Villanova (Donald Pleasence) and Adam Caine. Jaguar eventually sneaks into a meeting attended by the world's major drug dealers and learns that Estoban is actually his previously thought dead friend and partner Bret Barrett. Facing his former partner, Jaguar ends the rule of Bret's cartel as the police arrive to arrest the drug dealers.

**Commentary:** *Joe Lewis, considered as one of the greatest heavyweight American kick boxers in martial arts history, turned professional in 1970 and is one of only a handful of martial artists to defeat the legendary Chuck Norris in a match. However, unlike Norris, Lewis's film career never really took off after his debut in Jaguar Lives!, a good escapist ad-*

*venture with Lewis playing a globetrotting 007 type agent out to defeat evil villains. The film's James Bond influence does not end there though, because it features a number of actors that appeared in Albert Broccoli's Bond series, such as Joseph Wiseman (Dr. No), Donald Pleasence (Blofeld), and Christopher Lee (Scaramanga) as well as "Bond girl" Barbara Bach. Someone also managed to pull some strings as legendary director/actor John Huston appears in a small role as a shipping magnate. Despite the fact that Jaguar Lives! contains some distracting talk-filled interludes, it was after all made as a vehicle for Joe Lewis to show off his breathtaking skills as a master of the martial arts.*

*Pleasence plays General Villanova,* the egotistical dictator of Santa Fortuna, and in a neat twist, Pleasence portrays both the general and an actor/body double whom Jaguar grabs from a make out session in bed so as to obtain some information. Villanova is always self-promoting, from the photos of himself in grand poses spread throughout his mansion to his boasting on how his people love him and the U.S. government supported him. Dressed in a bright white military uniform, Pleasence puts in an over-the-top performance by walking with his head held high to accentuate his attitude. Villanova's last scene comes when Jaguar bests his men and takes off in his beloved new helicopter, resulting in the general almost crying like a baby.

# *The Pumaman* (1980)

**Cast:** Walter George Alton (Professor Tony Farms/Pumaman), Donald Pleasence (Kobras), Miguel Angel Fuentes (Vadinho), Sydne Rome (Jane Dobson), Silvano Tranquilli (Dobson). Directed by Alberto De Martino.

**Synopsis:** Paleontologist Tony Farms works at a museum cataloging dinosaur bones. One day, a stranger comes in and throws him out of a three-story window. The stranger then declares that Tony is the Pumaman and disappears. Confused at what has happened to him, Tony is happily surprised to meet a beautiful reporter named Jane Dobson who invites him to the Dutch Embassy, where her father is an ambassador. However, their pleasant evening is interrupted by the appearance of the mysterious Kobras (Donald Pleasence) and his henchmen. But what Tony does not know is that Kobras is fully aware that he is the Pumaman and is actually using the sacred Puma gold mask as a mind control device on Jane and others. Kobras has his men attack Tony and he narrowly escapes with the aid of the stranger who reappears with the Puma belt that gives Tony magical powers. The stranger reveals himself to be Vadinho, the Aztec high priest of the temple of the Pumaman, protector of his people with the blood of the gods in his veins and a visitor from the stars. As Puma Man, Tony engages in a battle with Kobras and his forces and with Vadinho's help, eventually defeats Kobras and frees Jane.

**Commentary:** *The Pumaman* is a laughably bad science fiction adventure made in Italy, the home of the low budget genre feature and untold rip-offs. There is not much going for this film, mainly because of the ridiculous plot and the even more ridiculous special effects of Pumaman flying around. Of course, most of this is due to a non-existent budget that inspired the producers to not put much effort into this project. *The Pumaman* was later spoofed on the comedy TV classic series *Mystery Science Fiction Theatre 3000* which is actually better than the original film version because it provides intentional laughs along with the original non-intentional hilarity.

As was the case with many older actors in the 1980s, choice roles were often few and far between, making it necessary to seek out television work and lower budget features to supplement their incomes. Pleasence's role in *The Pumaman* was clearly just to pay the bills and is truly a waste of his talent, not to mention embarrassing, considering that his name is not spelled correctly in the credits. Although sporting some interesting-looking clothes, including a black leather suit and a shiny green outfit, Kobras is mostly reduced to providing evil stares and sending his henchmen out to do his dirty work. Even for Pleasence fans, *The Pumaman* should be left out of their list of films for necessary viewing.

# *The Monster Club* (1981)

**Cast:** Vincent Price (Eramus), Donald Pleasence (Pickering), Carradine (R. CHetwynd-Hayes), Stuart Whitman (Sam), Richard Johnson (Busotsky's father), Barbara Kellerman (Angela), Britt Ekland (Busotsky's mother), Simon Ward (George), Valentine (Mooney), Patrick Magee

(Innkeeper), Anthony Steel (Lintom Busotsky), Geoffrey Bayldon (Psychiatrist), James Laurenson (Raven), Neil McCarthy (Watson, B-squad member), Lesley Dunlop (Luna). Directed by Roy Ward Baker.

**Synopsis:** In a deserted part of town late one night, horror writer R. Chetwynd-Hayes is bitten a vampire named Eramus. Upon finding out that he just bit the famous writer, Eramus confesses his admiration for Chetwynd-Hayes' work and takes him to the Monster Club with the promise of material for his next book. In the club, Eramus explains the monster genealogy to Chetwynd-Hayes, and then tells him three stories. In the first, George and Angela are a conniving pair who plan to steal antiques and money from a lonely man named Raven who happens to be a shadmock. Raven falls quickly for Angela, and she accepts his marriage proposal under the guise to steal his money. When she is found out and refuses his love, Raven unleashes his deadly power upon her. In the second story, a shy young boy named Lintom has trouble adjusting to his new school. Making matters more difficult for him is that his father is never around during the day and he is alone with only his mother to watch him. One day while being picked on by his classmates, Lintom is rescued by a clergyman named Pickering (Donald Pleasence) who inquires about Lintom's family. His suspicions become aroused when he hears that Lintom's father only comes out at night. Curious about this odd habit, Lintom sneaks down to the basement and discover his father sleeping in a coffin. He then runs out of the house into Pickering who reveals to Lintom that he is a government vampire hunter. Pickering stakes the father, but not before being bitten and then staked by his own men. Lintom's father then promptly rises and explains he is always prepared with a special vest in case he gets staked. In the last story, Sam, a horror film director, is scouting locations for his newest film. After finding an off the beaten path village, Sam is taken hostage by the innkeeper and the bizarre townspeople. It is only when Sam explores the village church that he learns the town is inhabited by ghouls who plan on making him their next meal. With the help of the innkeeper's daughter, Sam is able to escape but ends up in a police escort for the village elders who dutifully drive him back for supper. Back at the Monster Club, Eramus nominates Chetwynd-Hayes for membership as man himself via wars and devastating weapons turns out to be the most dangerous monster of all.

**Commentary:** *The Monster Club* is a tongue-in-cheek horror film mostly geared toward a young audience. Producer Milton Subotsky, in trying to recapture the horror anthology format which brought him so much success in the past, misses more then he hits with *The Monster Club*, his last film for Amicus, though it is enjoyable to watch. One of Subotsky's coups was bringing horror legends Vincent Price and John Carradine together to star in the linking story about the writer R. Chetwynd-Hayes (a real person who actually wrote the book that the film is based on) being introduced to the Monster Club by a vampire in the shape of Vincent Price.

The budget for *The Monster Club* appears to have been quite small, due to the patrons of the club wearing very cheap monster masks as if they were bought at a convenience store. Featured in between each of the three stories are songs by a musical group evidently influenced by the early 1980s new wave movement. For one of the songs, "Stripper," a woman at the Monster Club suitably strips right down to her own skeleton. The film takes a different approach in creating its own monster genealogy, though some of the hybrid monsters like the shadmock in the first story whose whistles are deadly seem more silly than scary. The best story is the last one *The Ghouls* that takes its subject matter seriously and features a very atmospheric village and the scene-stealing Patrick Magee as a ghoulish innkeeper.

Donald Pleasence stars in the segment *The Vampires*, executed in a comedic black humor style. Although Pickering himself is played in a more serious manner, his assistants act more like the Keystone Kops than vampire hunters. As an interesting take on a modern vampire hunter, Pickering works for the government to eradicate the undead and looking nifty dressed in black with a bowler hat, Pickering is a dutiful agent that tracks down his prey with much stealth. One feels sorry for him after he is bitten and then chased down and staked by his own men. An interesting tidbit is Lintom Busotsky who as an adult film producer shows his autobiographical film at the Monster Club—his name is an anagram of Milton Subotsky, the real producer of *The Monster Club*.

## *Escape from New York* (1981)

**Cast:** Kurt Russell (Snake Plissken), Lee Van Cleef (Hauk), Ernest Borgnine (Cabbie), Donald Pleasence (President), Isaac Hayes (The Duke), Harry Dean Stanton (Brian), Adrienne Barbeau (Maggie), Tom

Atkins (Rehme), Frank Doubleday (Romero). Directed by John Carpenter.

**Synopsis:** In 1997, due to an out of control crime rate in the United States, Manhattan Island has been transformed into a maximum security prison, and while en route to an important global summit, Air Force One is commandeered by hijackers and soon crashes in Manhattan. Police chief Hauk sends in his military team, only to discover that the President (Donald Pleasence) has been taken hostage which forces the team to withdraw over the risk that the President might be killed. Desperate to rescue the President and the important tape that he possesses for the global summit, Hauk strikes a deal with "Snake" Plissken, a lieutenant war hero whose about to be put away for robbing the Federal Reserve. Sent into Manhattan in a military glider, Snake is given less than twenty-four hours to rescue the President or an explosive charge embedded in his neck by the government will detonate. Once inside, Snake makes friends with Cabbie who then introduces him to Brain and his girl Maggie. Brain who works for the Duke, the dictator of the Manhattan Island prison, informs Snake that his boss has the President and plans on using him as a hostage to break out of Manhattan Island prison. Snake, Cabbie, Brain, and Maggie then work together to overcome the Duke's henchmen and free the President. But after attempting to escape from New York with the Duke in close pursuit, only Snake and the President make it alive to the wall that surrounds the entire prison. The Duke is shot dead and when the President shows a half-hearted thanks for those who died trying to rescue him, Snake slips him the wrong tape after the charges in his neck have been deactivated.

**Commentary:** Directed by genre master John Carpenter and considered as a cult classic and one of the best action films of the 1980s, *Escape from New York* is a combination of action, suspense, comedy, and political ideology. Reviews at the time were full of praise for its visionary style with one example declaring "It's a toughly told, very tall tale, one of the best escape (and escapist) movies of the season." [112] The main character is the anti-hero Snake Plissken, played by Kurt Russell in a breakout role from his days as a child actor for Disney. Carpenter previously worked with Russell in the TV biography of *Elvis* in which Russell portrays the legendary singer, but in *Escape from New York*,

Russell portrays a total nonconformist fighting the establishment at every turn. The Carpenter/Russell connection continued for two more films at which time Russell was considered as a bona fide Hollywood action star. Besides the look of the film, what really makes *Escape from New York* such a stand out production are the performances of Lee Van Cleef in his last great role, Ernest Borgnine as the comical cab driver, Harry Dean Stanton as the brilliant but devious Brain, and Adrienne Barbeau as Maggie who provides all of the beauty for such a dark and disturbing film.

Following his iconic role in *Halloween*, Pleasence's second film for Carpenter became another fan favorite, and through an unusual bit of casting, Pleasence plays the President of the United States. His British accent, however, is never explained but Pleasence excels as the top man that everyone wants. His first dignified appearance bidding farewell to his constituents before entering his emergency pod in the doomed plane, stands in harsh contrast to his tortured, excitable, and desperate attitude after being held prisoner by the Duke of New York. The President goes through a lot in the film like having his ring finger cut off, being regularly beaten, and continually mocked by being forced to wear a blonde wig. When Snake Plissken asks after bringing him to safety how he feels about the rest of his group dying to rescue him, the President provides a nonchalant thanks while checking his face in a mirror before appearing on TV, thus sealing his fate for the final embarrassment that Snake has in store for him.

# *Halloween II* (1981)

**Cast:** Jamie Lee Curtis (Laurie Strode), Donald Pleasence (Dr. Sam Loomis), Charles Cyphers (Sheriff Leight Brackett), Jeffrey Kramer (Graham), Lance Guest (Jimmy), Pamela Susan Shoop (Karen), Hunter con Leer (Gary Hunt), Dick Warlock (The Shape, Patrolman #3), Leo Rossi (Budd), Gloria Gifford (Mrs. Alves), Tawny Moyer (Jill), Ana Alicia (Janet), Ford Rainey (Dr. Mixter), Cliff Emmich (Mr. Garrett), Nancy Stephens (Marion), Nancy Kyes (Annie Brackett), Pamela Mc-Myler (Laurie's mother), Dennis Holahan (Laurie's father). Directed by Rick Rosenthal.

**Synopsis:** Laurie Strode has just survived a brutal attack by the knife-wielding Michael Myers. Dr. Loomis (Donald Pleasence) who saved Laurie by shooting Myers through a second floor window, rushes outside of the house, only to find that Myers has gotten up and disappeared. Later patrolling the streets in a police car, Loomis spots a man that looks like Myers aimlessly wandering through the streets. He runs after him with Sheriff Brackett in tow, but before they reach him, another police cruiser hits and pins him to a van, causing a huge explosion. While the police are content that they got their man, Loomis is not sure and still wants to continue the search. Meanwhile, Laurie is taken to Haddonfield Memorial Hospital for treatment of her wounds, where Jimmy, an EMT, develops a crush on her as he visits her in the hospital. While Laurie recovers in her room, Myers, who has managed to evade the neighborhood police, makes his way into the hospital and immediately begins to murder all of the hospital employees in his relentless pursuit of Laurie. Still on Myers' trail, Loomis discovers the Celtic term "Samhain" written by Myers in a schoolhouse and deduces that Myers is somehow tying the murders into part of a religious ritual of the dead. But Loomis' search ends when nurse Chambers arrives with a marshal to take him back to Smith's Grove, due to the hospital director's concerns that Loomis will further jeopardize their rehabilitation program. On the drive back to Smith's Grove, Chambers tells Loomis of a recently opened secret file on Myers which reveals that Laurie is his sister. Loomis quickly realizes the implications of this news and forces the marshal at gunpoint to drive back to the hospital, where Myers is now in hot pursuit of Laurie. They arrive just in time to prevent Myers from reaching Laurie in the parking lot. Myers then breaks into the hospital and corners Laurie and Loomis in the anesthesia room. Myers succeeds in stabbing Loomis before Laurie shoots him in the eyes, effectively blinding him. She then escapes as Loomis opens several valves, releasing pure oxygen into the room. With a flick of his lighter, Loomis turn the room into an inferno that quickly engulfs himself and Michael Myers.

**Commentary:** After the phenomenal success of John Carpenter's 1978 *Halloween*, it was only a matter of time before the appearance of a sequel. With *Halloween*, Carpenter effectively created the new "slasher film" genre which made it possible for the ongoing series *Friday* *the Thirteenth* in 1980 and the *A Nightmare on Elm Street* series that kicked off in 1984. Some notable differences in *Halloween II* was that Universal Pictures hopped on board to distribute the film, and Carpenter declined to direct (except for a few scenes) and instead gave the directing helm to newcomer Rick Rosenthal. *Halloween II* ingeniously takes place immediately after the first film, and is faster paced than the original with plenty of action. The addition of the empty hospital also provides a suitably creepy setting for Michael Myers to hide and kill at random without getting caught. Jamie Lee Curtis was by this time considered as a 'scream queen,' a title she would shed in later years after starring in a number of horror films, including Carpenter's *The Fog* (1980). Like any good sequel, *Halloween II* also reveals more on the background story, in this case, Michael Myers' connection to Laurie Strode and his never-ending pursuit.

Returning as Dr. Loomis, Pleasence is allowed to delve a bit more into his character. Already established was Loomis' desire to put Michael Myers away for good, but what the first film only hinted at is finally realized in the second—that Michael Myers is an unnatural force that can be stopped but not killed. The great opening scene highlights this when a neighbor complains of the noise being the death of the neighborhood; Loomis looks at the blood on his hands and counters, "You don't know what death is!" One continuing plot point is the police unfairly blaming Loomis for Myers' escape when in fact it was not his fault and had fought to keep Myers locked away for good. This sets Loomis up as the true hero of the series, especially when he sacrifices himself in the climax in order to stop Myers and save Laurie. But like all great heroes and villains, Pleasence did return for future sequels.

## *Race for the Yankee Zephyr* (1981)

**Cast:** Ken Wahl (Barney), Lesley Ann Warren (Sally), Donald Pleasence (Gilbert Carson), George Peppard (Theo Brown), Bruno Lawrence (Baker), Grant Tilly (Collector), Harry Rutherford-Jones (Harry). Directed by David Hemmings.

**Synopsis:** Gilbert "Gibbie" Carson (Donald Pleasence), a New Zealander who loves to drink, helps his friend Barney, a young helicopter pilot, to run a deer farm. One day while searching for deer, Gibbie gets dropped in the wilderness by accident and while wandering back home discovers the remains of a long lost World War II plane called the Yankee Zephyr. Inside the plane, Gibbie is delighted to find cases of liquor, along with military medals amid the crates. He brings the medals back home and pawns them off to a local collector who then calls his connections to sell the medals. This attracts the attention of wealthy treasure hunter Theo Brown and his henchmen. Excited that he received $75 apiece for the medals, Gibbie tells Barney who believes that his friend got ripped off. They return to the collector's store, only to be pursued by Brown's henchmen. Realizing that there is another party interested in the plane Gibbie found, Barney wants to get to the site first but his helicopter has broken down and is in need of serious repair. Gibbie then takes Barney to see his daughter Sally whose in charge of a trust that Gibbie's late wife left for him. Sally agrees to lend the money under duress, but before they can do anything, Brown arrives with his men demanding to know the location of the plane in order to retrieve 'confidential' information. Barney escapes with Gibbie and Sally in his faulty helicopter but not before one of Brown's men puts a tracer on the tail. Barney, Gibbie, and Sally eventually find the plane and discover why Brown wants it so badly—there are crates full of gold bullion onboard. Brown arrives with his men and chases them off but they accidentally destroy the floats attached to the plane and end up going down with the plane when it sinks. However, Barney and Sally are happy to be alive and become even happier when they realize that Gibbie is standing on an unopened crate of gold at the shoreline.

**Commentary:** *Race for the Yankee Zephyr*, a.k.a. *Treasure of the Yankee Zephyr*, is an enjoyable adventure film under the helm of actor David Hemmings during the directing phase of his career. It is unfortunate that Hemmings mostly stuck to directing television programs after *Race for the Yankee Zephyr* because he demonstrated great promise in his directing abilities. This film also benefits from its cast, resting heavily on Pleasence but also on George Peppard as the snooty martini-sipping businessman Theo Brown with his upper class accent, and relative newcomer Ken Wahl who gained fame later in his acting career in the television series *Wiseguy*. What really makes this film stand out though is the amazing aerial photography of New Zealand, big explosions, and spectacular stunt and action sequences, most notably a breathtaking helicopter chase and a boat chase. An unfortunate occurrence was the death of three of the jet boat drivers during filming to which *Race for the Yankee Zephyr* is dedicated.

Pleasence made quite a few films during his career in which he perfected portraying the happy drunk, among them *The Hallelujah Trial*, *Wake in Fright*, and his quite funny role in *Race for the Yankee Zephyr*. The scenes involving Gibbie in the local pub grossing out the patrons with his description of the native crocodile's eating habits and becoming a one-man wrecking crew when Barney arrives to fetch him, are classic. Gibbie is a happy-go-lucky chap who always seems to fall into good fortune, such as when Barney is forced to make a crash landing and Gibbie goes off to return the next morning with some friendly locals to help out. Also amusing is Gibbie leading Brown and his henchmen on a wild goose chase for the plane, set to the theme of *The Great Escape* that Pleasence had ironically also starred in.

# *Alone in the Dark* (1982)

**Cast:** Jack Palance (Frank Hawkes), Donald Pleasence (Dr. Leo Bain), Martin Landau (Byron "Preacher" Sutcliff), Dwight Schultz (Dr. Dan Potter), Erland van Lidth (Ronald "Fatty" Elster), Deborah Hedwall (Nell Potter), Lee Taylor-Allan (Toni Potter), Phillip Clark (Tom Smith/Skaggs), Elizabeth Ward (Lyla Potter), Annie Korzen (Marissa Hall). Directed by Jack Sholder.

**Synopsis:** Dr. Dan Potter has been hired to take over as the new psychiatrist at the Haven, a home for mental patients. There he meets Dr. Leo Bain (Donald Pleasence), the institution's director, who smokes a lot of herbs in his pipe and refers to the patients as his 'children' who are each on their own voyage. Potter is then introduced to the patients on the third floor—former veteran Frank Hawkes, Byron "Preacher" Sutcliff, Ronald "Fatty" Elster, and the mysterious Skaggs the "Bleeder," all murderous psychopaths under strict security lockdown. Hawkes believes that Potter has murdered their former psychiatrist Harry Burton and plans on killing them as well. In response, Hawkes, Sutcliff, Elster, and Skaggs hatch a plan to kill Potter as soon as they can and steal information on his address. At Potter's house, his wife Nell and daughter Lyla welcome Dan's visiting sister Toni who is recovering from her own mental problems. While the Potters talk and catch up with each other's lives, a massive blackout occurs, plunging everyone into darkness. Realizing that their chance has come, Hawkes, Sutcliff, and Elster kill the security guard and escape in a car while Skaggs runs off on his own. Believing that the blackout was caused by a local nuclear power plant, Toni drags Nell along to a protest where they get arrested, along with fellow activist Tom Smith. When the three return to the Potter house, they find that the police are there who tell them that one of the patients has encountered Lyla at home. In a panic, Potter asks Smith and Detective Burnett to stay for dinner hoping for protection in numbers. But Hawkes, Sutcliff, and Elster will not be scared away and as night approaches they begin to lay siege to the Potter house with deadly intent.

**Commentary:** *Alone in the Dark* is an underrated slasher film with a great veteran cast, made up of Pleasence, Jack Palance, and Martin Landau. All three ham it up and steal the scenes they appear in, thus creating much amusement for the viewer. One of Palance's most hilarious lines is when he introduces himself to Potter—"I'm here because I enjoy the social life. There are no crazy people; they are just on vacation." Reviewers were unusually kind to *Alone in the Dark*; one recognized this film as a commentary on the field of psychiatry—"The genre Mr. Sholder is sending up is more than ready for parody. *Alone in the Dark* is unobjectionable, even when it does not work, and certainly amusing when it does."[113] Coincidentally, newcomer Dwight Schultz as Dr. Potter would rise to fame in 1983 for providing his own take on a mentally disturbed character as "Howling Mad" Murdock in the popular TV series *The A-Team*. Another interesting aspect is the mystery killer known as the "Bleeder" whose face is never shown to the audience and is only described as a murderer who suffers from nosebleeds when dispatching his victims. *Alone in the Dark* also holds the distinction of being Jack Sholder's directorial debut and as the first feature film to be distributed by New Line Cinema.

As psychiatrist Dr. Leo Bain, Pleasence shines and is almost as bizarre as his own patients; in fact, this role makes his earlier take on the profession of psychiatry in *Watch Out, We're Mad!* look like a walk in the park and is also polar opposite to Dr. Loomis in Carpenter's *Hal-*

*loween*. Bain's nonchalant attitude concerning the dangerous nature of some of his patients horrifies Dr. Potter and the exchanges between them are often very comical. In one scene, Dr. Bain hands a book of matches to the "Preacher" who immediately sets his shirt on fire and starts swinging it around; Bain brings an end to this when he whispers to the "Preacher" that he will castrate him if he does not stop. This must have been an ongoing threat because the film's prologue shows the "Preacher" dreaming about going to Mom's diner where he encounters Bain as a mad meat cleaver-wielding chef who does indeed castrate him. Dr. Bain also tends to over-analyze everyone and makes excuses for his murderous patients to a fault that comes back to haunt him when he pays a visit to the Potter house.

# *Warrior of the Lost World* (1983)

**Cast:** Robert Ginty (The Rider), Persis Khambatta (Nastasia), Donald Pleasence (Prossor), Fred Williamson (Henchman), Harrison Muller Sr. (McWayne), Philip Dallas (Elder), Laura Nucci (Elder), Vinicio Ricchi (Elder). Directed by David Worth.

**Synopsis:** In a post-apocalyptic world, nations and governments have collapsed and law and order is maintained by an army known as the Omega under the control of the dictator Prossor (Donald Pleasence). His main opposition are the Outsiders who seek to create the New Way which will unite all the people under a fair and peaceful government system. Into this battle comes the Rider, a lone stranger on his supersonic talking motorcycle called Einstein. After being chased by the Omega and crashing, the Rider is healed by the secret Elders who advise the Outsiders. Seen as the "chosen one" that will defeat Prossor, the Rider is sent with Outsider Nastasia to rescue her father McWayne, an important scientist. After sneaking into the Congress of Omega, the Rider and Nastasia rescue her father from execution, but Nastasia ends up being captured during the escape. McWayne then takes the Rider into the wastelands where, after a test in battle, the Rider assumes his role as the "chosen one" and unites the different factions of warriors into an army which he leads back to the Congress of Omega to save Nastasia and defeat Prossor. After battling the entire Omega battalion and defeating their mega-weapon, the Rider and

McWayne confront Prossor in his war room. Prossor then reveals he has Nastasia under his mind control and orders her to fire on command, but after grazing the Rider, she overcomes the link and shoots Prossor dead. The Rider, Nastasia, and McWayne return to the Outsiders compound as heroes, yet the apparent defection of one of their most trusted members and Prossor's secret reveals that the war is not over.

**Commentary:** *Warrior of the Lost World* often gets picked on by its critics for its very low budget which might explain why it was parodied on *Mystery Science Theatre 3000*. Essentially a take-off on *The Road Warrior* with bits and pieces mixed in from the television series *Knight Rider*, *Warrior of the Lost World*, although creatively put together, is filled with car and helicopter chases and mandatory huge explosions. The post-apocalyptic, dystopic story is well suited for its particular genre, but because of its minuscule budget, the costumes are less than stellar, and the talking supersonic motorcycle is somewhat over the top. Still, *Warrior of the Lost World* does not take itself too seriously which makes it acceptable viewing for a low-grade apocalyptic tale.

Pleasence portrays the dictator Prossor, based somewhat loosely on his infamous Blofeld character from the Bond thriller *You Only Live Twice*. His voice is heard over loudspeakers before he is even shown in the film as a way of directing the people under his control to unconditionally obey him. When Prossor does appear, he nurses a disabled hand while directing his Omega militia to carry out his every whim; the conclusion also provides Pleasence with the opportunity to present a neat twist to the story. Over the course of his acting career, Pleasence played this type of megalomaniac character numerous times and this time as Prossor, he proves that you might not want to cross any of them or else face certain death.

# *The Devonsville Terror* (1983)

**Cast:** Suzanna Love (Jenny Scanlon), Robert Walker Jr. (Matthew Pendleton), Donald Pleasence (Dr. Warley), Paul Willson (Walter Gibbs), Mary Walden (Chris), Deanna Haas (Monica), Wally Flaherty (Priest). Produced and directed by Ulli Lommel.

**Synopsis:** In 1683 in the town of Devonsville, the townspeople hunt down and condemn three women to death as witches. One of the accused witches curses the townspeople as she is burned as the stake. Three hundred years later, Devonsville is still a simple backcountry town, but Walter Gibbs, a convenience store owner, tires of his ailing wife and smothers her to death. He then believes that he sees the ghost of the witch. Shortly after, three new women come to Devonsville—Chris, an environmentalist, Monica, a radio host, and Jenny Scanlon, the new schoolteacher. Jenny is romantically pursued by Gibbs and Ralph Pendleton, another local, but after she politely rejects them, they quickly view her with contempt. Jenny also meets Matthew Pendleton who urges her to leave the town as some people are starting to believe that the three new women are reincarnations of the original three witches killed in 1683. Troubled by haunting nightmares, Jenny goes to Dr. Warley (Donald Pleasence) who places her under hypnosis to delve into her past life. Ironically, the executioner during the Devonsville inquisition was Warley's ancestor, so Warley fittingly wishes to lift the curse from his family and from himself. When Jenny states under hypnosis that she is on a mission, Warley understands the significance and encourages her to continue. Convinced that murdering his wife opened the door for the witches' return, Walter convinces Ralph that something must be done before it is too late. Ralph and his friend proceed to kidnap and murder Chris and Monica. They then grab Jenny and tie her to a stake to burn, but before they can, lighting flashes in the sky, and Jenny, possessed by the witch, uses her powers to destroy Walter and Ralph.

**Commentary:** As the director of *The Devonsville Terror*, German actor Ulli Lommel was responsible for a huge output of films with his best-known most likely being *The Boogeyman* (1980) which made huge profits and boasted a neat supernatural slasher plot. Three years later, Lommel filmed his witch opus which starred his then wife Suzanna Love who also appeared in *The Boogeyman*. The resulting film overflows with dreary atmospherics and offers genuine suspense, along with some creative ways to die. Love plays the innocent-looking heroine avenger well as does Paul Willson as the slimy and murderous Walter Gibbs.

Pleasence appears as Dr. Warley, the Devonsville physician whose family is cursed with the bizarre disease of being eaten by worms. Warley is also affected by this curse and the film features some unsettling scenes of him picking worms out of his skin. As a result, he is determined to end the curse by setting things right. His office is also a showcase for his collection of Devonsville inquisition artifacts, prime source material for his studies on the history of the event. Warley is also part hypnotist that helps immensely in getting the townspeople to reveal what their ancestors did in 1683. Although featured in a small role and with scenes restricted to his doctor's office, Pleasence nonetheless provides an interesting character study.

## *Frankenstein's Great Aunt Tillie* (1984)

**Cast:** Donald Pleasence (Victor Frankenstein/Old Baron Frankenstein), Yvonne Furneaux (Matilda "Tillie" Frankenstein), June Wilkinson (Randy), Aldo Ray (Burgermeister), Zsa Zsa Gabor (Clara). Produced and directed by Myron J. Gold.

**Synopsis:** In the town of Mucklefugger, Transylvania, the town elders decide to claim the Frankenstein castle because the family has abandoned it and owes a large amount of unpaid taxes. But their plan is thrown into disarray when Victor Frankenstein (Donald Pleasence), the grandson of the original Frankenstein who created a monster, arrives back at the castle with his wife Randy and his great aunt Tillie. Their arrival creates a huge upheaval because aunt Tillie is a feminist who rallies all of the women to stand up for their rights and Victor finds his grandfather's original monster that he revives with the help of his wife. All in vain, the burgermeister attempts to stop the antics of the Frankensteins; he fails miserably and all-out chaos ensues.

**Commentary:** All around, *Frankenstein's Great Aunt Tillie* is a very embarrassing production. The film's plot is utter nonsense, the acting is horrendous, and it seems to go on forever. It is billed as a comedy but there is nothing really to laugh about unless you consider women spraying the police with seltzer water amusing. In fact, this film is just really bad. The monster is a bizarre sight, appearing as a type of blue Neanderthal. Among the recognizable cast members are Yvonne Furneaux who appeared in the Hammer version of *The Mummy*, June Wilkinson, Aldo Ray who plays the burgermeister seriously, and Zsa

Zsa Gabor. Pleasence actually plays a dual role as Victor Frankenstein and his grandfather in flashback sequences; both are a complete waste and Pleasence wears the worst hairpiece in his career. In one bizarre scene, Pleasence is shown wearing a dress while playing a flute to try and calm the monster. *Frankenstein's Great Aunt Tillie* actually makes *The Pumaman* look good. Therefore, avoid it at all costs.

## *The Ambassador* (1984)

**Cast:** Robert Mitchum (Peter Hacker), Ellen Burstyn (Alex Hacker), Rock Hudson (Frank Stevenson), Fabio Testi (Mustapha Hashimi), Donald Pleasence (Minister Eretz), Chelli Goldenberg (Rachel), Michal Bat-Adam (Tova), Ori Levy (Abe), Uri Gavriel (Assad), Zachi Nov (Ze'ev). Directed by J. Lee Thompson.

**Synopsis:** Peter Hacker, the American ambassador to Israel, is desperately trying to negotiate peace talks between the Israelis and the Palestinians. However, the Israelis and the PLO seem more determined to fight, especially after a PLO splinter group called Saika attacks both sides to make certain that the peace talks are impossible. To complicate matters, Hacker's wife Alex has been carrying on an affair with PLO leader Mustapha Hashimi. Their clandestine meeting is captured on film in Hashimi's apartment and Hacker is later contacted by a blackmailer demanding $1,000,000 or he will play the tape on television. Hacker refuses to pay the blackmailer but is told he will want to, due to it being Hashimi. Not knowing who Hashimi is, Hacker goes to Minister Eretz (Donald Pleasence) who informs him of Hashimi's PLO status. Racing against time, Hacker has Frank Stevenson, his chief security officer, try and track down the holder of the tape, and by using detective work, promises, and violence, Stevenson brings in the blackmailers but along the way discovers a more dangerous agenda—that the print is held by a KGB agent known as Stone who is looking to assassinate Hacker. Sensing an opportunity in the situation, Hacker patches things up with his wife and contacts Hashimi to arrange a meeting between Israeli and Palestinian students for peace talks. Hashimi agrees and they all meet, but Eretz learns that Saika is aware of the meeting, resulting in a bloodbath for both sides when they are ambushed before the arrival of the Israeli army. Hacker survives the attack and returns home to his wife. Stone lies in wait with a rifle but is spotted first and killed by Stevenson who recovers the tape. Hacker becomes depressed with all of the violence until a large gathering of students arrives at his house chanting for peace.

**Commentary:** *The Ambassador* is a well made action film by the team of Yoram Globus and Menahem Golan, responsible for a whole slew of 1980s genre films, including the *Death Wish* franchise with Charles Bronson. Unlike many of their other films, *The Ambassador* had a bigger budget and big stars to match with Hollywood bad boy Robert Mitchum as the title character and Rock Hudson in his last film role as Hacker's right hand man. Mitchum and Hudson provide ample assistance in conveying the chaos going on around them, but Hudson definitely looks ill throughout the film. While Mitchum seems a bit naïve in his quest for peace, he makes his character quite believable and realistic as well as the relationship between himself and his wife. The plot of this film is actually quite relevant today, due to the ongoing conflict between Israel and the Palestinians which appears to have no end in sight.

Along with *The Ambassador*, Pleasence appeared in one other production for Globus/Golan—*Hanna's War*—which also featured Ellen Burstyn acting alongside Pleasence. In *The Ambassador*, Pleasence portrays Eretz, the Israeli minister of defense, who clearly understands the dangers related to attempting to negotiate peace which he believes will never happen. The role of Eretz is a prime example of the "man in power" which Pleasence was often called upon to play during his acting career. Wanting assistance from Israeli's U.S. ally, Eretz goes to great lengths to try and defend Hacker. In one memorable scene, when Eretz discovers that his team is responsible for capturing the illicit video of the affair between Hashimi and Hacker's wife, he immediately gets into an argument about the dangers of the video and then brings everything to a boil when he screams "It is not your business to embarrass our government!"

# *Where is Parsifal?* (1984)

**Cast:** Tony Curtis (Parsifal Katzenellenbogen), Berta Dominguez D. (Elba), Erik Estrada (Henry Board II), Peter Lawford (Montague Chippendale), Ron Moody (Beersbohm), Donald Pleasence (Mackintosh),

Orson Welles (Klingsor), Christopher Chaplin (Ivan), Nancy Roberts (Ruth), Arthur Beatty (Jasper). Directed by Henri Helman.

**Synopsis:** Parsifal Katzenellenbogen is a businessman who lives in a large mansion with his artsy wife Elba and son Ivan, but because they have little money, they take in a host of oddball tenants. Parsifal's latest business scheme is a machine that he bought from an inventor that writes messages in the sky that he hopes to sell for millions to the right buyer. But there are a number of obstacles in Parsifal's way, such as Elba's outcast demeanor, a preaching Buddhist named Jasper, and a Scottish loan shark named Mackintosh (Donald Pleasence) who shows up wanting his money. After repeated attempts to sell his machine, Parsifal finally gets an interested buyer named Henry Board II who agrees to come for dinner with Montague Chippendale, his actor/spokesman for his weight loss product. However, the dinner does not go as planned when Elba's friend Morjack the magician does a disappearing act with Chippendale who disappears only to have Mackintosh appear in his place and start grabbing all of Parsifal's belongings as payment for the money owed to him. Mr. Board leaves quickly but gets interested in the machine again with a mysterious prospect named Klingsor who calls up and wants to see a demonstration of the machine. With the two bidders and the surrounding public in attendance, Parsifal has the skywriting machine set to display when Elba secretly takes control of the machine and puts in her own message about mastering fate through love. Both Klingsor and Henry are enticed by this and get in a bidding war negotiated by Mackintosh that results in a very happy Parsifal receiving five million dollars.

**Commentary:** *Where is Parsifal?* is an enigma in Pleasence's film career and is notable for being Peter Lawford's very last film and one of Orson Welles' last films as well, though the production appears to never have gotten a proper release and it was in fact thought to be a lost film for a period of time. *Where is Parsifal* appears to have been a vanity project written by Berta Dominguez D. who also stars in this film produced by her husband Alexander Salkind who went on to produce the 1978 blockbuster *Superman* with Christopher Reeve. Her artistic character is loosely based on her real life as an artist who knew Salvador Dali and Pablo Picasso, but other than the life imitates art angle and the inclusion of some well-known actors, the storyline is very weak and at times nonsensical. The best parts of this film involves Ron Moody as the German tenant Beersbohm who manages to steal all of his scenes by utilizing both physical comedy and a flair for the dramatic.

Pleasence portrays Macintosh, a rough and tough Scottish loan shark determined to get his money back from the crackpot Parsifal, and compared to other characters in this film, Pleasence's role is more thought out with a clear goal. Macintosh only appears a few times but allows Pleasence to display a Scottish accent and wear a kilt. His best scene has him popping out of a coffin during a magic act in the middle of dinner and immediately confiscating all of the silverware as payment for Parsifal's debt. But in the end, Parsifal settles his account with Macintosh by letting him serve as the negotiator for the bidding war for a "small" percentage.

# *A Breed Apart* (1984)

**Cast:** Rutger Hauer (Jim Malden), Powers Boothe (Mike Walker), Kathleen Turner (Stella Clayton), Donald Pleasence (J.P. Whittier), Brion James (Huey Peyton), John Dennis Johnston (Miller), Jayne Bentzen (Amy Rollings), Andy Fenwick (Adam Clayton), Dustin Lecate (himself). Directed by Philippe Mora.

**Synopsis:** As a resident of Cherokee Island, Vietnam veteran and eccentric outdoorsman Jim Malden survives off the land and cares for a number of wild animals that reside on the island. Malden makes the occasional trip to the local general store, where he has struck up a casual relationship with proprietor Stella Clayton and her young son Adam. Aware of Malden's island and its rare bird population is millionaire egg collector J.P. Whittier (Donald Pleasence) who hires out mountain climber Mike Walker to steal the eggs from a rare new breed of bald eagle for $200,000. Walker manages to befriend Stella and through her, he gains the trust of Malden who lets him stay on his island believing that Walker is a photographer. Malden, who has a difficult time conveying his interests in Stella because of his past, is jealous of Walker. Complicating matters is that a group of local redneck hunters continually try to hunt animals on Malden's island, prompting him to fight back and raise the stakes. Walker aids Malden in driving the hunters off his island, but the death of one of them draws in the local media, making it more difficult to get to the eggs. Knowing that Malden wants to start a relationship with Stella and her son, Walter encourages him to do so which gives him time alone to scale the base towards the eagle's nest, but after reaching the nest, Walter has second thoughts and decides not to steal the eggs. Instead, he sells the story of J.P. Whittier's illegal collection to the media while Malden enjoys time with Stella and Adam.

**Commentary:** *A Breed Apart* is an average adventure film starring cult favorite Rutger Hauer, looking exactly as his replicant character from the science fiction classic *Blade Runner* (1982). Also carrying over his replicant role from *Blade Runner* is Brion James as a redneck with a mean streak. *A Breed Apart* contains some disturbing images of shot birds, but also some wonderful aerial photography of bald eagles. But the main issue with this film is the lack of background material on Malden, due to hearing the sounds of helicopters and gunfire being replayed in his head which is not explained until the conclusion when a reporter reveals Malden's military background and the fate of his former family. The reason for this is quite simple—one of the original film reels was lost after completion, thus forcing the editor to piece it together with chunks of story missing.

Although integral to the plot, Pleasence only has a small role as a type of demented Daddy Warbucks and looking like him with a clean-shaven head. His character of J.P. Whittier is the real villain in this film because he does not stray from his expensive and illegal demands. Walker, who is also supposed to be somewhat villainous, appears as anything but and by the conclusion seems more like a hero; also, Malden, supposedly the film's hero, commits some violent acts of vigilante justice which seems to taint him a bit. Unfortunately, Pleasence's role in *A Breed Apart* is forgettable as part of a film plagued with issues.

# *Phenomena* (1985)

**Cast:** Jennifer Connelly (Jennifer Corvino), Donald Pleasence (Professor John McGregor), Daria Nicolodi (Frau Bruckner), Dalila Di Lazzaro (Headmistress), Patrick Bauchau (Inspector Rudolf Geiger), Fiore

Argento (Vera Brandt), Federica Mastroianni (Sophie). Produced and directed by Dario Argento.

**Synopsis:** John McGregor (Donald Pleasence), a professor of entomology or the study of insects, assists the police when they find a head of a missing tourist. Confined to a wheelchair and assisted by a chimpanzee named Inga, McGregor arrives at an approximate date for the murder of the Danish tourist. Meanwhile, Jennifer Corvino, the daughter of a famous actor, arrives in Switzerland to attend the prestigious Richard Wagner International School for Girls. Because Jennifer experiences episodes of sleepwalking and possesses the uncanny ability to communicate with insects, she quickly finds herself an outcast among her fellow students. One night, Jennifer's sleepwalking takes her out on the road, where she is struck by a car before being rescued by Inga in the woods and brought back to meet McGregor. Jennifer quickly makes friends with McGregor who is amazed by her ability to influence insects. Back at the school, Jennifer's roommate Sophia goes out to meet her boyfriend one night and is murdered by the maniac. Jennifer hears Sophia's screams and runs outside, only finds the killer's black glove with maggots in it. McGregor, wanting to find the maniac killer, gives Jennifer a sarcophagus fly that leads her to the site of one of the murders, but she is scared off by a real estate agent. The killer then tracks down McGregor and stabs him to death while Inga escapes and finds a straight razor in a garbage bin. With no one left to help her, Jennifer calls her father's lawyer for help who in turn contacts the school chaperone Frau Bruckner. Jennifer agrees to stay at Bruckner's house overnight and to be taken to the airport the next day. However, when Jennifer discovers maggots in the bathroom, Bruckner knocks her out and locks her in the house with her son, a mutated maniac with a hunger for decaying flesh. The son then chases Jennifer out of the house and onto a boat and attempts to kill her, but her screams for help draws a swarm of insects that attacks and kills him. Bruckner then tries to kill Jennifer to avenge her son's death but Inga kills her with the straight razor.

**Commentary:** Dario Argento, director, writer, and producer of *Phenomena* (presented in a cut version as *Creepers* in the US market), is widely hailed as one of the masters of Italian giallo films. Of his many films, *Phenomena* ranks among his best, along with *Deep Red* and *Sus-*

*piria. Phenomena* was also close to Agento's heart, due to the story of Jennifer Corvino's mother leaving the family one Christmas which actually happened to the director as a young boy. Like most of Argento's work, *Phenomena* features a mysterious killer on the loose, pretty young girls being horribly murdered, and the forces of the supernatural at work. *Phenomena* incorporates all of these features and does it with style; it also features the music of Agent's traditionally favorite band Goblin with that of some heavy metal groups like Iron Maiden and Motorhead. A big part of the success of this film is due to its young American star Jennifer Connelly (in only her second film role) who would go on to appear in many big Hollywood films. As Jennifer Corvino, Connelly creates an interesting and sympathetic character that truly helps to drive all of the suspense.

During his career, Pleasence starred in a number of Italian giallo films and *Phenomena* is his best. Much like his character in *Ground Zero*, Pleasence is confined to a wheelchair but manages to create a fascinating character whose knowledge on insects serves as the connecting link between the young heroine and the killer. There is also an angle of McGregor's former assistant Rita who apparently was also a victim of the killer that drives his determination to help the police solve the case and end the murders. An interesting aspect of *Phenomena* is the relationship between Pleasence's character and Inga the chimpanzee whose actual name was Tanga. Compared to other films that feature a human interacting with a chimpanzee, Inga does a convincing job expressing concern for McGregor and later the need for revenge over his murder. In typical fashion, Argento "borrowed" the idea of Inga the chimpanzee attacking and killing with a straight razor from Edgar Allan Poe's *Murders in the Rue Morgue* that features a razor-wielding orangutan.

# *Treasure of the Amazon* (1985)

**Cast:** Stuart Whitman (Gringo), Donald Pleasence (Klaus von Blantz), Bradford Dillman (Clark), Sonia Infante (Morimba), John Ireland (Priest), Emilio Fernandez (Tacho), Pedro Armendariz (Zapata), Jorge Luke (Jairo), Ann Sidney (Barbara), Clark Jarrett (Dick), Hugo Stiglitz (Riverboat Captain). Produced and directed by Rene Cardona, Jr.

**Synopsis:** In the 1950s, a tale is told of a legendary river of diamonds hidden deep in the Amazon rain forest. The lure of instant riches draws many adventurers to the Amazon, where they must face Tacho, an Indian who runs the local government with an iron first, and even worse, the Hibero, a tribe of natives with a penchant for collecting and shrinking the heads of their victims. Two new adventurers, Zapata and Jairo, ride a riverboat down the Amazon and soon meet Gringo, a grizzled expert on the Amazon and a member of a previously failed journey. They hire him as their guide and set off through the thick of the jungle. Competing against the trio are Barbara, Dick, and Clark who works for an oil company, and Klaus von Blantz (Donald Pleasence), a former Nazi officer with dreams of reviving Hitler's Third Reich. Barbara and Dick are the first to accidentally find the diamonds in the river, forcing Clark to take off in his plane to obtain more equipment. However, they are soon under attack by the Hibero with Dick left defenseless as Barbara runs for help and meets up with Zapata, Jairo, and Gringo. She then leads them to the river and upon seeing the diamonds in the river, greed and jealousy soon takes over the group and they split apart. Blantz, along with his Indian guide Morimba, also arrive to find the riches and encounter the deadly Hibero. After much violence in the Amazon jungle, Blantz makes it out alive only to be captured by Tacho and tortured to death for lying about his loot. Gringo and Barbara also make it out, and after telling the truth and handing over half their riches, Tacho allows them to leave the Amazon alive.

**Commentary:** *Treasure of the Amazon*, a low-budget imitation of the popular *Raiders of the Lost Ark* (1981), is not ashamed to throw every cliché in the book at the viewer. In this film, the adventurers face all sorts of trouble in the jungle, including headhunters, piranha, killer bees, and leeches. From the opening moments of a native on the riverboat getting his finger chopped off for attempting to steal to going overboard to be eaten by alligators, the audience knows they are in for a trashy film. However, *Treasure of the Amazon* is actually quite enjoyable, mostly due to its roster of veteran actors like Pleasence, Stuart Whitman, Bradford Dillman, and John Ireland. Another benefit is the direction of Rene Cardona Jr. who captures some impressive scenes of the Amazon landscape. The film also deserves its "R" rating for some quite brutal scenes of decapitation, topless native women, and a rather nasty death by crabs.

As former Nazi Klaus von Blantz, Donald Pleasence goes overboard with his deranged character. Blantz's background is somewhat fleshed out as having run a concentration camp during World War II and having made deals with Tacho who gave him Morimba, one of his topless wives, to act as his jungle guide. Although Blantz does not share many scenes with the rest of the characters, he is a major character in the film and his battles with the Hibero are well done. Spouting a German accent, Plcasence also provides some crazy dialogue, such as when he tries to convince Morimba to join his new Third Reich—"You could be part of that world. You are intelligent, like a Doberman." Blantz is also the most vicious of all the characters, such as when he mows down the natives with his machine gun and betrays Morimba. In the end, Blantz's crimes and final lies to Tacho earns him a well-deserved death.

## *Nothing Underneath* (1985)

**Cast:** Tom Schanley (Bob Crane), Renee Simonsen (Barbara), Donald Pleasence (Commissioner Danesi), Nicola Perring (Jessica Crane), Maria McDonald (Margaux Wilson), Catherine Noyes (Carrie Blynn), Cyrus Elias (Danesi's assistant), Anna Galiena (Diana), Bruce McGuire (Interpol Agent). Directed by Carlo Vanzina.

**Synopsis:** Bob Crane is a forest ranger working in Yellowstone National Park in Wyoming, and his twin sister Jessica is a runway model working in Milan, Italy. One day, Bob has a powerful premonition that his sister has come into great harm. A call to her hotel does not provide any answers, so Bob travels to Milan to investigate. After realizing that his sister is missing, Bob goes to Commissioner Danesi (Donald Pleasence) and pleads for him to open a case on his sister. But Danesi is skeptical about Bob's claim of empathetic communication with his sister and without concrete evidence, he is unable to do much to help. Bob then goes off on his own to try and find his sister. His travels put him in touch with another model named Carrie who seems to know something about what has been going on. However, the next night she is found murdered in her hotel room. Now satisfied that he can open the case with a body, Danesi contacts Bob and together they try to figure out who is responsible for Carrie's murder of Carrie and the disappearance of Jessica. Bob then receives a letter from his sister indicating that she has run off. Settling on the fact that his sister simply ran away, Bob decides to head back to Wyoming. However, Bob again feels a strong premonition and travels to an old apartment building. Upon sneaking inside, he finds Jessica's body nailed into a chair. Then, while hiding in a closet, Bob discovers that his sister's killer is Barbara, another model who was in love with Jessica. Barbara spots Bob and attacks him with a power drill before Danesi and his men break into the apartment and save him. In a fit of madness, Barbara grabs Jessica's corpse and jumps out of a window to her death.

**Commentary:** *Nothing Underneath* is an Italian giallo somewhat similar to the superior *Phenomena* in which Pleasence also appeared in 1985. By definition, Italian giallo films are crime and mystery stories with elaborate murder plots and were very popular in Italy. Thus, *Nothing Underneath* fits rather neatly into this sub-genre with telepathic links thrown in for good measure. Wielding a sharp pair of scissors, the killer is difficult to identify, thanks to all of the twists and turns in the storyline. The setting in the world of fashion also provides a seemingly never-ending parade of beautiful women, some of whom appear sans clothes so as to hold the viewer's interest. The title of this film refers to an explanation given to Bob by a photographer when asked to explain his sister's daily habits. The photographer states that he only knows the models for their skin deep beauty, and knows nothing underneath about their lives.

Pleasence plays Commissioner Danesi, a man preparing to retire in two weeks time and who takes Jessica's case as his very last one. While Bob's claim of a telepathic link to his sister would send most police running the other way, Danesi does not totally rule it out and even does research into the subject when another model turns up dead. He clearly is a man tired of dealing with murder. A great example occurs in a restaurant, where Danesi tells Bob, "You know, I've never much cared for sauces the color of blood." But Danesi is not one to fade away, for he doggedly pursues his last case as if it were his first. Running down his leads and having Bob followed when answers do not come fast enough are all part of his style. It is also interesting to see Pleasence attempt an Italian accent in this otherwise average giallo thriller.

# *Cobra Mission* (1986)

**Cast:** Oliver Tobias (Richard Wagner), Christopher Connelly (Roger Carson), Manfred Lehmann (Mark Adams), John Steiner (James Walcott), Ethan Wayne (Mike), Donald Pleasence (Father Lenoir), Gordon Mitchell (Colonel Mortimer). Produced and directed by Fabrizio de Angelis.

**Synopsis:** In a discussion with his fellow war buddies James and Mark, Vietnam veteran Roger Carson realizes that society does not care about their sacrifices made during the war. They then pay a visit to Major Morris, their former commander, who reveals that he was forced to retire, due to having sensitive information on American prisoners of war still being held in Vietnam. Upon deciding that something needs to be done, the trio locates Richard, another former soldier from their platoon, who is now in a mental hospital. After traveling to Vietnam, they come across Father Lenoir (Donald Pleasence), a French priest who provides them with weapons for their mission as well as a map to the area beyond the border under Vietcong control. Coming across one of the camps, Richard recognizes a soldier who tortured him during the war and shoots him which starts a violent firefight. The vets gain control of the camp and free a group of POWs whom they help to escape in a truck. However, after regrouping to rest, Mark ends up killed by a Vietnamese woman and the Vietcong army pursues and surrounds them. They are spared when Colonel Mortimer from the U.S. shows up in a helicopter to take them away, but they must leave the surviving POWs behind. Mortimer explains that the U.S. is aware of the POWs but in an agreement with the Vietcong, they must remain, as many are considered as war criminals. Roger, James, and Richard bitterly return home, only to realize one more act of betrayal by their government.

**Commentary:** *Cobra Mission*, a.k.a. *Operation Nam*, is one of many 1980s action films that delved into the travesty of American prisoners of war left behind in Vietnam. Writer/director Fabrizio de Angelis, best known for his numerous action and genre-based films, does provide many action scenes and explosions in *Cobra Mission*; however, two particulars set it apart from similar films. One is the inclusion of Ethan Wayne, son of the legendary John Wayne, as Mike, a fellow prisoner of war who gives his character a sympathetic background set against the horrors going on around him. The other is the downbeat ending with not only the mission failing but the "heroes" being targeted by their own government for their efforts to right a wrong. But unfortunately, due to its low budget and bad timing by the producers, *Cobra Mission* would play second fiddle behind another Vietnam inspired film released the same year—director Oliver Stone's *Platoon*

Donald Pleasence plays Father Lenoir, a French priest with a church stuck in the middle of the Vietnamese jungle, but along with preaching the word of God, Father Lenoir uses his spare time to amass enough weapons in his basement to fully stock a small army or in this instance four Vietnam veterans hell-bent on rescuing American prisoners of war. His philosophy on the POWs is that they have given up and abandoned God; thus, God has abandoned them, but he believes they can still be saved by the four American soldiers if they are successful in their mission and so he sends them on their way with a stockpile of weapons and a kind blessing.

## *Animali Metropolitani* (1987)

**Cast:** Donald Pleasence (Professor Livingstone), Ninetto Davoli (Scorcelletti), Maurizio Micheli (Coniglio), Leo Gullotta (Don Michele). Directed by Stefano Vanzina.

**Synopsis:** In the year 2030, two university professors at a conference on evolution propose that man will de-evolve back to the apes and to test their theory, they produce a documentary project called *Animals Metropolitan*, set in Rome during the twentieth century.

**Commentary:** This is a wacky Italian comedy that does not make much sense. Pleasence portrays Professor Livingstone who has set out to prove that man is actually devolving back to his ape ancestors. There are numerous women stripping down to lingerie and lots of crazy-eyed guys chasing them which is typical of this type of Italian low-budget fare. The plot manages to include a bunch of 1980s punk rockers and some gun-toting grannies for good measure. In one odd scene, while chatting with his colleagues at an outside restaurant table, Livingstone carefully and methodically examines each piece of pasta with a magnifying glass. Turns out he was wise to do so because when the group decides to take a look at what is going on in the restaurant's kitchen, they find the chefs putting some nasty surprises in the cooking pasta. In addition, Pleasence is dubbed by an Italian actor. A rather bizarre film, *Animali Metropolitani* can definitely be skipped by all Pleasence fans.

# *Warrior Queen* (1987)

**Cast:** Sybil Danning (Berenice), Donald Pleasence (Clodius), Rick Hill (Marcus), Josephine Jacqueline Jones (Chloe), Tally Chanel (Vespa), Samantha Fox (Philomena), Suzanna Smith (Veneria), David Brandon (Victo), Mario Cruciani (Roberto), Marco Tulio Cau (Goliath). Directed by Chuck Vincent.

**Synopsis:** In 79 AD in the Roman city of Pompeii, society has become depraved and wretched for its unfortunate villagers. Local men and women are kidnapped by traders and sold in the market for use as sex slaves. Chloe, a young beautiful blonde girl, is sold to Victo, a heartless noble who runs a brothel called the House of Venus. Visiting Pompeii is Empress Berenice who is not amused at the decadence occurring in the province. Berenice, along with famed gladiator Marcus, are the invited guests of Clodius (Donald Pleasence) who revels in debauchery as entertainment. Marcus is one of the main attractions who will be fighting in Clodius' arena during the gladiator games. His main competitor is Goliath, just as cruel as Victo, his friend and supporter. During the games, Marcus wins the affection of Chloe that enrages Goliath who wants her for himself. While on a romantic interlude, Goliath and his henchmen ambush Marcus to steal Chloe, but Berenice arrives and thwarts their plans. Already giving indications of its restlessness, Mount Vesuvius finally erupts and destroys Clodius' arena along with the city of Pompeii. After escaping with Marcus and Berenice, Chloe finds herself finally free.

**Commentary:** The success of *Conan the Barbarian* in 1982 kickstarted an entire slew of imitations throughout the 1980s; a few of them were good, but were mostly less than mediocre. *Warrior Queen* is unfortunately one of the latter—an embarrassingly awful, low-budget costume drama with plenty of naked women in an attempt to hold the viewers' interest. Produced by schlockers Harry Alan Towers whom Pleasence would appear for in a number of films, and Joe D'Amato, *Warrior Queen* was basically cut and pasted by Towers and D'Amato and is clearly a rip-off of 1985's *Barbarian Queen*; Rick Hill, who plays the hero Marcus, was also the hero of the similarly themed 1983 film *Deathstalker*. The heroine is played by cult favorite Sybil Danning who is not given the opportunity to do much except appear bored and show up every now and then to spoil the villains' plans. An interesting note is that the footage of an erupting Mount Vesuvius was taken directly from the 1959 film *The Last Days of Pompeii*. This film wholeheartedly embraces its cheesiness with a giant phallic symbol in the brothel and a multitude of ways to dispatch the unfortunate or fortunate depending on how one looks at it, including a most amusing scene involving deadly Frisbees.

Pleasence, who once admitted that later in his career he took jobs to simply pay the bills, would probably be the first to admit that *Warrior Queen* is a bad film. At least Pleasence seems to be having a bit of fun as Clodius, a clone of real-life Emperor Nero trying unsuccessfully to impress Berenice with various violent amusements while at the same time berating his cheating wife Philomena. It certainly is a sight to see Pleasence wearing an imperial breastplate, a red cloak, and a gold laurel wreath adorning his head as he catches doves with a net to amuse his honored guest. Clodius is last seen attempting to prevent the residents of Pompeii from fleeing from their burning city; he meets his demise by being run down and dragged through the streets by a horse-drawn chariot, a fitting punishment for appearing in this awful film.

## *Specters* (1987)

**Cast:** John Pepper (Marcus), Trine Michelsen (Alice), Donald Pleasence (Professor Lasky), Massimo De Rossi (Matteo), Riccardo De Torrebruna (Andrea), Lavinia Grizi (Barbara), Riccardo Parisio Perrotti (Gaspare), Laurentina Guidoitti (Maria), Erna Schurer (Catacomb guide). Directed by Marcello Avallone.

**Synopsis:** An archaeological team in Italy led by Professor Lasky (Donald Pleasence) is busy excavating under ancient Roman baths in search of undiscovered tombs. When workers drilling for a new subway above the ruins cause vibrations, a wall opens up in the excavation, revealing a 2,000 year-old vault. Lasky's main assistant Marcus is sent down into the vault where he discovers an ancient pagan sarcophagus and a sacrificial dagger. As Lasky's team tries to make sense of what they have found, Marcus' girlfriend Alice is warned at a nightclub that according to the alignment of the planets she may be in danger. Soon after, various people connected with Lasky's team are stalked one by one and then horribly murdered. As Marcus is called to a museum where he finds a fellow anthropologist dead, a demon from the vault seizes Alice and takes her back to its lair. After realizing everyone is either dead or gone missing, Marcus travels back to the catacombs where he finds Professor Lasky near death. Lasky came face to face with the demon and warns Marcus that he must close the catacombs before the evil escapes. As Marcus quickly sets up a charge of dynamite, he hears Alice screaming from deep within the catacombs. He rushes in and saves her, then stabs the demon with the sacrificial dagger before making their way to safety... or so they think.

**Commentary:** As a horror film, *Specters*, a.k.a. *Spettri*, the original Italian title, has plenty going for it but still fails to hit the mark. Although this film features real Italian catacombs, creepy to say the least, along with scenes in a museum, a pulsating music score, a pretty blonde heroine, and of course Donald Pleasence, everything else is a regrettable letdown. Things start to go bad with a blind catacombs guide who goes way over the top in being melodramatic; the rest of the cast (except of course for Pleasence) appears to have had very little acting experience which does not help matters. Some of the dialogue is painful to listen to, such as when Alice, after being warned about her safety, responds, "Okay, you're right. There will be a catastrophe if you don't make me a plate of spaghetti!" The only demon in the film that brings up the question as to why it was titled *Specters* is either represented by the wind, seen from its own point of view or by a claw until the climax when it is shown very briefly with lots of smoke around it, an obvious ploy to conceal it from viewers. Lastly, the producers of *Specters* apparently could not make up their minds as to which film they wanted to rip off the most—a *Creature from the Black Lagoon* look-alike on a horror film set, a *Nosferatu*-like shadow that frightens Alice, or the obvious *Nightmare on Elm Street* scenario of the demon's hands coming through the bed to grab Alice.

Much like Pleasence's role in the *Halloween* series, his appearance in Italian horror films started off on a high note but diminished with each successive film. Pleasence's role in Dario Argento's *Phenomena* is well acted and the film is impressive for its style; however, Marcello Avallone is no Argento, thus Pleasence is unfortunately wasted in *Specters*. Not having much to do besides translating a few inscriptions that warn the viewer of horrors to come, Pleasence looks suitably bored but cannot really be blamed because John Pepper and Trine Michelsen, the main stars in this production, exhibit pretty wooden acting skills that invariably harm the film. Pleasence's best scene comes before his demise when armed with a flashlight, he goes into the darkened mausoleum to investigate strange noises and spots ancient Roman statues before the demon with glowing green eyes appears before him.

# *Double Target* (1987)

**Cast:** Miles O'Keeffe (Robert Ross), Donald Pleasence (Senator Blaster), Bo Svenson (Colonel Galckin), Kristine Erlandson (Mary McDouglas). Directed by Bruno Mattei.

**Synopsis:** Southeast Asia has been experiencing a rash of terrorist attacks on US consulates and bases and after Robert Ross, a highly decorated Vietnam veteran, learns that his Vietnamese wife has died in a concentration camp, he attempts to track down their son who is still at the camp. But the Vietnamese government refuses to assist Ross and a shady group actually tries to kill him when he shows up to meet them. Rescued by American agents, Ross is taken back to the US base and informed that two Russian mercenaries are responsible for training the terrorists and the attempt on his life. The head of the Defense Department, Senator Blaster (Donald Pleasence), makes a deal with Ross to allow him to search for his son but only if he agrees to do surveillance on the Russians. Ross agrees and finds his son at the camp, but soon decides to meet force with force when the Russians come after him.

After waging an all-out war, Ross defeats the Russians and the terrorists before returning back to the US base with his son.

**Commentary:** *Double Target* is the product of schlock director Bruno Mattei who went under a number of aliases during his directing career. In what is basically an Italian rip-off of *Rambo: First Blood Part II*, *Double Target* follows the same formula of an outcast Vietnam veteran going back into action for the US government which would prefer that he simply disappear. Miles O'Keeffe who made his career as the action hero in a string of films dating back to the early 1980s, does a competent job as Robert Ross although all he really does is run around and punch, kick, and shoot the enemy. Pleasence as Senator Blaster seems to be based on the Marshall Murdock character in *Rambo: First Blood Part II* and does what he can with the role but is basically confined to his office while suffering from asthma and experiencing coughing fits in-between as he devises a plan to get rid of Ross and save his own political career. On top of this, the lip synching is totally off which makes for distracted viewing. The result is that *Double Target* is definitely a film to skip for Pleasence fans.

# *Ground Zero* (1987)

**Cast:** Colin Friels (Harvey Denton), Jack Thompson (Trebilcock), Donald Pleasence (Prosper Gaffney), Natalie Bate (Pat Denton), Burnham Burnham (Charlie), Simon Chilvers (Commission President), Neil Fitzpatrick (Hooking), Bob Maza (Walemari), Peter Sardi (Carl Denton), Marion MacKenzie (Mrs. Denton), Nigel Stock (Flight Lieutenant Denys Cavendish). Directed by Bruce Myles and Michael Pattinson.

**Synopsis:** Second generation cinematographer Harvey Denton goes about his daily life until one night he receives a mysterious message on his answering machine telling him to watch the news. He turns on the TV and sees that classified documents have been stolen concerning nuclear tests being investigated by the Royal Commission of Inquiry. The following night, Denton surprises two strangers in his apartment who knock him out and steal a bunch of his father's home movies. Returning afterwards to the television station where he works, Denton finds out that a story he worked on has been taken by intelligence officers. Denton goes to the agency, where he meets Trebilcock, an Australian government agent who informs him that a skeleton with a bullet wound to the head found in a buried plane is believed to be his father. Denton is shocked to hear this news, due to being told that his father had drowned. When he hears the mysterious voice again on a call-in news program, he finds out the man is Prosper Gaffney (Donald Pleasence) and goes off in search of him. Gaffney, a former British military officer now crippled and suffering from throat cancer, tells Denton that his father filmed the government experimenting with the effects of atomic radiation on aborigines and was murdered for doing so. Gaffney leads Denton to a radiated sacred aboriginal cave where his father hid the film negatives. After facing stiff opposition from government agents, Denton manages to place the negatives in the hands of the Commission President, only to be told that long-term exposure to radiation has erased the images. Bitter and paranoid, Denton returns to his apartment to find one more surprise from his deceased father.

**Commentary:** *Ground Zero* is a hidden gem and Pleasence's best film and performance of the 1980s. Based on actual nuclear tests done by the British government in Maralinga, South Australia, *Ground Zero* is a suspense-filled thriller that incorporates the actual events of the McClelland Royal Commission investigation into British nuclear testing in Australia; coincidentally, the results of the commission's findings were still actively going on during the filming of *Ground Zero*. This film also includes archival newsreel footage of the actual nuclear tests as well as sobering information about the victims during the closing credits. The inclusion of James Bond-like action scenes are a bit out of place but do not distract from the overall tone and the twist ending which is quite a stunner. An interesting note is that one of the main characters, played by Jack Thompson, made his film debut in Pleasence's first film made in Australia—*Wake in Fright* (1971). Although extremely well made and the recipient of numerous AFI awards, *Ground Zero* was not widely released in theatres.

 *Ground Zero* would be Pleasence's third and last film made in Australia. Speaking through an electrolarynx, Pleasence's mellow voice is distorted which perfectly suits his character of Prosper Gaffney, a disillusioned and crippled ex-military man suffering from a slow death sentence for his involvement in the nuclear testing. He at first tries to turn away Denton, denying that he called him, but then slowly reveals the secrets he has harbored since the events occurred many years earlier. Although confined to a wheelchair and dependent on an aborigine named Charlie for assistance, Gaffney is still fiercely independent to the point of dragging his body across the ground if needed and going toe-to-toe with military agents. What makes Pleasence's performance stand out as a highlight of his career is the depth of his character and how he fleshes him out. Pleasence was singled out in reviews of the film, "Also good is Donald Pleasence as the extremely odd hermit who lives in a desert cave and who has waited many years for the Maralinga tragedy to come to light." [114] For his powerful role as Prosper Gaffney, Pleasence earned a nomination for Best Actor in a Supporting Role by the Australian Film Institute in 1987.

## *Django Strikes Again* (1987)

**Cast:** Franco Nero (Django), Donald Pleasence (Gunn), Christopher Connelly ("El Diablo" Orlowsky), William Berger (Old Timer), Consuelo Reina (Dona Gabriela). Directed by Nello Rossati.

**Synopsis:** Legendary gunslinger Django has given up his violent past and now lives in San Domingo preparing to pledge his service in the local monastery. A woman from his past comes to see him; she is dying and asks Django to take care of her daughter Marisol when she is gone. When Django tries to refuse, she explains that Marisol is his daughter from their prior relationship. Rethinking his decision, Django travels to the woman's village only to find it destroyed and many of the villagers dead in the streets. A lone survivor of the village tells Django that Marisol and some other villagers were taken by "El Diablo" on the river. While searching the coast, Django spots a steamboat and goes aboard where he meets Captain Orlowsky, known as 'El Diablo' by the natives. Django's demand for the return of Marisol and the other village girls results in a beating and getting thrown in with his other prisoners. They end up at a silver mine where Django meets Gunn (Donald Pleasence), a Scottish entomologist once imprisoned by Orlowsky when he failed to find a mythical butterfly for his personal collection. Gunn helps Django to escape in a large cooking pot and after realizing that he must embrace his past to save Marisol, he goes to his own "grave" and digs up a machine gun before heading back to challenge Orlowsky. Django then finds an ally in a village boy who has vowed to avenge the death of his father at the hands of Orlowsky. Together, traveling in a horse-drawn hearse, Django and the boy enact violent justice against Orlowsky's men. Django then sets a trap for Orlowsky that backfires, resulting in Django and the boy being chained up on the steamship with Marisol. But Orlowsky's jealous African slave master frees them to get revenge on a countess and Django makes quick work of everyone onboard before tracking Orlowsky to his silver mine. With Gunn's help, Django destroys the mine, frees the slaves, and turns Orlowsky over to his former captives who show him no mercy.

**Commentary:** After the worldwide success of the classic Italian spaghetti western *A Fistful of Dollars* (1964) and its two subsequent sequels in the "Man with No Name" trilogy, hundreds of other spaghetti westerns quickly followed. One of the best of this new and popular genre was Sergio Corbucci's *Django* (1966), starring Franco Nero as the mysterious machine gun-toting, gunslinger lead hero, one of the most brutal and violent westerns ever produced. *Django* became a quick success and spawned an entire series of some thirty Django films; however, none of them were official sequels nor did they feature Franco Nero. But in 1987 when the era of the Italian spaghetti western was long past, the official sequel with Franco Nero on board finally came about and though it took a vastly different approach to the character, it still wound up as an enjoyable Django adventure. Like in the original *Django* film, the viewer must cast aside the improbability of the weapon that the gunslinger uses and just go along for the ride. In the first film, Django carries his machine gun in a coffin, but in this "sequel," he travels in style and carries the gun in a horse-drawn hearse. Django is also fond of dynamite and uses it quite liberally to blow up anything and anyone who might get in his way. The ending seems to leave open the possibility of yet another sequel, and although Nero is quite long in the tooth to reprise his role (seventy years old as of 2011), director Quentin Tarantino is taking a stab at the series in 2012 with *Django Unchained*.

Although featured in a small role, Pleasence seems to have had fun as the enslaved Scottish entomologist. He also provides Django with the important background information on Orlowsky, sets in motion the butterfly trap, helps Django escape from the silver mine, and enacts some revenge in the finale as he runs around tossing sticks of dynamite. Although stuck doing crippling and heavy manual labor, Gunn retains his sense of humor which probably helped him to survive. The one odd thing about Pleasence's character is his name of "Gunn" that seems contrary to his profession and is never explained. One Pleasence highlight is when Gunn goes to throw a lit stick of dynamite that slips down his shirt and into his pants; the look on Pleasence's face as he frantically searches for the dynamite is indeed a sight to behold.

# *Prince of Darkness* (1987)

**Cast:** Donald Pleasence (Father Loomis), Jameson Parker (Brian Marsh), Victor Wong (Professor Howard Birack), Lisa Blount (Catherine Danforth), Dennis Dun (Walter), Susan Blanchard (Kelly), Anne Marie Howard (Susan Cabot), Ann Yen (Lisa), Ken Wright (Lomax), Dick Blocker (Mullins), Jessie Lawrence Ferguson (Calder), Peter Jason (Dr. Paul Leahy), Alice Cooper (Street schizoid). Directed by John Carpenter.

**Synopsis:** A priest waiting for a meeting with the holy cardinal passes away at the church in his sleep while clutching a small box. Father Loomis (Donald Pleasence) ends up with the box, along with the priest's diary, and soon learns that the box contains a special key to a vault in an abandoned church in Los Angeles. After traveling to the church, Loomis uses the key to unlock the door to the basement where the secret sect that the priest belonged to kept a large container with a swirling green liquid. Contacting his friend Howard Birack, a professor of physics, Loomis seeks to have him investigate what exactly the liquid is and what it means in relation to the diary. Birack brings in his physics students to assist him, along with some biochemists and a Latin translator for the diary. However, the team is not prepared for what they find—the green liquid is actually the essence of Satan himself who seeks to release his father the Anti-God. In addition, a life form is growing out of the pre-embryonic fluid and has the psychokinetic power to control objects and people around it. Trapped in the church by the controlling and now murderous mass of homeless people outside, the members of the team are taken over one by one as Satan assumes the body of a chosen member. Loomis and the surviving members of the team must then do battle with the Evil One before he can bring his father the Anti-God into the world.

**Commentary:** *Prince of Darkness* marks director John Carpenter's grand return to independent filmmaking after finding the studio system not to his liking for various reasons. The result was a film totally under his control, even writing under the pseudonym of Martin Quatermass. As the second of Carpenter's apocalyptic trilogy (the others being *The Thing* and *In the Mouth of Madness*), *Prince of Darkness* is a frightening psychological horror film that oozes with doom and gloom, and boasting a great cast, including some familiar Carpenter faces like Pleasence, Victor Wong, and Dennis Dun, the story coasts along as the situation becomes bleaker the further the team progresses. There are some interesting elements here, including the mix of science and religion to combat evil and the premonitions sent to the team members from the future. Also in a small role is shock rocker Alice Cooper as one of the murderous and possessed homeless vagrants.

*Prince of Darkness* also marks the last teaming of Pleasence and John Carpenter, the man who made Pleasence forever tied to the Dr. Loomis character in the *Halloween* series. As a nod to that connection, Pleasence's character is named Father Loomis, a devout man who seeks to have his friend Birack use science to help prove and combat the evil which as he states can no longer be held secret. There are some great scenes with Pleasence and Victor Wong discussing the nature of the existence of God and Satan with the two looking for a way to meld their beliefs. Pleasence's Father Loomis is obviously a deeply religious man trying to come to grips with what he must eventually face. And when he does, it is a powerful scene with Loomis seizing an axe to square off against Satan himself. An interesting note is that Pleasence was to have appeared in one other Carpenter film, his 1982 remake of *The Thing*. Originally cast as Dr. Blair (the role that went to Wilford Brimley), Pleasence was forced to back out, due to scheduling conflicts.

# *To Kill a Stranger* (1987)

**Cast:** Angelica Maria (Christina Carver), Dean Stockwell (John Carver), Donald Pleasence (Colonel Kostik), Aldo Ray (Inspector Benedict), Sergio Aragones (Major Keller), Ken Grant (Tom). Directed by Juan Lopez Moctezuma.

**Synopsis:** John Carver is an American television journalist working in a South American country to expose corruption within its military. He invites his wife Christina to come visit him from the U.S. and provides a car for her upon arrival, but she gets involved in an accident along the way. Stranded at a desolate gas station, Christina accepts a ride from a kind stranger who drives her back to his home to phone John. At the stranger's house, Christina notices certain things that make her uneasy and her attempt to reach John on the phone is unsuccessful. The kind stranger then reveals his true self—a maniacal psychopath who tries to rape Christina. After being shot at and chased, Christina manages to get the gun away from the stranger and shoots him dead before dumping his body in a well and escaping. She then makes her way back to John's hotel, but instead of being relieved, she reads in the newspaper that the stranger was a national hero named Colonel Kostik (Donald Pleasence) and that the army is investigating his death. On top of this, local authority Inspector Benedict is conducting his own investigation into the case. Christina tells John what happened and together they try to evade both the army and Benedict while hiding Kostik's body. But Benedict is a clever man and quickly figures out Christina's involvement. Major Keller and the army eventually track down Christina with the help of information from a witness and are about to execute her when Benedict arrives and intervenes. An inspection inside of a bag reveals a woman's body that leads everyone back to the well where more women and Kostik's body are found. With the horrible truth about Kostik exposed, Christina is allowed to leave with John.

**Commentary:** *To Kill a Stranger is a low budget effective thriller that provides some relevant commentary on the power and corruption of military rule in places like South America. Directed by* Juan Lopez Moctezuma, known for a few horror films shot in his native Mexico, the first half of *To Kill a Stranger* is infused with some of those elements and is all the better for it. The segment with Christina stranded alone in a foreign country and then trapped in the house of a murderous rapist provides much tension and some real scares. Also in the cast is American actor Dean Stockwell who does a fine job as Christina's journalist husband and Sergio Aragones (noted *Mad Magazine* artist and creator of Groo the Wanderer) in one of his only roles as the hardliner Major Keller.

*Pleasence portrays the title character* in To Kill a Stranger and while he is only featured in the first half of the film, he more than leaves a lasting impression. At the beginning of the film, it is implied that his Colonel Kostik was involved in the killing of a popular news journalist, but when he is finally revealed, he seems to be the savior of Christina while stranded at the gas station. Kostik drives her to his home and even comes up with a well thought-out backstory that his wife is an American and would love to meet Christina. But as soon as Christina enters the home, things quickly begin to go downhill. The walls are plastered with guns and swords and Kostik's "wife" is apparently not feeling well and went to bed early. When Kostik calls the hotel where John is staying and quickly leaves a fake message before he can pick up, the viewer knows that Kostik's transformation from a kind stranger and into a homicidal maniac is just around the corner. When the change does arrive, is like night and day—Kostik gives Christina a glass of wine, then tries to jump on her on the couch, but when rebuked, he retrieves a shotgun and proceeds to fire at Christina both inside and outside of his house. The battle between Christina and Kostik provides some nail biting drama and Pleasence does his best as a complete maniac who also happens to be a beloved national hero.

# *Phantom of Death* (1988)

**Cast:** Michael York (Robert Dominici), Edwige Fenech (Helene Martell), Donald Pleasence (Inspector Datti), Mapi Galan (Susanna), Fabio Sartor (David), Renato Cortesi (Agent Marchi), Antonella Pnonziani (Gloria Datti). Directed by Ruggero Deodato.

**Synopsis:** Robert Dominici is a classically trained pianist adored by the critics and female fans alike. Right before one of Robert's concerts, a doctor is brutally murdered which leads to Inspector Datti (Donald Pleasence) missing the performance with his daughter Gloria, due to being assigned to the case. After speaking to a witness, Datti knows that the killer is in his thirties and begins his search. Soon after, Robert's girlfriend Susanna is also murdered and Datti arrives to question him, although Datti is suspicious of Robert's best friend David who was having an affair with Susanna. Following Susanna's murder, admirer Helene Martell pays a visit to Robert and offers to comfort him. Meanwhile, Datti with no solid leads is shocked when the killer calls his house and brags that he will never be caught and can kill as often as he wishes; he even mentions Datti's daughter. Feeling unwell and losing his hair, Robert visits a doctor who tells him he has Hutchinsons, a very rare, fatal genetic disease, and Gilbert's syndrome which will rapidly age him and affects his psyche. Robert, who previously killed Doctor Pesenti before she could fully explain his condition, becomes enraged that he will be cut down in the prime of life. Complicating matters is that Helene calls Robert to let him know she is pregnant with his child. He tries unsuccessfully to kill her to terminate her pregnancy but is scared off. Helene then tells Datti that the attacker was in his 50s. Now obsessed with killing the young and old in frustration over his situation, Robert begins a deadly game of cat and mouse with Datti, taunting him as he continues his murderous spree with the goal of killing Helene and his unborn child.

**Commentary:** Much like Dario Argento, director Ruggero Deodato is also widely known by fans for his genre films which tend to be more on the gory side with titles like *Cannibal Holocaust, House on the Edge of the Park*, and *Body Count*. Deodato's *Phantom of Death* (originally titled *Un Delitto Poco Commune* in Italian which translates into the more appropriate title *A Crime Uncommon*), is a hit and miss affair. The premise of the rapidly aging killer is an interesting concept and Michael York really sells his character, eliciting sympathy for an otherwise murderous individual. The film also concludes with the killer being stopped in a most unique fashion via a heart attack from old age. Where this film misses includes the rather ridiculous premise of Robert Dominici receiving martial arts training while dressed as a ninja, and when he dons a phantom of the opera type mask while traveling through Venice, an obvious link-up to the film's US title.

Pleasence's appearance as Inspector Datti appears at first glance to be yet another role as a police chief, but there is some added depth via his continuing frustration as well as his concern for his daughter Gloria. The look on Pleasence's face when the killer first mentions Gloria perfectly reflects that of a protective father. Later on in the film when Datti thinks he has safely sent his daughter to Rome to escape, he once again receives a phone call from the killer which truly compounds his fears. Datti reaches his breaking point after one of his officers is murdered in broad daylight and requests a transfer to a distant precinct, but like any good cop, Datti is drawn back in through a simple clue that leads to his big break.

## *The Commander* (1988)

**Cast:** Lewis Collins (Major Colby), Lee Van Cleef (Colonel Mazzarini), Donald Pleasence (Henry Carlson), Manfred Lehmann (Mason/Hiccock), Brett Halsey (McPherson), Chat Silayan (Ling), Hans Leutenegger (Gutierrez), Christian Bruckner (Frank Williams), Frank Glaubrecht (Lennox). Directed by Antonio Margheriti.

**Synopsis:** Colonel Mazzarini, a major arms supplier, is deeply involved in trading guns for drugs with a ruthless general in Thailand, but when negotiations go bad, the general steals a disc containing valuable source information on contacts. In response, Mazzarini puts together a team of mercenaries led by Major Colby to attack the general's stronghold in order to take over his operations. Also on the team is Hiccock, a secret agent for government head Henry Carlson (Donald Pleasence) who gets plastic surgery to mimic another mercenary named Mason. Hiccock's goal is to retrieve the disc and deliver it to Carlson so he can track a leak in his department. Colby then leads his men into Thailand and uses his contacts to arrange vehicles, arms, and support for their mission. Along the way, the team finds some friends like Ling, a beautiful but deadly Thai mercenary, and enemies like Duclo, a Frenchman who sells out the team for money. After fighting their way through the jungle, Colby, Hiccock, and the rest of the team reach the general's drug compound, where they learn that Mazzarini has also betrayed them. With their lives on the line, the team begins an all out war to destroy everything in sight. While a number of team members are killed, their mission is successful with Hiccock retrieving the disc which he then uses to blackmail Mazzarini. A meeting is set up to sell the disc, but one other major backstabbing and double cross is about to take place.

**Commentary:** *The Commander*, a.k.a. *Der Commander*, is a low-budget action adventure set in a remote Asian jungle with Italian genre director Antonio Margheriti using the pseudonym of Anthony M. Dawson. This is actually the third part of Margheriti's trilogy of jungle adventure films, the first two being *Codename: Wildgeese* (1984) and *Commando Leopard* (1985). One interesting connection between these three films besides the director is Lewis Collins as the hero. *The Commander* plays out predictably with no real surprises along the way, but the big draw are the battle scenes that are average at best with lots of gunfire and a few explosions. Adding some star power along with Pleasence is Lee Van Cleef, best known for his Italian spaghetti westerns. *The Commander* was one of Van Cleef's last films of his career that stretched back to *High Noon* in 1952. During his heyday, Van Cleef was *the* leading spaghetti western villain, and in *The Commander*, Van Cleef once again found himself playing the villain—a rose growing, gun-selling, sly as a snake character who of course eventually receives his just desserts.

Pleasence portrays Henry Carlson, a government leader who likes to chain-smoke cigars while being followed around by his lackeys. It is not a very involved role but Carlson does pop up every now and then to keep an eye on his secret agent Hiccock. Pleasence's character can best be described as a man in charge, a role that Pleasence could do backwards with his eyes closed at this point in his career. Carleon does get to have a bit of fun toward the climax, turning up while Hiccock and Colby sit in their convertible with a briefcase full of cash. Prepared for his own vacation via a bright yellow shirt with a sun hat and camera, Carlson gives them his full blessing to enjoy themselves after a hard fought but successful mission.

# *Last Platoon* (1988)

**Cast:** Richard Hatch (Sergeant Chet Costa), Donald Pleasence (Colonel B. Abrams), Milene Thy-Sanh (Mey Ling). Directed by Ignazio Dolce.

**Synopsis:** Sergeant Chet Costa is a decorated soldier that in the past led a number of missions deep into Vietnam to combat the enemy and rescue American POWs. One morning, Costa's fiancée, Mey Ling, disappears and he discovers that she has crossed over into enemy territory. Chet's boss, Colonel Abrams (Donald Pleasence) sends him on a new mission—to destroy a bridge being used by the Vietcong to transport supplies along the Ho Chi Minh trail. Costa is given a squad of soldiers, made up mostly of criminals who are hoping to get pardons once the mission is completed. After being dropped off by helicopter in the middle of the jungle, Costa and his men make their way to his contact, a Vietnamese freedom fighter who has organized his village to assist the soldiers. Once there, Costa finds Mey Ling who reveals that she ran off to help save her mother who has already been killed by the Vietcong. Mey Ling then helps Costa plant explosives and they blow up the bridge, only to be chased by hundreds of Vietcong. Once the soldiers realize it is a suicide mission, they start getting ideas about turning on Costa and escaping. Mey Ling is then taken hostage by the Vietcong and Costa fights his way into the camp to free her, but Mey Ling ends up being killed before they can get back to the base.

**Commentary:** *Last Platoon* is yet another of Pleasence's "jungle films" released during the 1980s, and like those that came before it, lacks a solid plot except for a short, doomed love angle between Costa and Mey Ling. Compared to *Double Target*, *The Commander*, and *Operation Nam*, *Last Platoon* falls pretty much even with *Operation Nam* only slightly above the rest. In the lead role as Sergeant Costa is Richard Hatch whose claim to fame was playing Captain Apollo in the popular science fiction TV series *Battlestar Galactica*. Pleasence portrays Costa's boss and his only friend and dressed in military fatigues, he actually is allowed to do a bit more than just stay in his office by actively participating in Costa's rescue after completing his mission. Called a "mother hen" by the general, Pleasence conveys a worried demeanor about Costa, his best soldier, which provides the bulk of emotion in this film.

# *Vampire in Venice* (1988)

**Cast:** Klaus Kinski (Nosferatu), Christopher Plummer (Professor Paris Catalano), Donald Pleasence (Father Alvise), Barbara De Rossi (Helietta Canins), Yorgo Voyagis (Dr. Barneval), Anne Knecht (Maria Canins), Elvire Audray (Uta Barneval), Maria Cumani Quasimodo (Princess). Produced and directed by Augusto Caminito.

**Synopsis:** Professor Paris Catalano, the world's leading authority on vampirism, is tracking the vampire Nosferatu, last seen in Venice during the plague of 1786. In the city, Catalano follows up a lead and travels to the house of Canins which is supposed to have a vampire in the family tomb. Upon arrival, Catalano is shunned by the Princess who owns the home and receives no help from either Father Alvise (Donald Pleasence) nor Dr. Barneval. But Helietta Canins and her younger sister Maria believe the stories and call for a séance to rid the home of Nosferatu's power. The séance proves to be effective but only to call forth Nosferatu who then makes his way to the Canins house where he dispatches the Princess to her death. Nosferatu's power proves too great for the combined efforts of Catalano, Alvise, and Dr. Barneval and he soon chooses Helietta as his new vampire mistress. However, when Nosferatu sees Maria trying to jump from a building in a suicide attempt, he saves her and they fall in love. Just so happens that love is the only thing that can kill Nosferatu. Longing for death, Nosferatu takes Maria back to the desolate island where he resides, but before Nosferatu can truly die, Dr. Barneval arrives with help and shoots Maria by accident. Enraged, Nosferatu kills Dr. Barneval and carries Maria away from civilization.

**Commentary:** *Vampire in Venice, a.k.a. Nosferatu in Venice, is a pseudo-sequel to Werner Herzog's Nosferatu the Vampire (1979), a sort of reimagining of F. W. Murnau's 1922 Dracula inspired Nosferatu. However, the only real linking feature between Herzog's film and its sequel is the character of Nosferatu, bearing a completely different look, due to Kinski reportedly not wishing to go through the painful heavy make-up process to play the vampire once again. Kinski also reportedly clashed with a few directors working on the film which eventually led to producer Augusto Caminito taking over directorial duties, resulting in a some-*

what uneven continuity because he had little experience. *Vampire in Venice* almost succeeds on atmosphere alone with hauntingly beautiful scenes of the canals of Venice and fog-enshrouded streets. In the title role, Kinski does an admirable job portraying an ancient being longing for death; Christopher Plummer also puts in a good performance as what can only be described as one of the most inept vampire hunters in history.

*Pleasence portrays* Father Alvise, a man of the cloth who aids the elderly Princess and helps her pray for atonement. As what can be described as part of the new order of priests, Alvise does not believe in the story of Nosferatu and dismisses it as a local superstition. But when the dreaded vampire does arrive, Alvise acts upon the best idea of the lot by locking himself behind a gate in the house and not interfering. His only role in combating the vampire is figuring out that Nosferatu inhabits the island because of its plague victims and letting Dr. Barneval go off on his ill-fated mission. After failing to stop Nosferatu, Professor Catalano exclaims that even with the power of God, the vampire cannot be stopped. He is then thrown out of the house by Alvise who rages in anger that he would put himself on a level with God.

# *Halloween 4: The Return of Michael Myers* (1988)

**Cast:** Donald Pleasence (Dr. Sam Loomis), Ellie Cornell (Rachel Carruthers), Danielle Harris (Jamie Lloyd), George P. Wilbur (Michael Myers), Michael Pataki (Dr. Hoffman), Beau Starr (Sheriff Ben Meeker), Kathleen Kinmont (Kelly Meeker), Sasha Jenson (Brady), Gene Ross (Earl), Carmen Filpi (Reverend Jackson Sayer), Jeff Olson (Richard Carruthers), Karen Alston (Darlene Carruthers). Directed by Dwight H. Little.

**Synopsis:** It has been ten years since Michael Myers went on a murderous rampage trying to kill his sister Laurie Strode. Now locked up in Richmond Federal Sanitarium, Myers is being transferred back to Smith's Grove under the orders of Dr. Hoffman, the medical administrator, who no longer feels Myers is a threat to society. Dr. Loomis (Donald Pleasence), Myers' former doctor, is upset at hearing of the transfer and warns Dr. Hoffman of the dangers that Myers is capable of producing. Hoffman ignores him until he receives a phone call explaining that the ambulance carrying Myers has crashed and that he may not be among the dead. Knowing that Myers might head back to Haddonfield where his niece resides, Loomis immediately takes off towards town. Meanwhile, Jamie Lloyd, the daughter of Laurie Strode, is having a difficult time adjusting to life with her foster family in a town that punishes her for her family's past. Her foster sister Rachel has reluctantly agreed to babysit her on Halloween because their parents will be attending an important meeting. At the discount mart where she picks out her Halloween costume, Jamie believes that Myers is pursuing her. Loomis, who has reached town on the heels of Myers, convinces Sheriff Meeker of the threat to Jamie and they go out on patrol to find her. During trick or treating, Rachel sees Myers trying to pursue Jamie but is able to get her away; they end up being picked up by Meeker and Loomis, then go back to Meeker's house to hole up until the state police arrive. But Myers does not give them the chance; he breaks into the house and kills anyone who stands in his way. Jamie escapes the house and is taken by Loomis to the schoolhouse with Myers in hot pursuit. Still unable to escape him, Jamie and Rachel leave in a pickup truck hoping to get out of town, but Myers is hiding in the back of the truck and kills the men before Rachel shakes him loose and hits him full force with the truck. Jamie examines the body of her uncle who jumps up before the police arrive and proceeds to shoot Myers dead. Safe at home, Jamie is waiting to take a bath when she stabs her foster mother with a pair of scissors.

**Commentary:** After the failure of *Halloween III* which featured a horror story separate from the previous two films, producers realized that if the series was to continue, they would have to bring Michael Myers back from the dead. Also coming back for the sequel would be the heroic Dr. Loomis, played by Donald Pleasence. The fact that they both perished in a fireball explosion at the end of *Halloween II* was explained simply by saying that they survived with severe burns. *Halloween* creator John Carpenter had written a psychological story treatment for the fourth film, but it was rejected in favor of the standard "slasher" plot, so he opted out of the production. With Jamie Lee Curtis also missing as Laurie Strode, child actor Danielle Harris replaced her as the subject of Michael Myers' murderous obsession. The rest of the film follows the predictable plotline of Myers escaping and killing everyone who tries to prevent him from reaching his target—poor little Jamie Lloyd. However, the film's conclusion provides a neat twist to the series via the idea that Michael Myers can actually form a psychic link to continue his evil.

Back after an eight year gap from *Halloween II*, Pleasence returns in fine form as the trench coated Dr. Loomis with his face burned on one side from the explosion and crippled by a bad limp; nonetheless, the good doctor still manages to foil Myers' evil plans. One main difference this time around is that Loomis seems to have more respect and authority, and even though Dr. Hoffman goes behind his back to get Myers transferred, when things go wrong, Loomis is not challenged in pursuing Myers back to Haddonfield. Loomis also is more accepted by the sheriff's office and his advice is more heeded whenever a decision needs to be made. Once more, Pleasence gets to philosophize on the presence of pure evil as exemplified in a discussion with Hoffman—"We are not talking about any ordinary prisoner, Hoffman. We are talking about evil on two legs." Pleasence's character is also more physical, such as when he dives out of the way to avoid being run over by Myers and is later thrown through a glass window by Myers in an attempt to defend the terrified Jamie. But his best scene is the last when he comes to the horrible realization that Myers has somehow passed on his evil to the innocent Jamie. His repeated screaming of "No!" and his attempts to shoot Jamie while physically restrained is certainly enough to bring shivers to the viewer.

## *Hanna's War* (1988)

**Cast:** Ellen Burstyn (Katalin), Maruschka Detmers (Hanna), Anthony Andrews (McCormack), Donald Pleasence (Captain Thomas Rosza), David Warner (Captain Julian Simon), Vincent Riotta (Yoel), Christopher Fairbank (Ruven), Rob Jacks (Peretz), Serge El-Baz (Tony), Eli Gorenstein (Aba), Joe El Dror (Yonah), Ingrid Pitt (Margit), Jon Rumney (Uncle Egon), Magda Faluhelyi (Aunt Ella). Directed by Menahem Golan.

**Synopsis:** In Hungary during the summer of 1937, young Anniko Senesh hears of the Nazi Germany propaganda against her fellow Jews being spread in the newspapers. She experiences this persecution first-hand when Hungarian soldiers interrupt a meeting of the literary society and strip her of her newly-elected title as grade representative due to her being Jewish. Upset at what is going on in her country, Anniko decides to attend an agricultural school in Palestine, where she can learn to help others and concentrate on her writing. While in Palestine, Anniko changes her name to Hanna and finds happiness yet is still worried about her mother back in Hungary whom she has not heard from. In 1943, Hanna sees her opportunity to return home when a British officer approaches her about joining a British-trained Hungarian team to go behind enemy lines and set up escape routes for captured British airmen. However, on her first mission Hanna is caught with a hidden radio transmitter by enemy soldiers. After being brought before Hungarian authorities, Hanna is interrogated and tortured by Captain Thomas Rosza (Donald Pleasence) who wants to know her real name and the code she uses to send message on the transmitter. Her state appointed lawyer Captain Julian Simon also tries to get her to give up her secrets, but even after bringing in Hanna's mother and threatening to kill her, Hanna will not give in which forces Rosza to turn her over to the High Court of Budapest under the charge of treason. At her trial, Hanna declares that the judges and captains will be held responsible for their actions against Hungarian Jews; Captain Simon, who knows that the Germans are being forced out of Hungary by advancing Russian troops, decides to take matters into his own hands in an attempt to save himself.

**Commentary:** Based on *The Diaries of Hanna Senesh* and the biographical novel *A Great Wind Cometh* by Yoel Palgi, one of Hanna's fellow officers, *Hanna's War* is a well-made biopic that reveals one woman's heroic fight against the Holocaust. Native Israeli Menahem Golan who wrote, produced, and directed *Hanna's War*, is best-known for working with his cousin Yoram Globus to form Golan-Globus Productions which was responsible for a slew of low budget films from the late 1970s through the 1980s. Although at times a bit weak in dialogue, strong performances from Maruschka Detmers as the heroic yet tragic Hanna, Ellen Burstyn as Hanna's mother, Donald Pleasence as Captain Rosza, and

David Warner as the Hungarian captain who tests Hanna's will, makes up for it. But what truly makes their performances so powerful is that they were all based on real people and events. The real Hanna Senesh is now considered as a hero of the Zionist movement and as one of Israel's most esteemed poets; there are also foundations and a school named after her because she continues to be an inspiration for others.

Pleasence's role as Captain Rosza serves as a bookend to his appearance as 'Forger' Colin Blythe in *The Great Escape*, two powerful performances that show both captive and captor of World War II. Rosza is a truly villainous character who blinks at nothing while torturing young Hanna and yet attempts to bizarrely demonstrate a soft side in between. At times uncomfortable to watch, Pleasence's Rosza beats Hanna bloody with his fists, has guards use a high pressure water hose on her, and deprives her of food and sleep as he tries to break her spirit. The scene in which Rosza examines Hanna's pulled fingernails and sings "yours were so pretty" is quite unnerving to say the least. But at the same time, Rosza frees Hanna's mother from prison and attempts to protest when Captain Simon wants to rush Hanna's judgment. This villainous role certainly caught the eye of reviewers—"The villains provide what zest there is, an example being Donald Pleasence doing his nutty number as a sadist with a soft streak," [115] and "You do have to give Pleasence credit for working up so much sheer repulsiveness."[116] Historically, the real Captain Thomas Rosza escaped from Budapest and was never seen nor heard from again.

## *House of Usher* (1989)

**Cast:** Oliver Reed (Roderick Usher), Donald Pleasence (Walter Usher), Romy Windsor (Molly McNulty), Rufus Swart (Ryan Usher), Norman Coombes (Mr. Derrick), Anne Stradi (Mrs. Derrick), Philip Godawa (Dr. Bailey). Directed by Alan Birkinshaw.

**Synopsis:** Ryan Usher and his fiancée Molly have been invited to the estate of his wealthy uncle Roderick whom he has never met. While driving to the estate, they get lost and while looking at the directions, Molly suddenly sees two children on the road. Ryan swerves to avoid hitting the children with the car and crashes into a tree. Molly staggers out of the car and discovers that Ryan is unconscious from a bleeding head injury. She then walks up ahead and reaches the Usher estate, where she explains the accident to Clive Derrick and his wife, servants at the Usher estate. Molly is told to wait in the house and rest while they get Ryan to the hospital. That night Molly is introduced to Roderick, who explains the Usher family misfortunes, including the fact that the estate is slowly sinking into the marsh before inquiring about her own family. That night, Molly hears the voices of the children which leads her through a secret passage, where she discovers a hidden family crypt with the body of Ryan laid out. Outraged at having been lied to by Roderick, Molly is told that nothing could be done anyway even though she hears scratching from inside Ryan's coffin. She is later drugged and Roderick has her examined before trying to take advantage of her, due to his need to find a bride to continue the Usher line of descent. After trying to escape from the house, Molly finds Roderick's insane brother Walter (Donald Pleasence) locked up in the attic. Walter soon escapes and kills Clive's wife and daughter. In the confusion, Molly slips into the crypt and frees Ryan, but before they can escape, Roderick, Clive, and Walter appear and begin fighting to the death as the house crumbles and burns around them. Ryan manages to holds back Roderick to allow Molly to escape from the dreaded House of Usher as it quickly goes up in flames.

**Commentary:** Edgar Allan Poe's 1839 classic short story *The Fall of the House of Usher* has been filmed several times, most notably director Roger Corman's 1960 adaptation with Vincent Price as Roderick Usher. This 1989 version is considered as an 'updating' of the story with new characters but fails miserably for several reasons. One of the most problematic issues is the screenplay that contains many plot holes and weak dialogue. The fact that Molly is a hairdresser from Los Angeles stands out like a sore thumb from the rest of the characters and the expression on Oliver Reed's face when Molly explains that her mother sells Avon is priceless. But Reed himself is also to blame for some of the problems because his acting in this film is way over the top in a bad way. A much better production with Pleasence and Reed is the television production *The Black Arrow* (1985). Although *House of Usher* does provide some suitably creepy settings and decent gruesome effects, it is ultimately disappointing, especially because of its very confusing and nonsensical ending.

Even in poor films like *House of Usher*, Pleasence still managed to create interesting characters as he does here in his hammy performance as Walter Usher. Locked away in the attic and bound to a wheelchair with his wispy long hair and a bizarre drill contraption strapped to his hand, Walter Usher at first seems to be a pathetic victim and a bit off his rocker, but once he escapes, things take a turn for the worse, especially when we realize that Walter is a maniac killer, such as when he beheads Mrs. Derrick and turns her head into a centerpiece before moving on to kill her daughter. Walter also reveals himself to be Ryan's father which is confusing because Ryan never mentions this fact to Molly. One of Pleasence's best bits occurs when Molly runs into him again and sees that he is no longer in his wheelchair to which he replies with an astonishment smirk, "I've made a miraculous recovery!"

## *Ten Little Indians* (1989)

**Cast:** Donald Pleasence (Judge Lawrence Wargrave), Frank Stallone (Captain Philip Lombard), Sarah Maur Thorp (Vera Claythorne), Herbert Lom (General Brancko Romensky), Brenda Vaccaro (Marion Marshall), Warren Berlinger (Detective William Blore), Yehuda Efroni (Dr. Hans Werner), Paul L. Smith (Elmo Rodgers), Moira Lister (Ethel Mae Rodgers), Neil McCarthy (Anthony Marston). Directed by Alan Birkinshaw.

**Synopsis:** Ten strangers have been invited to a free African safari by a Mr. Owens. Captain Lombard greets the guests as they arrive and leads them to the camp, where they are scheduled to meet their host. Among the guests are Judge Wargrave (Donald Pleasence), Dr. Werner, private investigator William Blore, playboy Anthony Marston, secretary Vera Claythorne, Marion Marshall, husband and wife Ethel and Elmo Rodgers, and Serbian General Brancko Romensky. The group crosses a ravine in a wooden lift which is promptly cut down by the natives, leaving the group stranded and unable to get back. Nervous but with no other choice, the group continues on, and after reaching their camp, they discover that their mysterious host Mr. Owens is not there. That night, the group meets for dinner and notices a tray holding ten Indian statues. They also find a recording left by Mr. Owen in which he explains that he has invited them to charge each one with a murder they committed and got away with in the past. Marston is the first to die, and more of the guests quickly follow him, all according to the poem "Ten Little Indians." With just a handful left, the survivors come to the realization that the mysterious Mr. Owens is actually one of them. Cut off from the outside world, with nowhere to go, the survivors start turning on each other in a desperate attempt to survive until the real Mr. Owens reveals himself—or herself.

**Commentary:** Numerous film adaptations of Agatha Christie's novel "Ten Little Indians" have been produced, and this 1989 version stands out as the best of the lot. The cast is overall good, though the setting and some of the dialogue differs from the original source material. Producer Harry Allen Towers obviously liked Christie's story a great deal because he previously produced two other film versions in 1965 and 1974; Towers was also responsible for changing the film's ending, going with a more upbeat theatrical version rather than Christie's rather bleak conclusion. Another connection to past productions of *Ten Little Indians* is Herbert Lom who played Dr. Werner in the 1974 version. In this film, Lom provides a great performance as General Romensky.

With top billing in this production, Pleasence gets to shine as Judge Wargrave who acts as the voice of reason among the guests while also spreading distrust; he also transforms from being calm to overly excited during which he starts popping pills like candy. His conversions with Dr. Werner are quite good and a past history between the two is hinted at early on. Even at his age, Pleasence's Judge proved to be quite a match for Philip Lombard, the young hero played by Frank Stallone.

# *River of Death* (1989)

**Cast:** Michael Dudikoff (John Hamilton), Robert Vaughn (Wolfgang Manteuffel), Donald Pleasence (Heinrich Spaatz), Herbert Lom (Colonel Ricardo Diaz), L.Q. Jones (Hiller), Sarah Maur Thorp (Anna Blakesley), Cynthia Erland (Maria), Foziah Davidson (Dalia). Directed by Steve Carver.

**Synopsis:** During the last days of World War II in Germany, and in order to avoid being captured, Nazi doctor Wolfgang Manteuffel and his backer Heinrich Spaatz (Donald Pleasence) plan on escaping to South America with their ill-gotten riches, but at the airstrip, Manteuffel has other ideas and shoots Spaatz in the knee before taking off in his plane. Twenty years later in the Amazon jungle, tracker John Hamilton is leading a doctor and his daughter Anna to a mysterious lost city, where they hope to find the source of a deadly disease that has been killing the native population. As they near the lost city, they are attacked by a group of savages who kill the doctor and take Anna captive before Hamilton is able to escape back to an outpost. There, he tries to convince Colonel Diaz that they must go back to the lost city to rescue the girl, but his pleas are dismissed. Hamilton then goes to his friend Hiller who puts him in touch with Bergens, a wealthy businessman eager to finance the mission. After agreeing to take Bergens and his mistress Maria along for the ride, Hamilton puts together a team and they begin their journey by helicopter. Along the way, they encounter river pirates and are later captured by a group of cannibals, but Colonel Diaz shows up with a machine gun and saves them. However, Hamilton and his team's hopes are dashed when Diaz turns them over to Nazi soldiers guarding the lost city. There, they meet Dr. Manteuffel who has been continuing his horrific experiments and as it turns out is responsible for the killer disease. Hamilton is then thrown in a jail, where he discovers that Anna has also been infected with the disease. After breaking out of jail with the help of some native prisoners, Hamilton kills the Nazis and heads back to the laboratory where Bergens reveals himself to be Spaatz and is about to kill Manteuffel. As they struggle over a gun, Maria pulls a flare gun on them. Her father was apparently killed by Manteuffel while Spaatz looked on, so she kills them both and destroys the laboratory. Hamilton then heads back into the jungle to return home.

**Commentary:** *River of Death* was the second film (third if you count the 1979 television production *Gold of the Amazon Women*) that Pleasence starred in involving a search for treasure in the Amazon. But compared to the zany and over-the-top fun of *Treasure of the Amazon*, *River of Death* plods along at a snails pace with much less action. Based on the book by famed novelist Alistair MacLean, *River of Death* falls flat, although not for a lack of trying, as *River of Death* was obviously made on a decent budget and features a great opening war scene and some great aerial photography of the Amazonian landscape (actually the jungles of Africa). On hand to provide some interesting portrayals are Herbert Lom as the scheming colonel and Robert Vaughn as a nasty Nazi doctor. But one of the main problems with *River of Death* is its lead actor Michael Dudikoff, known at the time for his role in the *American Ninja* film series. Here, Dudikoff provides one of the most wooden performances captured on film. Literally devoid of emotion, his John Hamilton is a complete bore, only made worse by the fact that he narrates via a voice-over what is on his mind during various scenes.

Pleasence gets to play a sort of master of disguise in *River of Death* that is actually quite funny since it only involves him changing hairpieces. After being shot in the knee by Wolfgang Manteuffel whom he jokingly calls Wolfie, Spaatz swears revenge for the doctor, and being good to his word, he hangs around in South America for years waiting for his chance while passing himself off as a businessman with a brown wig. Spaatz later goes back to basic bald at the beginning of the mission prior to donning a white wig before entering the lost city. This switching of simple disguises apparently worked as Wolfgang Manteuffel is shocked when Spaatz pulls off his wig to reveal his true identity. An unintentionally hilarious *Pink Panther* scenario occurs in *River of Death* with Herbert Lom playing another chief of police and Pleasence playing a pseudo undercover agent.

# *Paganini Horror* (1989)

**Cast:** Daria Nicolodi (Sylvia Hackett), Jasmine Maimone (Kate), Pascal Persiano (Daniel), Maria Cristina Mastrangeli (Lavinia), Michel Klippstein (Elena), Donald Pleasence (Mr. Pickett). Directed by Luigi Cozzi.

**Synopsis:** Desperate for a new hit album, an Italian pop music group purchases an original unpublished score by Niccolo Paganini, the famous violinist who supposedly sold his soul to the devil for fame and fortune. The group decides to pass off the music as their own and along with their manager head to a haunted house owned by Sylvia Hackett to make a music video. However, once at the house, bizarre things begin to occur and soon Paganini himself returns from the dead to hunt down the group members one by one and murder them with his violin blade. The last victim meets the true owner of Paganini's score, Mr. Pickett (Donald Pleasence) who is actually the devil in disguise and has forced Sylvia to lure people to the house for punishment of their sins.

**Commentary:** *Paganini Horror* is an occasionally entertaining but often confusing Italian horror film based very loosely on the life of Niccolo Paganini, rumored to have had an association with the devil, due to his refusal to accept the last rites from a priest, thinking that it was a bit premature which proved to be dead wrong. The film takes this rumor and runs wild with it, making Paganini a sort of undead hit man for the devil. Sporting a gold mask reminiscent of Lon Chaney's *Phantom of the Opera* skeletal makeup, Pagaini pop ups every now and then to dispatch his victims with his unique gold violin that conceals a giant switch blade. Although this is a somewhat novel idea, many parts of the film are confusing and downright silly, such as when the group encounters a *Star Wars* style force field around the house that prevents them from escaping and when Paganini plays one encore too many and is vanquished by the sunlight to turn to ash in the shape of a musical note.

Pleasence, who previously played the devil in *The Greatest Story Ever Told*, is back as Old Scratch, although he is now more of a business man running a roach motel sort of hell. Mr. Pickett/Satan is first seen selling the Paganini score to a band member, decked out in a sweeping trench coat and presenting himself like an antique dealer. He later takes the money from the sale and travels to the top of a tower, where he throws the money up in the air, calling it little demons in what is presumed to be how the curse is put into effect. At the film's climax, Mr. Pickett appears as a well-dressed business man who explains to Kate, the lone survivor before stabbing her, that Sylvia, whom viewers are supposed to guess was the little girl who murders her mother in the film's prologue, is his "agent" responsible for bringing new victims to the house to be punished by Paganini. Hands down, Pleasence's previous role as the devil in *The Greatest Story Ever Told* tops this convoluted Satanic affair.

# Halloween 5: *The Revenge of Michael Myers* (1989)

**Cast:** Donald Pleasence (Dr. Sam Loomis), Danielle Harris (Jamie Lloyd), Ellie Cornell (Rachel Carruthers), Beau Starr (Sheriff Ben Meeker), Jeffrey Landman (Billy Hill), Tamara Glynn (Samantha Thomas), Jonathan Chapin (Mikey), Matthew Walker (Spitz), Wendy Foxworth (Tina Williams), Betty Carvalho (Nurse Patsey), Don Shanks (Michael Myers/Man in Black). Directed by Dominique Othenin-Girard.

**Synopsis:** After having been shot by the police, Michael Myers falls through a mineshaft and manages to crawl out through a tunnel opening by the river and escapes. Badly injured, he makes his way to the cabin of a local and falls into a coma only to awaken a year later to continue where he left off. Jamie, who was psychically linked to Michael when she touched him, has been rendered mute by the experience and is recovering at the Haddonfield Children's clinic. Dr. Loomis (Donald Pleasence) is aware of Jamie's psychic link to Michael and when she begins having convulsions, he knows that Michael is back intending to kill Jamie. Loomis becomes frustrated because Jamie cannot help him to locate the whereabouts of Michael who has already set out on another killing spree. Complicating matters is the arrival in Haddonfield of a mysterious man in black with a tattoo on his wrist of a thorn that is identical to that of Michael Myers. When Jamie senses that Michael is trying to kill her friend Tina, she runs out of the clinic with her friend Billy to try and stop him. Jamie is successful and finally agrees to help Loomis. A trap is set in Michael's childhood home with Jamie as the bait. Michael creates a diversion to lure away the police and then goes into the house for Jamie. Loomis seemingly turns on Jamie by offering her to Michael, only to trap him in a chain net before beating him unconscious with a board. Michael is taken to the police station and thrown in jail; however, Jamie knows that he cannot be stopped which proves to be correct when the man in black makes his appearance and begins slaughtering the police force and setting Michael free.

**Commentary:** After the success of *Halloween 4*, it should not come as a surprise that the producers decided to continue the series. But after setting up an interesting angle with Jamie being controlled by Michael Myers through a psychic link, *Halloween 4* simply kept the link and once again focused on Myers. It seems that director Dominique Othenin-Girard tried a bit too hard to change the series, resulting in a disappointing film with only a few good bits and plenty of plot holes, such as Myers apparently lying in a coma for a full year in some man's cabin who thinks nothing of letting a masked stranger stay there without calling the authorities, then waking up the day before Halloween, only to kill the man and begin his trail of vengeance again. In addition, unlike previous *Halloween* films in which Myers only killed those who blocked his path to his intended target, *Halloween 5* has him chasing after a bunch of horny teenyboppers while knowing that Jamie is in the clinic; also, the police act like the Keystone Kops, complete with clown music, all which helped the franchise to take a serious nosedive. There are a few interesting ideas, such as Michael donning a different fright mask to fool a victim's girlfriend and Jamie appealing to her uncle's humanity. This film also introduced a new character—the mysterious man in black who shares the same tattoo as Michael and who frees him in the end. But all he basically does in this film is to serve as a link or a foreshadowing device for *Halloween 6*.

According to several interviews with Pleasence during the filming of *Halloween 5*, this was to be his last turn as the heroic Dr. Loomis, and although Pleasence admitted that the first film was the best in the series, he explained why he kept taking the Loomis role—"If that turns out to be the case, I'm definitely going to miss him. It's hard to play a continuing character like Loomis for nearly eleven years and simply wash your hands of him. It seems a pity."[117] Pleasence also mentioned that he was opposed to director Dominique Othenin-Girard's take on his character via a more heavy and serious tone than in previous *Halloween* films. That being said, Pleasence was probably unable to alter too much of his character's dialogue, for Loomis does appear more heartless in some respects, especially toward the young Jamie who Loomis wants to use to track down Michael Myers. When Loomis supposedly ends his role in the franchise by beating the stuffing out of Michael Myers with a wooden board before falling on top of him from a heart attack or stroke, this seems a perfect way for him to fade out— but then again, never say never with *Halloween*.

# Casablanca Express (1989)

**Cast:** Jason Connery (Alan Cooper), Francesco Quinn (Captain Franchetti), Jinny Steffan (Lieutenant Lorna Fisher), Manfred Lehmann (Otto von Tiblis), Jean Sorel (Major Valmore), Donald Pleasence (Colonel Bats), Glenn Ford (Major General Williams), John Evans (Winston Churchill). Directed by Sergio Martino.

**Synopsis:** At the Allied Headquarters in North Africa during 1942, plans are being made to transport British Prime Minster Winston Churchill to an important meeting with US President Franklin Roosevelt in Casablanca. However, the Nazis are aware of Churchill's location and are planning to kidnap him and bring him back to Berlin. British Colonel Bats (Donald Pleasence), French Major Valmore, and US Major General Williams decide to sneak Churchill onto a cargo plane to the meeting, but British espionage agent Alan Cooper, along with Captain Franchetti and Lieutenant Lorna Fisher, discover that Otto von Tiblis, Germany's head of intelligence in Africa, has discovered their plan. A last minute change is decided that places Churchill instead on a train to throw off the Nazis. With Churchill safely aboard the train, Cooper conducts a security check and discovers the presence of a spy within the Allied forces who alerted the Germans of the new change of plans. Tiblis gets aboard the train and with a battalion of German paratroopers, takes everyone hostage. The Allies are helpless to attack because Tiblis has the train wired to explode as he waits for a German plane to take them away. Reaching a desperation point, the Allies allow Cooper to stage a last ditch effort to save Churchill, and together with Franchetti and Lorna, Cooper carries out his operation that results in the train being demined, the killing of Tiblis and the German soldiers, and freedom for Churchill. However, upon returning to Allied headquarters, Cooper learns that all of the lives lost in the process actually went to protecting Churchill's double. It seems that the real Churchill went along with the original plan and arrived safely in Casablanca by plane.

**Commentary:** *Casablanca Express is the first of two films that Pleasence did for director Sergio Martino and is far superior to American Tiger. The story is similar to the classic The Eagle Has Landed, although told from the Allied point of view. The cast is made up of several film* *veterans like Glenn Ford and two of the sons of veterans—Jason Connery (Sean Connery's son) and Francesco Quinn (Anthony Quinn's son). The result is a fairly well-made adventure yarn with good tension, plenty of firefights and action, but is burdened by some less than stellar dialogue and inaccurate technical aspects. Pleasence plays* Colonel Bats in a supporting role that does not give him a lot of screen time but is important nonetheless. Bats is Cooper's boss and all of the major decisions go through him to Churchill. Plus, it is Bats who gives the order to kill Churchill if he cannot be rescued from the Germans. Besides this important segment, viewers get to see Pleasence in uniform in a take charge role, done with class more than once during his acting career.

## *Buried Alive* (1990)

**Cast:** Robert Vaughn (Gary), Donald Pleasence (Dr. Schaeffer), Karen Witter (Janet), John Carradine (Jacob), Ginger Lynn Allen (Debbie), Nia Long (Fingers), William Butler (Tim), Janine Denison (Shiro), Arnold Vosloo (Ken Wade). Directed by Gerard Kikoine.

**Synopsis:** Janet is a young teacher who has accepted a position at Raven's Croft health facility for girls after being impressed by its director Gary Julian. However, soon after arriving at her new job, Janet begins to experience horrific visions and nightmares of people trying to grab her through the ground and a living brick wall. Janet is told by Gary that she will become accustomed to the place which his assistance Dr. Schaeffer (Donald Pleasence) confirms, but things do not get any better and soon some of the girls go missing which attracts the attention of Sheriff Ken. One night after confronting one of the girls, Janet is told that there is a labyrinth of tunnels in the basement and one of the missing girl's belongings somehow ended up there. Exploring for herself, Janet eventually finds a large hidden room with padded walls and chair restraints, but is surprised by Dr. Schaeffer who tries to grab her as she runs out. After talking with the mother of one of the missing girls, Janet learns that Dr. Schaeffer was once a patient at the facility. Fed up with the entire situation, Janet confronts Gary about Schaeffer and the disappearances but he instead proposes to her, and when she tells Gary that she is leaving and will contact Sheriff Ken, Gary flips out and starts chasing her through the house with the expressed purpose of walling her up alive in the basement.

**Commentary:** Supposedly based on the short story by Edgar Allan Poe, *Buried Alive* barely resembles Poe's masterpiece of the macabre *The Premature Burial*; instead, what is presented is a slasher-type film set in a girls' school which conveniently allows some of the girls to be seen getting undressed. A black cat living in the house is also a weak attempt to link the film to another Poe tale—*The Black Cat* that has absolutely nothing in common with *The Premature Burial*. The dialogue is mostly terrible and the acting by the girls is not much better. This film even features Robert Vaughn and John Carradine in his last role before his death (the film was completed in 1988 but was shelved for two years). Vaughn does not do much with his role as the director of Raven's Croft/maniac killer who dons a Ronald Reagan mask; Pleasence is wasted, and Carradine is in a blink and you miss him role. What is even more confusing is the TV production by director Frank Darabont, also called *Buried Alive* which was released in 1990; however, Darabont's version is actually suspenseful and well-crafted as opposed to Gerard Kikoine's wasted effort.

*Buried Alive* was the second Edgar Allan Poe film adaptation that Pleasence appeared in for producer Harry Alan Towers, the first being *The House of Usher*. Unfortunately, both *Buried Alive* and *The House of Usher* are sub-par and it is probably a good thing that Pleasence did not appear in any of Towers' films following this debacle. As Dr. Schaeffer, Pleasence simply plays a red herring so as not make it obvious that Gary is the killer. His character pops up every now and then in the storyline sporting a really bad toupee and mostly just stares at Janet and eats from his bag of candy when not distributing the mail to the girls at the school. It is also unfortunate that Pleasence was not given the opportunity to share some scenes with Carradine because it was his final film appearance. However, Pleasence does make a bold attempt to deepen his character by trying to help save Janet, but he is killed off for his efforts, probably not a bad thing considering the quality of *Buried Alive*.

# *American Tiger* (1990)

**Cast:** Mitchell Gaylord (Scott Edwards), Daniel Greene (Francis), Victoria Prouty (Joanna Simpson), Donald Pleasence (Reverend Mortom), Michi Kobi (Old Madame Luna), Glenn Maska (Daniel). Directed by Sergio Martino.

**Synopsis:** Scott Edwards is an average Florida college student who helps pay for his tuition by working as a rickshaw runner. One day, he gives a ride to an old Chinese woman who is impressed when Scott mentions that he was born in the year of the dragon. Scott later gets lured into a bizarre taped sex encounter and steals what he thinks is the videotape from the filmmaker who turns up dead and is revealed to be the son of the televangelist Reverend Mortom (Donald Pleasence). Soon after, an assassin working for Mortom kills Scott's roommate and frames him for the murder of the reverend's son. With no one to turn to, Scott kidnaps Joanna Simpson, the girl from the sex video, who believes and helps him find an important missing key. Following a mysterious cat, Scott discovers that its owner is Madame Luna, the old Chinese woman that he carried in the rickshaw who turns out to be a powerful being with the secret of eternal youth. Scott then gets caught up in an ancient battle of good versus evil and after defeating the assassin and returning the stone of evil, Madame Luna becomes young once again and exposes the Reverend Mortom for the devil that he truly is.

**Commentary:** *There are bad films and then there is American Tiger, a.k.a. American Risco. Directed by Sergio Martino who had previously directed Pleasence in Casablanca Express and starring 1984 gold medal winner Mitch Gaylord, American Tiger fails in all respects and then gets downright weird. The film starts out as what is perceived to be a crime thriller with some gratuitous nudity thrown in at the expense of Victoria Prouty as Joanna. Then old Madame Luna shows up like an ancient Carrie and starts causing fires with her mind and making a cobra snake appear to scare off an assassin whenever necessary. Things get even more bizarre with some mumbo jumbo about returning the stone of evil placed inside the urn of wisdom.*

*Pleasence should have run as far away as possible from this film. He attempts a southern accent for his televangelist Reverend Mortom and quickly is up to no good after first appearing on TV. American Tiger also presents Pleasence as you have never seen him before, made up in green Kabuki makeup and being double-teamed in a cat and cobra wrestling match. To top things off, Pleasence begins making pig noises just before being shot and transformed into an ugly boar creature as his final humiliation. In effect, American Tiger can definitely be skipped even by diehard Donald Pleasence fans.*

## *Millions* (1991)

**Cast:** Billy Zane (Maurizio Ferretti), Lauren Hutton (Cristina Ferretti), Carol Alt (Betta), Jean Sorel (Leo Ferretti), Alexandra Paul (Giulia Ferretti), Roberto Bisacco (Osvaldo Ferretti), Catherine Hickland (Connie), John Stockwell (David Phipps), Donald Pleasence (Ripa). Directed by Carlo Vanzina.

**Synopsis:** Leo Ferretti, the CEO of a multimillion dollar corporation, is involved in a helicopter crash that puts him in a coma. His disjointed family is at odds on what to do; Leo's ex-wife Cristina has him transferred to Geneva where she hopes he will be saved, while his nephew Maurizio begins plotting on how he can take over the family business. Osvaldo, Leo's brother and Maurizio's father, names the more experienced Lomberto Razza as the interim president of Ferretti Industries, a decision that infuriates Maurizio who believes that he is the rightful heir to the family business. Through some unscrupulous means, Maurizio uncovers a secret project that Leo was planning as a way to transform the firm into a new holding company and go public. After deciding to take on the project himself, Maurizio sleeps with his father's CEO to find dirt on him and then uses blackmail to get named as the new interim president of the company. He then goes forward with the project and tries to convince Ripa (Donald Pleasence), Leo's bank investor, to lend him the six hundred million necessary for the project's success; however, Ripa turns him down flat. But a ray of hope is seen by Maurizio when his brother's wife puts him in touch with Piero Costa, a multimillionaire of the business world. But this connection to Costa will put Maurizio in a hostile competition to control Ferretti Industries.

**Commentary:** One wonders why *Millions* was even made. All of the characters are basically greedy with the possible exception of Leo's ex-wife, but then again she may have been just trying to get back in Leo's good graces for the money. In fact, viewers will find it difficult to root for any of the main characters—especially Maurizio who seemingly has no morals, due to blackmailing his own father, stealing the family business from his uncle, and sleeping around to the point where he gets his own cousin pregnant. Add on top of this some truly horrendous dialogue, very shaky acting, and ridiculously outdated car phones and you have a really bad R-rated Italian soap opera.

By the 1990s, Pleasence's film appearances were for the most part small, something rather common for older actors. His role as bank investor Ripa fits into this category, although his character is central to the plot because Maurizio, Costa, and Leo all vie for him to invest in their schemes. Speaking at times with a raspy voice and holding his ear for some reason, Pleasence may at first give the impression that Ripa is not quite up to playing in the big leagues with Maurizio's devious plans, but he quickly sees through the young man's façade and sends him on his way. In contrast, Ripa's approval of a possible takeover by one of Leo's business enemies demonstrates his underhandedness and cleverness. Even when Ripa comes clean about his dealings with Costa, Leo still offers to include him on another project. Basically, the money that Ripa has at his disposal as an investment banker makes him a hot commodity with the greedy characters in *Millions*.

## *Shadows and Fog* (1992)

**Cast:** Kleinman (Woody Allen), Killer (Michael Kirby), Hacker (David Ogden Stiers), Vigilante (James Rebhorn), Vigilante (Victor Argo), Vigilante (Daniel von Bargen), Irmy (Mia Farrow), Clown (John Malkovich), Marie (Madonna), Doctor (Donald Pleasence), Prostitutes (Lily Tomlin, Jodie Foster, Kathy Bates, Anne Lange), Student Jack (John Cusack), Police Chief (Greg Stebner), Mr. Paulsen (Philip Bosco), Hacker's followers (Fred Gwynne, Robert Silver), Vigilantes (Tom Riis Farrell, Ron Weyand), Magician (Kenneth Mars). Directed by Woody Allen.

**Synopsis:** In a small town, a strangler is on the loose killing the locals. Max Kleinman, a mild-mannered clerk, is awakened in his apartment by his neighbors who have formed a vigilante group to track down and capture the strangler. Already saddled with stress over trying to get a promotion at work, Kleinman is forced to agree to help but is not told his role in the "plan." Meanwhile, in a nearby traveling circus, Irmy, a sword swallower, wants to settle down with her boyfriend who performs as a clown, but he is reluctant, and Irmy later finds him cheating with another performer and leaves the circus in disgust, heading for the town. Kleinman, who is trying to find out his role in the "plan," visits his doctor (Donald Pleasence) who is more concerned with the nature of the strangler to be of any real help. Finally reaching town, Irmy has nowhere to stay but is helped by a prostitute who takes her back to the local whorehouse. There, she meets Jack, a local college student who wants to sleep with her. Jack finally convinces Irmy after offering her $700, but she winds up arrested later on for soliciting without a license. Kleinman has his own problems, like being forced to steal a piece of incriminating evidence from police headquarters that might link him to the death of the doctor who was strangled to death. Kleinman and Irmy then decide to stick together on the fog-enshrouded streets as the danger continues to mount, due to the vigilante group splintering into different factions and the strangler still his victims.

**Commentary:** *Shadows and Fog* is a fine tribute by Woody Allen to German Expressionism, and although classified as a comedy, it is more of a dramatic mystery with comedic undertones. Allen, who wrote and directed the film and stars as Kleinman, provides a variation on his usual neurotic characters. The story itself is based on an earlier play written by Allen called *Death*, which in turn was a parody of the work of Franz Kafka.

The film starts out well with twists and turns, but by the conclusion, it all seems a bit convoluted with a couple of loose ends. Allen packed this film with a lot of big name actors and it is enjoyable to look for all the familiar faces in various roles. It is also beautifully shot in black and white that greatly benefits the overall look and feeling of the film. But the real beauty of *Shadows and Fog* are the philosophic discussions debated by a number of the characters with most taking place in the whorehouse.

Pleasence's role as the Doctor in *Shadows and Fog*, his last big budget film, is small but very amusing. Allen obviously wished to play up Pleasence's horror film connection by having him explain to Kleinman that he needs to discover the nature of evil, a clear link to Dr. Loomis in *Halloween* trying to figure out the nature of his homicidal patient Michael Myers. The Doctor's office looks more like a laboratory out of a *Frankenstein* film, replete with medical beakers and corpses for dissection. Pleasence plays an excellent straight man to Allen's Kleinman, for when he sees body parts lying around the lab, he exclaims, "I guess the maid doesn't get in that often to straighten up." Although Pleasence appears in only two scenes, his role is an important one as a glass of wine he presents to Kleinman is used to accuse him of being the strangler. But perhaps the best bit about Pleasence's role is a little nod that Allen makes to one of Pleasence's greatest performances—as the strangler corners the doctor in an alley way, keen-eyed viewers can make out on a wall behind Pleasence the first half of a sign for a *Cul-de-sac*.

*Shadows and Fog* received some unfair negative reviews and was chosen by the late film critic Gene Siskel as one of the worst films of 1992. Possibly, critics had been told about the film's plot and expected something more in the vein of an outright in-your- face horror comedy like Mel Brooks' *Young Frankenstein* which featured Kenneth Mars (the Magician in Allen's film) as the one-armed Inspector Kemp. Although both of these films were shot in black and white, the comparison ends here, for Allen's film is much more cerebral and concerned with pushing its various messages related to paranoia, love, and society in general.

Also like *Young Frankenstein*, there are some very funny moments in *Shadows and Fog*. For example, Allen's Kleinman makes a number of hysterical observations, such as when he tells his neighbor who has provided some pepper to use against the strangler, "Very good, I'll ward him off with a seasoning," and then proceeds to use the pepper later on against the vicious mob that mistakenly believes that he is the strangler. Another issue is Allen's approach to filmmaking which in the case of *Shadows and Fog* caters to more sophisticated tastes than the average ticket buyer. In an article that attempts to dissect the immense popularity of Woody Allen in France, it is noted that the inspiration for Allen's latest film *Shadows and Fog* "seems more European than any Allen film because his homages to Ingmar Bergman" via *Interiors* in the late 1970s. [118]

# *Dien Bien Phu* (1992)

**Cast:** Donald Pleasence (Howard Simpson), Patrick Catalifo (Captain Jego de Kerveguen), Jean-Francois Balmer (L'homme de 'AFP), Ludmila Mikael (Beatrice Vergnes), Francois Negret (Corporal), Maxime Leroux (Artillery lieutenant), The Anh (Ong Cop/Mister Tiger), Christopher Buchholz (Captain Morvan), Long Nguyen-Khac (Mister Vinh). Directed by Pierre Schoendoerffer.

**Synopsis:** The French military is being pounded by the Vietnamese during the 1954 battle at Dien Bien Phu. Howard Simpson (Donald Pleasence), a Pulitzer Prize winning war correspondent for the *San Francisco Chronicle*, is covering the events of the war in Vietnam. Sometimes, Simpson holds conversations with the French soldiers who are dutiful but realistic; Mister Vinh, a Vietnamese nationalist running their newspaper; and Ong Cop who runs a betting parlor taking bets on when each French-occupied area will fall to the Vietminh. Among the French soldiers is Captain Jego de Kerveguen, who leads his battalion to defend Dien Bien Phu from the approaching Vietminh army. Despite supplies being airlifted in, Keveguen's battalion becomes decimated, due to a lack of reinforcements from other units. Eventually told by his commander to order a retreat, Keveguen refuses to obey and his soldiers fight on. Keveguen is denied any backup and informed soon after that a ceasefire has finally been called between the two warring forces. Ordered to destroy their weapons, Keveguen and his surviving troops march out of Dien Bien Phu as France recognizes its defeat in Vietnam.

**Commentary:** *Dien Bien Phu* is a powerful film that chronicles the 1954 battle in which France, due to a series of military mistakes, was defeated by the Vietminh. Director/writer Pierre Schoendoerffer had first-hand experience in Vietnam as a cameraman with the French army, and as a result, *Dien Bien Phu* is not your typical heroic tale but instead is akin to a documentary showing war as it truly is—brutal, violent, and unpredictable with the goal being to simply survive. Running at about two hours, Schoendoerffer's paean to the horrors of Vietnam conveys a feeling of utter relief for the French soldiers who are depicted as having a great sense of honor even as they slowly realize the futility of the war as the Vietminh close in with superior numbers. There are also many haunting images, such as bombs lighting up the Vietnamese hills with classical music playing in the background and a French paratrooper landing in a pit filled with the bodies of his fellow French soldiers.

*Dien Bien Phu* provided Pleasence with the last big role of his long film career. His character is based on the real-life Howard Simpson, a US war correspondent in Vietnam who would go on to write a number of books including *Dien Bien Phu: The Epic Battle America Forgot*. Unfortunately, Pleasence's role is rather limited, for he mostly spends his time being driven around in a rickshaw while sporting a white suit and smoking cigars non-stop. His best scenes include discussing the war with the local newspaper boss Mister Vinh and the gambler Ong Cop who share their philosophies on how the war is going and its eventual effect on the nation of Vietnam. Simpson also takes advantage of his contacts to get his articles sent to San Francisco without being censored. As he had done throughout his career, Pleasence makes use of his eyes to convey his feelings when dealing with other characters and situations. An interesting note is that *Dien Bien Phu* is in French with English subtitles—and Pleasence speaks French fluently throughout.

## *The Princess and the Cobbler* (1993)

**Cast:** Vincent Price (ZigZag), Anthony Quayle (King Nod—original version), Hilary Pritchard (Princess YumYum—original version), Joan Sims (Mad Holy Old Witch—original version), Windsor Davies (Chief Roofless), Felix Aylmer (Narrator—original version), Paul Matthews (Mighty One Eye—original version), Clinton Sundberg (Dying Soldier), Donald Pleasence (Phido the Vulture). Directed by Richard Williams.

**Synopsis:** In a kingdom run by the perpetually sleepy King Nod, invaders look to conquer it, especially the Mighty One Eye with his army and massive war machine. A prophecy foretells that the kingdom will remain safe as long as the three golden balls remain on top of the minaret. One day, a gold-craving thief sneaks into the cobbler's shop while he sleeps and attempts to rob him. The cobbler wakes up and during a struggle, they tumble out of the store with the cobbler dropping his shoe tacks in the street. At that moment, ZigZag, the king's vizier, comes through the town and steps on one of the tacks. Enraged, ZigZag's guards seize the cobbler and take him back to the palace, where he is brought before the king with ZigZag demanding permission to execute him for the offense. However, the king's daughter Princess Yum Yum takes pity on the cobbler and saves his life by breaking her shoe and asking her father to spare the stranger's life so that he may work for her. The king agrees and an infuriated ZigZag storms off. At the same time, the thief has made his way into the palace and after numerous attempts manages to knock the three golden balls off the top of the minaret. In the chaos and confusion, ZigZag has his henchmen steal and hide the golden balls; he then approaches the king with his vulture Phido (Donald Pleasence) and offers to find the golden balls in return for Princess Yum Yum's hand in marriage. When the king refuses it is up to the cobbler to stop ZigZag and the Mighty One Eye and return the golden balls and win the affection of Princess Yum Yum.

**Commentary:** As an animated feature that took twenty-eight years to complete, *The Princess and the Cobbler*, a.k.a. *The Thief and the Cobbler*, has a most fascinating and complex history. In 1964, Canadian animator Richard Williams began the project based on the folklore of the wise fool Mulla Nasruddin. Williams had to take on side projects to fund *The Princess and the Cobbler* that underwent a number of title changes over the years. Williams was a big fan of horror star Vincent Price who was one of the first actors to be hired to record dialogue for this film; ironically, due to taking so many years for the film to be completed, *The Princess and the Cobbler* became Price's last work to be released before his death. For the next twenty years, the project languished with work being completed at a snail's pace until Williams directed the hit animated feature *Who Framed Roger Rabbit* (1990) and used his success to get Warner Bros. interested in funding and releasing *The Princess and the Cobbler*. However, this deal fell apart when Williams failed to complete the film according to the deadline and ended up being kicked off his own project. The film was then taken over by the Completion Bond Company and under orders to finish it quickly and cheaply, new producer Fred Calvert re-edited the film. In 1993, it finally appeared in theatres overseas under the title *The Princess and the Cobbler* and in 1995 in the US under the title *Arabian Knight*.

Pleasence lent his voice as Phido the vulture for the original production and most probably did the recording back in the early 1970s. His character is quite comical, clumsily crashing about while attempting not to sleep, and when ZigZag fails to keep his promise to feed his pet that backfires in the end, Phido makes a tasty snack of his head in a darkened pit. While *The Princess and the Cobbler* provided Pleasence with the opportunity to appear in his first and only animated film, his role was not large and unfortunately was limited to only sounds made by the vulture sans dialogue. This is unfortunate as Phido was the pet of ZigZag (voiced by Vincent Price) and Pleasence could have shared dialogue with Price, another great actor known for his villainous roles. Making matters worse is that Pleasence's voice was totally cut from the 1995 Miramax version, replaced by Eric Bogosian who did share some dialogue opposite Price's ZigZag.

## *The Advocate* (1993)

**Cast:** Colin Firth (Richard Courtois), Ian Holm (Albertus), Donald Pleasence (Pincheon), Amina Annabi (Samira), Nicol Williamson (Seigneur Jehan d'Auferre), Michael Gough (Magistrate Boniface), Jim Carter (Mathieu), Lysette Anthony (Filette d'Auferre), Sophie Dix (Maria). Written and Directed by Leslie Megahey.

**Synopsis:** During the fifteenth century, court advocate Richard Courtois and his clerk depart from the city of Paris for the simple country life in Abbeville. Upon arriving there, Richard finds that he has traded big city corruption for a country court system that intertwines religion and calls for animals to be subjected to the same laws as people. Working as an advocate for the defense, Richard ends up locking horns with prosecutor Pincheon (Donald Pleasence) who knows all of the ins and outs of the system. Frustrated by what he sees, Richard is shocked when told that he will be defending a pig in the death of a young boy. At first wanting to refuse, Richard is drawn when a gypsy woman named Samira who owns the animal pleads for his help. Attracted to Samira, Richard reluctantly takes the case that angers the Seigneur Jehan d'Auferre who runs the town. In order to learn the ways of the court, Richard seeks out the advice of Albertus the local priest. As Richard delves into the case, he realizes something far more sinister is at work behind the killing. Fighting the court system, locals, and the Seigneur himself, Richard decides on a most unorthodox approach to vindicate his swine client and expose Abbeville's justice system.

**Commentary:** *The Advocate, a.k.a. Hour of the Pig, is a clever and very well made courtroom drama played out under most unusual circumstances. Based on real life cases, including State of Ponthieu vs. the Porker, the film delves into little known and obscure French country laws of the Middle Ages that allowed animals to be tried at court along with humans. Obviously lending itself to humor, The Advocate fully embraces this and manages to seamlessly mix together laughs, drama, and tension. Future Oscar winner Colin Firth shows a great range in one of his early film roles as* Richard Courtois, a man of conviction who realizes that he will have to get down and dirty in order to bring justice to his case. Other notable performances include acting veterans Michael Gough as Magistrate Boniface and Ian Holm as Albertus, a man of the cloth who likes to mix religion with the secular life.

*Arguably Pleasence's last great role, court prosecutor* Pincheon is at first presented as a simple man whom Richard feels stands no chance against his big city courtroom experience, but Pincheon proves to be more than his match as an expert in the town's laws and a lawyer that derives pleasure from seeing his new competition fall flat on his face. One notable scene has Pincheon asking Richard if he reads all of the town books before a court case, but Richard ignores him, resulting in a guilty verdict and the hanging of his swine client. Pincheon has one of the best moments in the film when he announces in court that the charge against the pig is compounded because it supposedly ate a portion of the victim that violates the church's decree of no meat eating on a Friday. Pleasence's once smooth voice is now quite raspy, which lends him the aura of a lifetime of wisdom which he dispenses to the new advocate in a powerful scene upon telling Richard that he should leave town before he too becomes a worn out old man.

# *The Big Freeze* (1993)

**Cast:** Bob Hoskins (Sidney), Eric Sykes (Mr. Blick), Eila Roine (Matron), Donald Pleasence (Soup Slurper), Raija Laakso (Louise), Sonja Lumme (Pretty Nurse), John Mills (Dapper Man), Spike Milligan (Der Schauspierler), Sylvi Salonen (The Flapper). Directed by Eric Sykes.

**Synopsis:** A retirement home for actors has been experienced plumbing issues and so the matron calls Blick and Sons, the local plumbing business, for assistance. Mr. Blick and his assistant Sidney arrive but are woefully unprepared to deal with the plumbing nightmare in the home. Working around a resident's birthday party, Blick and Sidney try to repair a frozen bathtub and faulty faucets; however, their incompetence only makes the situation worse when they cause the bathtub to fall through the bathroom floor onto the floor below. The Dapper Man, working in conjunction with the nurse, has Blick and Sydney wait in the lobby while he organizes the residents to repair all the problems with the plumbing system. When the matron returns from her outing, she is pleased to see everything is fixed. Blick and Sydney return to their store, only to find it completely flooded from a leak.

**Commentary:** Actor/comedian Eric Sykes wrote, directed, and acts in *The Big Freeze*, a simple yet wonderfully funny tale in the vein of a Laurel and Hardy one reeler. Like Sykes previous shorts *The Plank* and *Mr. H is Late*, *The Big Freeze* is mostly a silent film that focuses on the antics of incompetent plumbers Blick and Sydney. While Sykes is very enjoyable, Bob Hoskins really steals the show, due to his mannerisms and physical comedy that are unmatched by any other character. There are some great sight gags, such as Blick and Sydney trying to set up a ladder in a tiny bathroom, and a blowtorch that accidentally sends a flame up the toilet. Of the various residents of the home, John Mills as the Dapper Man seems to be in charge. The look on Mills' face as he observes the chaos created by Blick and Sydney is truly priceless. Mills also sort of plays himself as when Sydney spots him for the first time and exclaims, "It's John Mills!" *The Big Freeze* also features the final film role of Spike Milligan who puts in a hilarious performance as a Hitler impersonator.

Pleasence has a small role in the film and like most of the characters does not have any dialogue. Dressed as a sort of cross between Doctor Who and Daniel Boone, Pleasence's character is stubborn and single-minded in the pursuit of his next bowl of soup, hence his name the Soup Slurper. This results in a number of funny scenes, such as when he attempts to pour his soup against a strong breeze coming through an open window, and when he finally gets the chance to enjoy his soup, the bathtub fall inches above his head of which he is completely unaware.

## Safe Haven (1995)

**Cast:** Allie Byrne (Kate), Miranda Pleasence (Rachel), Jeremy Sheffield (Sean), Donald Pleasence (The Sailor). Produced and directed by Debbie Shuter.

**Synopsis:** Four friends decide to rent out a remote cottage on an island off the coast of Scotland for a holiday. Alone and isolated, one of the four becomes psychotic, placing the lives of the others in grave danger.

**Commentary:** *Safe Haven* is truly the last film that Pleasence completed before passing away. He had previously shot his scenes for *Fatal Frames* and died during post- production of *Halloween: The Curse of Michael Myers*. In addition, Pleasence was able to appear in a film with his daughter Miranda which makes it more of a shame that this low budget thriller disappeared into obscurity not long after it was released. Filmed around the Summer Isles in the North West Highlands of Scotland, *Safe Haven* is highlighted by some beautiful scenery and in a small role, Pleasence plays the old sailor who takes the four friends to the cottage on the deserted island.

## Halloween: The Curse of Michael Myers (1995)

**Cast:** Donald Pleasence (Dr. Sam Loomis), Paul Rudd (Tommy Doyle), Marianne Hagan (Kara Strode), Mitch Ryan (Dr. Terence Wynn), Kim Darby (Debra Strode), Bradford English (John Strode), Keith Bogart

(Tim Strode), Mariah O'Brien (Beth), Leo Geter (Barry Simms), J.C. Brandy (Jamie Lloyd Carruthers), Devin Gardner (Danny Strode), George P. Wilbur (Michael Myers). Directed by Joe Chappelle.

**Synopsis:** It has been six years since Jamie Lloyd and Michael Myers have disappeared from Haddonfield on Halloween night. Unbeknownst to the townspeople, both were taken by the man in black to an underground secret facility where a cult worshiping a rune symbol called Thorn resides. Jamie, who has just given birth, escapes the facility and returns to Haddonfield with Michael in pursuit. She reaches a bus station and calls a radio station asking for Dr. Loomis' (Donald Pleasence) help before Michael shows up and after another pursuit eventually kills her in a barn. Michael then discovers that Jamie's baby is not with her. Back in Haddonfield, Tommy Doyle, who had his own encounter with Michael as a child, hears Jamie's message and goes looking for her. Tommy finds Jamie's baby and contacts Dr. Loomis to explain that Michael is back. In addition, a new family related to the Strode family is now living in the Myers' house. Their daughter Kara has a young boy named Danny who has been seeing the man in black in his dreams. With the bogeyman returning to his hometown of Haddonfield, Kara, Tommy, and Dr. Loomis will have to work together to stop Michael, the Thorn, and the man in black once and for all.

**Commentary:** *Halloween 5* and *Halloween: The Curse of Michael Myers* a.k.a. Part 6, set up and end the cult of Thorn storyline. Filling in the back-story of why Michael Myers kills his family members, could not die and has incredible strength was a worthwhile idea, though the resulting film was plagued with issues. The biggest was disagreements between the director and producers, which led to three different versions of the film. The theatrical version was reviewed for this book, though there was also an unrated theatrical cut and more interestingly a producer's cut which was the original version that Pleasence signed on for. The producer's cut, never made available officially but out on bootleg, offers a more in-depth understanding of what is going on along with a totally different ending. Unlike the theatrical version, the original producer's cut stuck with the Thorn plotline until the end; Tommy (Paul Rudd in fine form for his film debut) stops Michael by performing a good rune ritual to counter the curse. After Tommy escapes with Kara, Danny and the baby, Dr. Loomis goes back inside and removes Michael's mask to see it is Dr. Wynn who grabs his wrist saying "Michael's gone. Your game now, Dr. Loomis." Loomis looks at his wrist which now has the mark of Thorn and screams while a new man in black, apparently Michael, walks away down a hallway.

*Halloween: The Curse of Michael Myers* would be Pleasence's swan song. Pleasence had filmed his scenes for *Fatal Frames* previously, and passed away shortly after principle shooting on the new *Halloween* ended. This presented a problem to the distributor as reshoots were demanded to change the ending based on a test screening. As a result, some of Pleasence's scenes were cut out from the version that fans saw in the theatres. For that reason alone, the producer's cut is the one that Pleasence fans should seek out when watching this film. In his final role as Dr. Loomis, Pleasence is in good form, with a weaker voice but still the same dominant spirit and excellent acting. Now retired from the medical field, Loomis seems at peace but when he hears Jamie's plea for help the old fire immediately lights in his eyes and he once again sets off to do battle with true evil. Loomis also has another villain to contend with in the persona of Dr. Wynn, a former colleague. But even two villains are not enough to stop the good doctor. Upon watching the two different film endings one can reflect that either Dr. Loomis got his final revenge on Michael for the theatrical version or continued on with a new battle against Thorn for the producer's version. It seems fitting either way that Pleasence got to end his career portraying one of his most famous characters. *Halloween: The Curse of Michael Myers* was dedicated in memory of Donald Pleasence.

## *Fatal Frames* (1995)

**Cast:** Stefania Stella (Stefania Stella), Rick Gianasi (Alex Ritt), David Warbeck (Commissioner Bonelli), Ugo Pagliai (Commissioner Valenti), Leo Daniel (Daniel Antonucci), Alida Valli (Countess Alessandra Mirafiori), Donald Pleasence (Professor Robinson), Angus Scrimm (Artist/Man in Graveyard). Directed by Al Festa.

**Synopsis:** American director Alex Ritt is hired to shoot the new music video for Italian singer Stefania Stella and after agreeing to the job, Alex travels to Italy where he meets Stefania and the crew. He is pleasantly surprised to meet Rebecca, a fellow American working as a dancer for the video. That night, they make plans to meet but Rebecca is accosted and slashed to death by a machete wielding masked killer. Alex runs for the police but when they arrive at the crime scene, all the evidence including Rebecca's body has vanished. Although the police first disbelieve Alex, they soon take him seriously when other women go missing and the killer starts sending them videotapes of his killings. Assigned to lead the case, Commissioner Bonelli focuses on Alex as his prime suspect and while delving into the history of the killings, he learns that similar killings were committed in America in the past. With the help of the FBI, a parapsychologist, and numerous leads, Bonelli intensifies his manhunt until he discovers via an elaborate trap set up by the father of Alex's slain wife that Alex is indeed the killer.

**Commentary:** Although *Fatal Frames* is listed as Pleasence's last film, he actually filmed his part before *Halloween: The Curse of Michael Myers*. While boasting several known actors, such as Pleasence, David Warbeck, and Alida Valli, *Fatal Frames* is a hodgepodge of stylized editing, 1980s style music and video shoots, and horrendous acting. Rick Gianasi as Alex Ritt is one of the main culprits, followed closely by Stefania Stella who portrays herself. As actors, they are woefully bad and their scenes together are laughable. Also, it is not difficult to guess the ending and the proceedings seem to drag on forever at 125 minutes running time.

Pleasence portrays Professor Robinson, a specialist working for the FBI tracking down serial killers. He is quite convinced that Alex is the video killer but is not given much to do besides playing tapes of the killings. Pleasence uses a cane and looks quite old which might explain why the producers decided to have a much younger man do a voiceover for Pleasence. In addition, when Robinson calls Bonelli after the Italian police think they have caught their killer, he says that he must get home to America before Halloween. Oddly enough, John Carpenter's score to *Halloween* can be heard playing in the background.

# AFTERWORD

The first time I met Donald Pleasance was at a party, probably some-time in 1955. We didn't have much to say to each other, mainly because he spent the evening standing on his head in the corner. Five years later, he asked me to be his agent. He had no memory of our earlier meeting, probably because he stood on his head at parties all throughout that period.

Our first film together was *The Flesh and the Fiends* in 1960, a re-working of the Burke and Hare story with George Rose and Peter Cushing. This is an early example of the Pleasance trademark—slightly mad, pushing to the boundary and with a wonderful streak of dark, lunatic humour. Our relationship lasted through nearly two hundred productions until his death in 1995. Very few actor/agent relationships last as long in these days. In the theatre too, Donald was a major star. Harold Pinter's *The Caretaker* in 1960 with Alan Bates helped cement Pinter's reputation as a major literary voice, and later when it trans-ferred to Broadway won Donald his first of four Tony nominations, followed a couple of years later by his extraordinary Adolf Eichmann-like performance in *The Man in the Glass Booth* in London and on Broadway. A wonderful career followed as Blofeld in *You Only Live Twice* (the inspiration for Mike Myers' Dr. Evil in three *Austin Powers* films) and the *Halloween* series with John Carpenter. He was always working and in those forty five years, he was often averaging more than three films a year, together with dozens of TV guest star spots.

Representing a highly castable and personally popular star like Donald was a most wonderful privilege—the people one met because he was on everybody's guest list and during the Golden Age of screen actors. I'll never forget one fabulous afternoon lunching with him and

Danny Kaye, Yul Brynner and Katharine Hepburn on Sam Spiegel's yacht when they were making *The Madwoman of Chaillot*. Those days are gone, and the stars and the producers are simply not like that anymore and we were so lucky to have been around to share them.

Personally, Donald was a very great friend, a generous man as his friends and family would certainly testify, and always pragmatic and positive about his career choices. In many ways, he was a Renaissance man. He wrote a book for children called *Scouse the Mouse* and on the recording of which, I'm ashamed to say, he included a song called "Snow Up Your Nose for Christmas." But that was Donald, amusing himself by seeing just what he could get away with. Researching these few remarks led me to an Internet site of 70,000 fans that contribute to it daily, seventeen years after his death. Reading this book brought back such a flood of memories. I truly miss him.

– Joy Jameson

# ENDNOTES

1. Railway Employment Records, Kew, Surrey, England, The National Archives.

2. "Personal Profile: Donald Pleasence." *The Theatre Magazine*, June 1991.

3. November 22, 1964.

4. *The Los Angeles Times*, February 9, 1975.

5. Bomber Command War Diaries and Edward T. Peters' Logbook. Courtesy of Brian Peters.

6. Interview with Gerald Potterton, 2012.

7. Interview with Don Calfa, 2012.

8. Jeff Dawson, *Empire*, 1994.

9. Passenger and Crew Lists of Vessels Arriving at New York, New York, 1897-1957.

10. Tom English, "Case of Five British Actors Discussed." *NYT*, December 11, 1955.

11. "Pleasence's Villainy, an Act that Pays Off." *Chicago Tribune*, December 19, 1976.

12. Christopher Gullo, *In All Sincerity, Peter Cushing* (Xlibrix, 2004), 146.

13. Michael Codron & Alan Strachan, *Putting It On: The West End Theatre of Michael Codron* (Gerald Duckworth & Co., Ltd, 2010), 122.

14. "British Stars Say U.S. Show Biz is Not Biz for Them." *Newsday*, Dec.1, 1961.

15. "Donald Pleasence." *The New York Times*, December 10, 1961.

16. Interview with Shirley Eaton, 2011.

17. Interview with Jeremy Bulloch, 2012

18. Interview with Dolores Hart, 2012.

19. Donald Pleasence, "Taking the Pick." *Films and Acting*, August 1962.

20. Interview with Joy Jameson, 2011.

21. Interview with John Mayall, 2011.

22. "Pleasence Without Makeup." *The New York Times*, November 22, 1964.

23. Interview with Howard Grey, 2012.

24. Jeff Dawson, *Empire*, February 1994.

25. Interview with Joy Jameson, 2011.

26. *Ibid.*

27. "Mad Dogs and an Englishman." *The Los Angeles Times*, February 9, 1975.

28. John Bratby, "The Two Faces of Donald Pleasence." *Annabel*, February, 1969.

29. Maurice Yacowar, *The Great Bratby, A Portrait of John Bratby RA* (Middlesex UP, 2008), 182.

30. "Some Gentle Evil." *Starlog*, June 1995.

31. Interview with Joy Jameson, 2011.

32. *Ibid.*

33. Interview with Ira von Furstenberg, 2012.

34. "Donald Pleasence—the Mild-Mannered Menace." *Film Review*, July 1975.

35. "'The Man in the Glass Booth" with Donald Pleasence Arrives." The New York Times, September 11, 1968.

36. Interview with Gerald Potterton, 2012.

37. *TV Times*, December 19, 1976.

38. Interview with Don Pedro Colley, 2012.

39. Interview with Lawrence Douglas, 2012.

40. "Wise Child." *The New York Times*, 1972.

41. Interview with Gerald Potterton, 2012.

42. Interview with Don Calfa, 2012.

43. Interview with Kevin Connor, 2011.

44. Interview with John Dark, 2012.

45. Interview with Gonzalo Suarez, 2012.

46. Interview with Robert Weinback, 2012.

47. Interview with Renée Glynne, 2012.

48. Interview with Jeff Bridges, 2011.

49. Interview with David Birney, 2002.

50. Interview with Gerald Potterton, 2012. Pleasence had begun plans on a sequel called *Scouse in New York* but the project was never completed.

51. Interview with Martyn Burke, 2011.

52. Interview with John Carpenter, 2002.

53. Interview with John Carpenter, 2011.

54. Interview with Sylvester McCoy, 2012

55. Interview with John Carpenter, 2011.

56. John Gullidge, "I Bet He Reads Samhain!" *Samhain Magazine*, 8/1990.

57. Interview with Dick Warlock, 2011.

58. Interview with Annie Korzen, 2011.

59. "Barchester Chronicles, From Trollope's Novels." *The New York Times*, October 26, 1984.

60. Interview with David Worth, 2012.

61. Interview with Ulli Lommel, 2011.

62. Interview with Oliver Tobias, 2011.

63. Interview with Joy Jameson, 2011.

64. Interview with Michael Pattinson, 2012.

65. Ibid. "On Ilkla Moor Baht 'at (On Ilkley Moor without a Hat")" is a popular folk song from Yorkshire, England and is sung in the Yorkshire dialect.

66.  Interview with Frank Stallone, 2011.

67.  "Personal Profile: Donald Pleasence." *The Theatre*, June 1991.

68.  Annalena McAfee, "Sidcup or Bust?" *The London Evening Standard*, 1991.

69.  Interview with Joy Jameson, 2011.

70.  "Sweeping the Boards: Donald Pleasence." Carol Allen, *The Theatre*, June 1991.

71.  "Donald Pleasence." *The Daily Mail*, July 2004.

72.  Interview with Donald MacDonald, 2012

73.  Interview with George Wilbur, 2012.

74.  "Masterly Pleasence Recalled as Friend." *The Times (London)*, October 6, 1995.

75.  Interview with Don Calfa, 2012.

76.  Interview with Gerald Potterton, 2012.

77.  Interview with Joy Jameson, 2011.

78.  Interview with John Carpenter, 2011.

79.  "Beachcomber Opens at the Normandie." *The New York Times*, January 17, 1955.

80.  "Screen: Briton's Protest," *NYT*, September 16, 1959.

81.  *Ibid.*

82.  William Roughead, ed. *Burke and Hare* (William Hodge & Company, 1920), 23.

83.  Dictionary.com

84.  Interview with Melvyn Hayes, 2001.

85.  "Hell Is a City," *The New York Times*, January 19, 1961.

86.  Interview with Joy Jameson, 2011.

87.  "Screen: Stylish Shocker," *The New York Times*, September 1, 1960.

88.  "Screen: Tepid Passions," *The New York Times*, August 3, 1960.

89.  "The Risk in Premiere at 52nd Trans-Lux," *The New York Times*, September 25, 1961.

90. *Ibid.*

91. "Screen: P.O.W.'s in "Great Escape," *The New York Times*, August 8, 1963.

92. *Return to the Great Escape*, documentary, 1993.

93. "Polanski's Wild Swing: Story of a Thug and a Weird Couple," *The New York Times*, November 8, 1966.

94. "Screen: "Eye of the Devil" Begins Run," *The New York Times*, December 7, 1967.

95. "Screen: "Fantastic Voyage" Is All That," *The New York Times*, September 8, 1966.

96. "Sayonara, 007: Connery is at it Again as Whatshisname," *The New York Times*, June 14, 1967.

97. Internet Movie Database (IMDB.com), 2011.

98. "Heston in Western," *The New York Times*, April 11, 1968.

99. Charlton Heston, *Charlton Heston: In the Arena* (Simon & Schuster, 1995), 391.

100. BFI National Archive.

101. "Candice Bergen Stars in Violent Western," *The New York Times*, August 13, 1970.

102. "Lucas' "THX 1138": Love is a Punishable Crime in Future," *The New York Times*, March 12, 1971.

103. "The Jerusalem File Arrives," *The New York Times*, February 3, 1972.

104. "Wedding in White Views a 40s Family," *The New York Times*, April 30, 1973.

105. "Black Windmill Comes to Music Hall," *The New York Times*, May 18, 1974.

106. "Hollywood Has an Appealing New Star—Old Gooseberry," *The New York Times*, July 25, 1976.

107. "Possessed Infant Turns into Killer in British "Devil," *The New York Times*, June 24, 1976.

108. "Two Films that Are Worth Adjusting To," *The New York Times*, October 12, 1975.

109. "The Last Tycoon," *The New York Times*, November 18, 1976.

110. "Eagle Has Landed on Screens with Lively Splash of Adventure," *The New York Times*, March 26, 1977.

111. "Cheap and Profitable Horror Films are Multiplying," *The New York Times*, October 24, 1979.

112. "Escape from New York." *The New York Times*, July 10, 1981.

113. "Screen: "Alone in the Dark," *The New York Times*, November 19, 1982.

114. "A Nuclear Cover-Up in Australia," September 23, 1988.

115. "A Woman's Martyrdom," *The New York Times*, November 23, 1988.

116. "Hanna's War Gives Trite Reading of a Saga that Deserves Better," *The New York Times*, November 23, 1988.

117. *Fangoria*, issue #89, 1990. Marc Shapiro, "A Farewell to Halloween."

118. "Woody Allen: France's Monsieur Right," *The New York Times*, April 15, 1992.

# INDEX

Lightning Source UK Ltd.
Milton Keynes UK
UKOW06f2135091214

242911UK00019B/1020/P